The Illustrated History

# CRIME Comics

•THE TAYLOR•

HISTORY OF COMICS

NUMBER 5

# The Illustrated History

# CRIME Comics

## MIKE BENTON
### Author of *The Comic Book in America*

TAYLOR PUBLISHING COMPANY
DALLAS, TEXAS

Published by
Taylor Publishing Company
1550 West Mockingbird Lane
Dallas, Texas 75235

Designed by David Timmons

**Library of Congress
Cataloging-in-Publication Data**

Benton, Mike
    The illustrated history of crime comics / by Mike
Benton.
        p.      cm. — (The Taylor history of comics ;
    no. 5)
        Includes bibliographical references and index.
        ISBN 0-87833-814-4
        1. Comic books, strips, etc. — United States —
History and criticism. 2. Crime — Comic books,
strips, etc.   I Title.    II. Series.
    PN6725.B3832    1993            92-37159
741.5'0973'09045—dc20                  CIP


Printed in the United States of America
10  9  8  7  6  5  4  3  2  1

Interior photography by Austin Prints For Publication
Jeff Rowe,  photographer

*The author gratefully acknowledges the help of the following people who have aided in the development of this book: Jerry Bails, Laura Benton, Scott Deschaine, Mike Dudley, Martin O'Hearn, Steve Rowe, Mike Roy, and Robin Snyder.*

*And a special thanks to the Gang at Taylor Publishing: "Mad Dog" Max Lakin, Holly "The Moll" McGuire, "Diamond" Jim Green, Carol "Crazy Legs" Trammel, and Lynn "Da Boss" Brooks.*

# CONTENTS

Facing Page: *Crime Detective Comics* © 1951 Hillman Periodicals

The Illustrated History

# CRIME
## *Comics*

•THE TAYLOR•

HISTORY OF COMICS

NUMBER 5

# COMIC BOOKS WITH BULLET HOLES

"**I**'ll never give up! *Never*! You dicks have one minute to leave! Then I start *blastin'*!"

"One more drink an' I gonna split that fifty-cent Romeo into nickels and dimes!"

"Wait, papa! Lemme put the finishing slug into him! He killed my brother! Take this, you rotten copper!"

Bloody murder, one-way rides, cement overshoes, and bullets to the brain.

Welcome to the world of crime comic books, where private eyes and public enemies rule. A world of gumshoes, gun molls, gangsters, flatfoots, hit men, and hoodlums, where life is cheap and the only maxim is crime may not pay, but it's sure damned exciting.

The crime comic book, with its crudely printed cartoon stories of lurid violence, is America's most notorious contribution to the field of mystery and detective entertainment. The most maligned of the comic book genres, crime comics attracted so much criticism during their peak years of publication (1947 to 1954), that there was a public backlash against the industry that almost drove comic book publishers out of business.

The origins of the crime comic book can be traced back to the late fifteenth century, when the invention of printing allowed for the publication of public broadsheets detailing the events of executions and crimes. Since the population was mostly illiterate, the text on the single sheets of paper was accompanied by illustrations of the grisly details of the crime or punishment. By the seventeenth century, the public was eagerly buying broadsheets which purportedly related the heinous crimes committed by condemned criminals, and their subsequent confessions written on the eve of their execution (invariably repentant and entirely ghostwritten). One of the best-selling English broadsheets detailed a string of gruesome killings in 1635 by a pair of lovers: "Murder Upon Murder Committed by Thomas Sherwood (Alias, Countrey Tom) and Elizabeth Evans (Alias, Canbrye Besse)."

In the late eighteenth century, James Catnach of London began the infamous Seven Dials Press, which specialized in publishing details about sensational crimes of the period from 1792 to 1841. The publications were widely circulated and many contained dramatic accounts of such infamous highwaymen of the early eighteenth century as Dick Turpin and Jack Shepherd. Murder and body-snatching were the most popular topics, and the last dying speech and confession of one murderer sold over a million copies. When news of lurid crimes was slow, Catnach made up horrible new murders, or simply changed the locale of old murders to suit whatever neighborhood in which his cheap magazines were sold. He also had a large number of woodblocks to illustrate well-known scenes of hideous crimes and public executions. Catnach's

cheap crime papers were eventually replaced by the penny newspapers of the mid-nineteenth century, which satisfied the public's appetite for the details of violent crimes.

In 1841, Edward Lloyd of London published *The People's Police Gazette*, one of the first popular periodicals devoted to re-creating crimes and police detective work. Four years later, *Police Gazette* began in the United States with true stories of nineteenth-century lynchings and train robberies. By the end of the nineteenth and beginning of the twentieth century, hundreds of stories about

*Crime and punishment for gambling in the 15th century. Illustrations from* The Origin of Dice *(1489).*

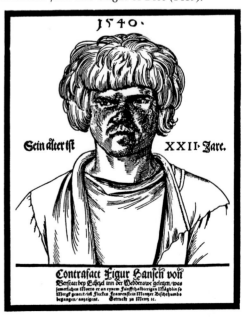

*Left: Sixteenth century broadsheet from Germany (1534). The illustration shows the tortured confession and punishment of a criminal who admitted to killing two priests and cutting the throat of his cook.*
*Right: Broadsheet illustration from 1540 of a twenty-two-year-old German who murdered a five-year old child.*

real-life western badmen and early bank robbers appeared in American boys' magazines, which sported garishly colored covers.

The true detective magazines of the late 1920s and 1930s continued the tradition of popularizing crime and criminals for public entertainment. Using a combination of purple prose salted with facts and grainy police photographs mixed with staged pictures of posed models, the true detective magazines dished up stories fresh from the headlines of big-city tabloids.

The newspapers of the early 1930s, with their daily stories of gangster warfare and violence that grew under Prohibition, also fed the imagination of a Chicago-area cartoonist. Sensing the growing anticrime sentiment of the time, Chester Gould created Dick Tracy, the first crime-fighting detective, for the newspaper comic strips. In addition to portraying police procedural and detective work, "Dick Tracy" was also the first newspaper strip to introduce brutality, gun play, and torture to the comic page. Bullets entered and exited bodies and heads, and the grotesque violence in the strip was as much a draw as the heroics of the detective himself.

"Dick Tracy," along with other detective and G-Men comic strips, were reprinted as features in the early comic books of the late 1930s. Other action detective heroes were soon created especially for the new comic book medium, but by 1941, the plainclothes detectives in the comic books were surpassed in popularity by a new batch of costumed crime-fighters: the superheroes.

At the beginning of World War II, there were nearly a hundred comic books devoted to costumed superheroes like Batman, Captain America, and the Black Hood. There was only one true crime comic book: *Crime Does Not Pay*. By the end of the decade following the war, there were fewer than thirty superhero titles and over forty crime comic books.

During the late 1940s, crime comics had surpassed the superhero characters to become the best-selling genre of the industry and were read by more adults than any other type of comic book. As *film noir* came of age and hard-boiled detective novels be-

*Famous Crimes #1 © 1948 Fox Features Syndicate*

*Parole Breakers #3 © 1952 Realistic Comics*

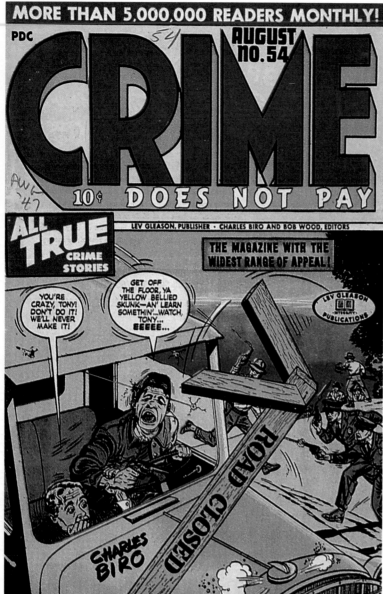

*Crime Does Not Pay #54 © 1947 Comic House. Art by Charles Biro.*

*Crime Does Not Pay #57 © 1947 Comic House. Art by George Tuska.*

came bestsellers, the popularity of crime comics soared. There was a growing market of adult comic book readers in the postwar years who were looking for a little violence, a little sex, and a little seasoning of cynicism in their entertainment.

The adult content of the crime comics—murder, betrayal, greed, depravity, lust, and hate—was in sharp contrast to the high-minded fisticuffs of superheroes and innocent high jinks of funny animals which had previously dominated the comic books. Parents, the clergy, social workers, and self-appointed guardians of public morals found crime comics objectionable and possibly detrimental to the well-being of children.

As crime comics increased in popularity in 1947, an anti-comic book campaign also began. Fueled by fears of juvenile delinquency and the possible harmful effects of violent media upon children, crime comics came under attack and were the subject of congressional investigations in 1950 and 1954. With the 1954 release of Dr. Fredric Wertham's *Seduction of the Innocent*, a popular and sensationalistic attack on crime comic books, public sentiment and congressional

*All-True Detective Cases #3 © 1954 Avon Periodicals. Art by Everett Raymond Kinstler.*

pressure forced the comic book publishers to adopt an industry code of standards which regulated crime comic books out of existence by the beginning of 1955.

Comic books based on detective television shows became popular in the 1960s, but few crime comics were produced then or even after some provisions of the Comics Code were relaxed in 1971. During the 1980s, comic books were given greater latitude to deal with crime and violence because of a proliferation of independent publishers who were not subjected to review and regulation by the Comics Code. For the most part, however, by the 1990s, true crime television shows had replaced the crime comic book for the ultimate in graphic realism.

During the height of their popularity in the late 1940s, however, crime comics were America's Most Wanted Comic Books and were read by more people each month than any other magazines. At the same time, concerned with the morals of our youth, critics nationwide branded crime comics as Public Enemy Number One. Their bloody history deserves a telling.

*Famous Crimes #1 © 1948 Fox Features Syndicate*

# SQUARE-JAWED DETECTIVES AND COMIC STRIP G-MEN

A young man visits his fiancée and her family on an October evening in 1931. The girl's father paid off the family's mortgage that day and has a thousand dollars left, which he keeps in a box under his bed. As the family and young couple celebrate their good fortune, the front door is kicked open by two masked men:

"Stick 'em up—alla yu!"

"And keep 'em up! We're after that dough—where is it?"

The girl's dad resists the robbers. "You want my money—my life savings? Why you—who are you to take what I have slaved years to get—"

BANG—BANG. The old man falls down, shot in the chest. The robbers slug the boyfriend with brass knuckles, grab the money, and escape with the girl, whom they'll use as a hostage. When the young man revives, he sees the bullet-riddled corpse of his girlfriend's father: "Over the body of your father, I swear I'll find you and avenge this thing—I swear it!"

Murder and kidnapping. Robbery and gun play. Newspaper headlines of the day screamed about the brutal violence that had taken over American cities by 1931. Prohibition had given rise to organized crime and ruthless mobs. Bootleggers shot each other in the streets. *Reader's Digest* reported that 486 gangsters were murdered in one year in Chicago alone.

The robbery, murder, and kidnapping which occurred that day in October made its way into several newspapers. There were plenty of front-page stories just like it: a hatchet murder of a grape truck driver, the gangland slaying of an undertaker-turned-bootlegger, and the police's running gun battle with child-killer Vincent Coll. The only thing that made this particular murder stand out from the other headline crimes was that it happened in the "funny" papers in a comic strip.

Chester Gould, a thirty-year-old Chicago newspaper staff artist and aspiring cartoonist, had finally hit paydirt. He had spent ten years of his life "knocking on doors with my head" in an attempt to interest Captain Joe Patterson of the Chicago Tribune Syndicate in his gag newspaper strips. Although Gould had drawn *The Radio Catts*, *The Girl Friends*, and several other funny strips for local papers, the captain showed only the

---

Facing Page: *Dick Tracy Large Feature Comic #15* © *1939 Tribune Media Services*. Art by Chester Gould.

*Original Dick Tracy #5 © 1991 Tribune Media Services.* Art by Chester Gould.

barest interest in Gould's dozens of submissions. Then Gould tried something different—a serious comic strip about a plainclothes detective.

"My wife Edna and our daughter had gone to bed," Gould recalled years later. "On the couch lay the daily paper where I had thrown it in disgust and frustration—its headlines screamed of another crime massacre. A spring breeze whispered at the window, and as I sat there leaning back from the drawing board, my mind grappled with the situation. Who could solve this crime problem? As I thought, my hand automatically began sketching. Yes, he'd be a sharp-looking young man with a firm, square jaw showing determination, the aquiline nose of a searcher, and analytical eyes. Suddenly, there he was on paper, keen visage staring across the page. Now to put him to work! As enthusiasm flooded me, my pencil sketched furiously. Strip after strip of daily panels seemed to fly off my easel."

Gould anxiously submitted his crime-fighting detective strip, whom he dubbed "Plainclothes Tracy," for Captain Patterson's consideration. The captain thought the strip had "possibilities" and summoned the artist to a meeting at the Chicago Tribune Tower.

"The name 'Plainclothes' is too long," the captain told him. "Call him Dick—like a

detective, you know. And have him become a cop to avenge the death of his girlfriend's father. We'll need two weeks of daily strips ready by the first."

Gould bought a nickel cigar and soda pop to celebrate, and then he returned to his suburban Chicago home to turn "Plainclothes Tracy" into "Dick Tracy." The first daily strips appeared on October 12, 1931. Full of hoodlums, gunsels, and murderers, "Dick Tracy" was the perfect comic strip for its time.

"What was taking place then," Gould recalled, "was the last stage of big-time gangsterism in Chicago." Like many people,

*Dick Tracy Monthly #8 © 1948 Chicago Tribune.* Art by Chester Gould.

Gould was disgusted by mob rulers and criminals who escaped the law because there "was too much red tape." What the public wanted, Gould surmised, was a heroic crime-fighter—someone who could take "direct action . . . shoot them right down on the spot."

As the Roaring Twenties disappeared into the Great Depression, the public's morbid fascination with big-shot gangsters was insatiable. Al Capone, whose recent biography sported the unabashed subtitle "The Biography of a Self-Made Man," was cheered as a hero by Boy Scouts at Chicago baseball games. Audiences flocked to movies about gangsters, such as *Little Caesar* and *Public Enemy*. By the time *Dick Tracy* appeared, crime movies were at their height of popularity, with forty titles released in a single year. Movie theaters, newspapers, popular magazines, and radio were full of real and fictional exploits of bad men who had somehow become folk heroes.

In the wake of growing criticism about the glorification of gangsters by Hollywood and the media, "Dick Tracy" was described in early 1932 by the Chicago Tribune Syndicate as the "antidote to maudlin sympathy with society's enemies—he creates no glamor for the underworld. Children love this character, and parents and teachers approve of him."

The sentiment was right for a spunky crime-fighter like Dick Tracy: "Put 'em up, hoods! Grab air, you babies—or I'll squeeze this thing—and I don't mean maybe!" (February 5, 1932).

Although Gould's "Dick Tracy" anticipated the anticrime crusade of the early 1930s, a comic strip with an action detective for a hero was still a bold innovation. Most newspaper comics of the time were "funny" strips, like "Mutt and Jeff," "Bringing Up Father," and "Krazy Kat." Only a few comic strips, such as "Little Orphan Annie," "Tarzan," "Tailspin Tommy," and "Buck Rogers," were adventure serials with heroes and villains.

Before Dick Tracy, comic strip detectives and crime-fighters were played for laughs. Charles Kahles's "Clarence the Cop" (1900) was an addled Irish policeman who spent his time avoiding practical jokers, chas-

*Dick Tracy Monthly #3*
*© 1934 Chicago Tribune.*
Art by Chester Gould.

ing juvenile mischief makers, and anguishing over his lot in life ("Transferred agin, be the great jumpin' jingo!"). Most early twentieth-century comic strip crime-fighters, such as "Alex the Cop" by Eddie Esks, "Mr. Wiseguy the Detective" by Hugh Doyle, and "Hawkshaw the Detective," a Sherlock Holmes parody by Gus Mager, were mostly amusing incompetents. Chester Gould's square-jawed detective, however, was deadly serious and thoroughly efficient:

"Come out of there, mug—or I'll fill that place so full of tear gas, you'll catch cold from wet clothes!" (July 22, 1932).

Chester Gould once recalled that he "always thought of Tracy as being just about six feet tall and an ordinary guy with a good build on him . . . an individual who could toss the hot iron right back at them along with a smack on the jaw thrown in for good measure."

Gould's Dick Tracy, however, was more in the tradition of Arthur Conan Doyle's Sherlock Holmes and less like a hard-boiled detective. "In drawing the character," Gould explained, "it has been the idea to picture

*Dick Tracy Monthly #3*
© *1934 Chicago Tribune.*
Art by Chester Gould.

him as a modern Sherlock Holmes, if Holmes were a young man living today, wearing a snap-brim fedora instead of a deerslayer hat."

Gould disallowed influences from the American pulp magazine writers of detective stories or the burgeoning gangster movies of the day. In researching his strip, the cartoonist said he "followed the newspapers almost exclusively—the police news and all the information about the operation of gangsters and the war against them. . . . I read and reread the Sherlock Holmes stories. I always found some inspiration in them."

According to mystery writer Ellery Queen, Gould's fondness for Holmes's deduction and police methods made Dick Tracy "the world's first procedural detective of fiction, in the modern sense." Tracy, Queen observed, is "a thinking detective who combines the intellectual school with the physical . . . a proficient craftsman of true-life police techniques."

Dick Tracy may have been a "thinking" detective, but it was bullets and blood that made the strip a roaring success. For the first time in the comic strip medium, Gould showed the world of crime as violent and ugly.

Characters were murdered—an almost unheard of occurrence for the funny pages. Brutal torture was the strip's mainstay. Blowtorches, branding irons, and skull-crushing vises were ingeniously employed to maximize the pain suffered by the strip's hapless victims. Even the criminals were painful to look at. The Mole, B-B Eyes, Little Face, and other villains were grotesque monstrosities, physically repulsive and psychically deformed.

Gould recalled that "from the very beginning I would receive letters saying what a 'horrible' strip I was doing. I once received a letter from a person asking, 'Why do you make your criminals so ugly?' I never looked at them as being ugly, but I'll tell you this. I think the ugliest thing in the world is the face of a man who has killed. His face to me is ugly." He dismissed his critics with a single maxim: "We need more graphic portrayals of where crime leads."

Evidently, the public agreed. Shortly after Dick Tracy's debut, the strip appeared in two or three new papers every day for several weeks. "It grew like wildfire," Gould recalled. Although Gould's still-stiff art and nascent storytelling had plenty of rough energy and raw charm, "Dick Tracy"'s early success was likely due to the growing anti-crime climate and activism of the early 1930s.

The exploits of Baby Face Nelson, Pretty Boy Floyd, and Clyde Barrow had already shaken citizens who felt powerless and un-protected by local police. The final straw came on March 1, 1932, when the infant son of famed aviator Charles Lindbergh was kid-napped and later murdered. It was "the crime of the century" and the public demanded action at all levels against kidnappers, mur-derers, and gangsters.

From child to congressman, there was a sense that by the time Franklin D. Roosevelt took office in 1933 there had to be an all-out war on crime. The new president turned the Justice Department's tiny Bureau of Investi-gation into what he called "a super police force to check the growth of organized crime." John Edgar Hoover was made the head of this new government crime bureau, whose agents would fight racketeers and kidnap-pers. The Federal Bureau of Investigation soon became the symbol of the nation's battle with lawlessness. Government detectives and federal lawmen were the new heroes in the war on crime.

The popularity of the "Dick Tracy" strip, along with the emergence of the govern-ment agent as crime-fighter, provided the inspiration for another comic strip detective. In 1933, a one-issue comic magazine from the Humor Publishing Company of Chicago featured the exploits of *Detective Dan, Secret Operative 48*. A government agent who goes after counterfeiters, kidnappers, and Orien-tal masterminds, Detective Dan Dunn was created by Norman Marsh, another Chicago-area cartoonist. In September 1933, Marsh's suspiciously square-jawed detective returned in a daily comic strip called "Dan Dunn, Secret Operative 48." The strip was meant as competition for "Dick Tracy" ("an obvious copy," sniffed Chester Gould). As a secret detective, Dunn also worked with other gov-ernment operatives of various names and numbers.

In January 1934, another secret gov-ernment agent appeared in the comic strips. "Secret Agent X-9," written by famed mys-tery writer Dashiell Hammett and drawn by Alex Raymond for King Features Syndicate, was created as competition for Dick Tracy.

*Famous Funnies #13 © 1935 Publishers Syndicate.* Art by Norman Marsh.

*The Funnies #6 © 1937*
*Dell Publishing Co.*

Agent X-9 (who remained mysteriously nameless throughout the 1930s) was a sophisticated detective in the tradition of Hammett's Continental Op and the Thin Man. Hammett wrote the first four story episodes over a sixteen-month period before he left the strip over difficulties meeting deadlines. Rich in characterization and wisecracking banter, the comic strip was Hammett's last published detective work during his lifetime.

In March 1934, another comic strip detective joined Secret Agent X-9 at King Features. Sports cartoonist Will Gould (no relation to Chester) created "Red Barry," a redheaded undercover cop and hard-boiled wise guy. Borrowing from sources like the *Black Mask* pulp magazine (home of such mystery writers as Hammett and Carroll John

Daly) and the Warner Bros. gangster movies, Gould's Red Barry was touted to newspaper readers as a "two-fisted hero" who wages a "relentless war on the underworld."

During the month that "Red Barry" appeared, a real-life, relentless war on the underworld was in full swing. John Dillinger escaped from his escape-proof jail and began an interstate bank robbery spree which made him "public enemy number one." Melvin Purvis, the agent in charge of the FBI office in Chicago, led a raid against the Dillinger gang in April 1934 in which an agent was killed by Baby Face Nelson. In July 1934, Purvis and the FBI agents caught up with Dillinger and allegedly killed him in a blazing gun battle.

Rex Collier, a crime reporter who had gained the friendship of J. Edgar Hoover in Hoover's dealings with the press, wrote a series of magazine and newspaper articles in July 1934 about the FBI and its pursuit of John Dillinger. Collier used the Dillinger case to create an image of the FBI as fearless national heroes. Collier even popularized a name for Hoover's battling government agents. They were G-Men.

The public excitement generated by Hoover's crime-fighters was not lost on Chester Gould. By the end of 1934, Dick Tracy was called to Washington, D.C., and enlisted by the government as a G-Man. As a G-Man, Tracy could cross state lines in pursuit of such criminals as Boris Arson, Cutie Diamond, and "Cut" Famon—all loosely based on gangsters Baby Face Nelson, Pretty Boy Floyd, and Al "Scarface" Capone.

While Gould's "Dick Tracy" played to the public's fascination with the FBI's war on crime, it was a movie that made the G-Man a cultural icon. In April 1935, Warner Bros. studio announced it had made the "first great story of the men who waged America's war on crime." James Cagney, star of the 1933 movie *Public Enemy*, was now a crime-fighting hero in *The G-Men*, the story of the Justice Department's Bureau of Investigation. The movie was a tremendous success, and Cagney's portrayal of the honest and dedicated G-Man became the role model for dozens of radio, pulp magazine, and comic strip heroes.

In the fall of 1935, radio producer Phillips H. Lord produced the *G-Men* radio show with the help of J. Edgar Hoover and the FBI. The show lasted until the end of the year, when Lord grew tired of accommodating the FBI's demands for changes in story lines.

Two new pulp magazines, *G-Men* (October 1935) and *The Feds* (December 1935), also chronicled the real-life exploits of America's newest heroes in series like "The Famous Cases of J. Edgar Hoover." *G-Men* also ran a three-page comic strip feature called "Public Enemies," which grimly detailed the demise of such bad guys as Baby Face Nelson ("Sixteen bullets had perforated his legs and a seventeenth had pierced his stomach, spleen and liver! Finis . . . Baby Face").

Meanwhile, back in the comic strips, the Hearst newspaper chain offered the adventures of government agent Jimmie Crawford in *The G-Man*. Other syndicates whipped up their comic strip version of FBI agents as well. In 1936, Dick Blair and Milt Youngren created *G-Men on the Job,* which followed the daily activities of a government agent called Bill. The strip was a behind-the-scenes look at how the FBI used modern procedures to crack crime cases.

By early 1936, Secret Agent X-9 was also emerging as a bona fide FBI agent under the direction of a new artist and a new writer, Charles Flanders and Max Trell, respectively. Reporting to Washington, X-9 now got his assignments from "the Director," who was a not-too-subtle caricature of J. Edgar Hoover. The strip presented the FBI as merely the support staff for X-9's heroics, and the director followed the agent like a puppy dog. The real director of the FBI, J. Edgar Hoover, was not amused.

Hoover was an ardent reader of the comic strips and had written to Chester Gould, expressing his admiration for Dick Tracy's anticrime efforts. The FBI director was on record as believing that the comic strip detectives had a "highly important influence in creating a public distaste for crime" and that he derived "a keen inward satisfaction from seeing their flinty-jawed heroes prevail over evil."

With the outpouring of comic strip G-

Men by 1936, however, Hoover was concerned that the image of the FBI might be trivialized by such freelance operatives as Secret Agent X-9, Dan Dunn, and Jimmie Crawford, the G-Man. Hoover wanted the public to perceive his FBI as a well-organized team of crime-fighters who worked quietly together. There was no room in his organization for individual glory-grabbing. Hoover dismissed most of the movies, radio shows, pulp magazines, and comic strips about his G-Men as "boom-boom things that have no other purpose than to act as a thriller." He decided to fight fire with fire—or comic strips with comic strips.

In 1936, Hoover contacted Rex Collier, a journalist who was rewriting FBI-supplied stories for the media, to write a comic strip about his agency called "War on Crime."

*Famous Funnies #46*
*© 1936 Ledger Syndicate.*
Art by Kemp Starrett.

The Clock. *Funny Pages #8 © 1937 Comics Magazine Company.* Art by George Brenner.

The comic strip, it was emphasized, would not contain "lurid tales of a fictitious underworld but actual case histories." Hoover already had an artist for the strip, Kemp Starrett, and a distribution agreement with the Philadelphia Ledger Syndicate. Based on materials supplied by the Crime Records Division of the FBI, Collier developed the scripts for Hoover's proposed comic strip.

"War on Crime," which made its debut in May 1936, told the story of the "courageous men of the FBI—the G-Men" and their real-life battles with public enemies like Machine-Gun Kelly and John Dillinger. The comic strip was based on "actual case histories showing the actual people involved! Real names—real people—real places—real cases!" Hoover and FBI Associate Director Clyde Tolson reviewed every line of dialogue and

every drawing in the strip. Collier often had to rewrite scripts to satisfy Hoover's insistence on anonymity for the comic strip's field agents.

The nameless agents in the strip, however, could not compete with Dick Tracy, Secret Agent X-9, or the other more colorful and personable comic strip G-Men. The FBI's restrictions on portraying any individual agent as a hero made "War on Crime" somewhat lackluster, and it disappeared from the newspapers by the end of 1936.

There were still plenty of other comic strip G-Men, detectives, and crime-fighters by the mid-1930s. "Radio Patrol," which made its debut in April 1934, was the first adventure comic strip to star uniformed police officers. Sgt. Pat, his partner Stuttering Sam, and plainclothes policewoman Molly O'Day chase after pickpockets and shoplifters via radio patrol cars which allow them to talk back and forth while in hot pursuit—an exciting premise for the day.

Other cops-and-robbers strips of the 1930s included "Inspector Wade" by Lyman Anderson (loosely based on Edgar Wallace's Scotland Yard detective from the 1929 novel *The India Rubber Men*); "Jim Hardy" (a small-town reporter/detective) by Jim Moores; "Detective Riley" by Jack Kirby (under the name of Richard Lee); and "Be a Detective" by Bruce Patterson. Almost every American newspaper had one or more detective comic strips on its comic pages.

The growing popularity of all newspaper comic strips by the summer of 1934 prompted the publication of *Famous Funnies*, the first modern newsstand comic book. It consisted almost entirely of reprinted Sunday comic strips from popular features such as "Mutt and Jeff," "Tailspin Tommy," "Joe Palooka," and "Dixie Dugan." Norman Marsh's "Dan Dunn, Secret Operative 48" was added to the lineup of newspaper strip reprints with the February 1935 issue. Dick Tracy followed Dan Dunn into the comic books a year later in *Popular Comics* (February 1936), another reprint anthology of popular newspaper comic strips. Despite the fact that Gould never drew an original Dick Tracy story for the comic books, reprints of the newspaper strip adventures alone were enough to keep his detective constantly on the comic book racks for over twenty-five years.

Other early crime and detective newspaper comic strips soon found their way into the comic books. J. Edgar Hoover's "War on Crime" was reprinted in *Famous Funnies* (October 1936) just months after its newspaper debut. By 1936, however, comic books like *New Comics* and *More Fun Comics* were using new artists and writers to create original characters and stories.

The first detective series created especially for a comic book appeared in the January 1936 issue of *New Comics.* Jerry Siegel and Joe Shuster, who were trying, without success, to interest publishers in a character called Superman, came up with a comic book series about government detectives called "Federal Men," starring G-Man Steve Carson.

Siegel and Shuster had already developed one of the first G-Man comic strips, "Bruce Verne, G-Man of the Future," for a 1935 advertising supplement. For "Federal Men," Siegel and Shuster came up with a fan club in which G-Man Steve Carson urged young readers: "I want you and every other real American boy to join my Junior Federal Men's Club. Waste no time! Get your friends to enroll at once so we can drive terror into the heart of gangland!"

For the same publisher (which would later be known as DC Comics), Siegel and Shuster created another cops-and-robbers comic strip, "Calling All Cars" (*More Fun Comics,* July 1936). The series was retitled "Radio Squad" and turned over to other artists and writers after Siegel and Shuster became busy with Superman following his debut in *Action Comics* (June 1938).

The first masked crime-fighter in comic books was George Brenner's detective, The Clock. In the November 1936 issue of *Funny Pages,* Brian O'Brien, a former district attorney and part-time playboy, dons a blue tuxedo and a black silk mask to become The Clock. O'Brien chose his name because he wanted to remind crooks that their last few minutes of freedom were "ticking off." He also left calling cards behind after he made his captures, which read: "The Clock Has Struck." O'Brien was purposefully vague and

mysterious in his veiled role as The Clock, even hiding his motives from the police: "Perhaps I am the big bad wolf and then again I might be Little Red Riding Hood." Brenner's freelance crime-fighter was more in the tradition of pulp heroes like the Shadow and the Phantom Detective rather than Dick Tracy.

The Clock appeared in *Funny Pages* and *Funny Picture Stories* from Comics Magazine Company. In December 1936, the same publisher launched the first comic book to be devoted entirely to stories about detectives: *Detective Picture Stories.* The Clock, as well as a host of other gumshoes and detectives, appeared in "picture stories," which were lengthier than the typical two-to-four-page adventure comic story of the time.

The young artists who wrote and drew for *Detective Picture Stories* were, for the most part, just out of their teens. Will Eisner, Bob Kane, George Brenner, Bert Christman, Ed Moore, and other journeyman comic book artists brought forth efforts like "The Case of the 4 Haircuts," "Roadhouse Racket," "Murder in the Blue Room," and "The Case of the Missing Heir." Borrowing heavily from the pulp detective magazines, the detective comic book concentrated on "vivid action and gripping stories." Like nearly every comic book about crime and criminals which followed it, *Detective Picture Stories* promised that its stories would show readers why "crime does not pay."

A few months later, the first issue of *Detective Comics* (March 1937) offered "bang-up adventure yarns in thrilling pictures by your favorite artists!" The new title, planned in late 1936, had been delayed while its publisher Major Malcolm Wheeler-Nicholson scurried to find funding for his two other floundering titles, *More Fun Comics* and *New Adventure Comics.* After forming a partnership with pulp magazine publisher Harry Donenfeld, the major brought *Detective Comics* to the newsstands. A year later, Donenfeld would own the major's comic book company, under the name Detective Comics, Inc.

The first issue of *Detective Comics* featured a "tough private detective" (Slam Bradley); a "crack amateur sleuth" (Bruce

*Detective Picture Stories #3 © 1937 Comics Magazine Company.* Art by J. M. Wilcox.

*Detective Comics © 1937 DC Comics, Inc.* Art by Craig Flessel.

*Detective Comics #27*
© *1938 DC Comics, Inc.*
Art by Fred Guardineer.

had all the "slambang stuff which we knew would be in *Superman* if and when we got *Superman* launched."

*Detective Comics*, under the editorship of Vincent Sullivan, was the lead title of the young comic book company by early 1938. Sullivan asked his boyhood friend, Gardner Fox, to try his hand at writing a new series for the comic. Fox, a young lawyer at the time, came up with "Steve Malone, District Attorney" for the August 1938 issue.

Other comic book detectives and G-Men appeared from other publishers as the 1930s ended. "Tom Traylor, G-Man" began in *Crackajack Funnies* (June 1938) while "G-Man Jim" operated in *The Comics* (March 1937). The crime and detective radio shows of the 1930s also inspired adaptations for the comics. The 1936 *Gang Busters* radio show was turned into a comic book feature for *Popular Comics* (April 1939), and the crime-busting hero of the radio series *Mr. District Attorney* began his comic book career in *The Funnies* (September 1939).

The Crimson Avenger, a masked crime-fighter drawn initially by Jim Chambers, joined *Detective Comics* in 1938. The caped

Nelson); a "master of disguise" (Cosmo); an "ace investigator" (Speed Saunders); a secret service agent (Bart Regan—"Spy"); and even a "range detective" (Buck Marshall). The artists and writers, who included Jerry Siegel, Joe Shuster, Creig Flessel, Tom Hickey, and Major Wheeler-Nicholson himself, imbued these early detectives with qualities borrowed from pulp fiction heroes, popular movie stars, and animated cartoon characters.

Jerry Siegel and Joe Shuster supplied two features for *Detective Comics*: "Spy" and "Slam Bradley." Professing an admiration for the "super-strength and action" of the early Max Fleischer Popeye cartoons, they made Slam Bradley into another hard-punching and wisecracking hero. Bradley, according to Siegel, was a "dry run for Superman" and

The Crimson Avenger. *Detective Comics #27* © *1938 DC Comics, Inc.* Art by Jim Chambers.

detective (who was secretly Lee Travis, publisher of the *Daily Globe Leader*) was similar to the Green Hornet, a popular radio hero. Both masked men were newspaper publishers, maintained a secret identity, and had Oriental valets as confidants. A few months later, another costumed crime-fighter made his debut in the May 1939 issue of *Detective Comics*. Batman, later joined by Robin, soon became the title's star, and the older detectives were pushed into the background. Although there were dozens of secondary detective series in comic books by 1940, such as Jane Drake, Detective (*Crash Comics*), Dan Williams, Private Eye (*Exciting Comics*), and G-Man Dalton (*Startling Comics*), the costumed hero took center stage with the arrival of Batman.

The January 1940 issue of *Pep Comics* featured the debut of the Shield, a red-white-and-blue-uniformed superhero billed as the "G-Man Extraordinary." That year, more costumed comic book heroes were created than at any time in history. By 1941, the superhero was the dominant force in the comic book industry and costumed vigilantes had replaced plainclothes detectives. Comic book readers preferred their crime-fighters in colorful masks and capes, with secret identities and boy sidekicks. Detection took a backseat to action. Consequently, the early comic books never produced a detective hero comparable to Dick Tracy or Secret Agent X-9.

Crime fiction, however, is more than about the detective who solves the crime. It is also about the criminal and the crime. While the popular gangster movies of the early 1930s had already exploited the dark side of the genre, comic books had chosen to emphasize the heroics of the crime-fighter over the deviant behavior of the criminal.

By 1942, however, this was no longer true.

Gang Busters. *Popular Comics #54* © 1940 Phillips H. Lord, Inc.

# CRIME DOES TOO PAY

"**I** train a lot of murderers in my routine! I tempt them with a different bait—some with hatred, frustration, love, or the vain desire to be called a tough guy!"—Mr. Crime

Twelve million comic books a month were flying off the nation's newsstands in 1942. Two dozen publishers in the New York City area were turning out nearly 150 titles. Captain America, Wonder Woman, Plastic Man, and hundreds of newly created superheroes spilled forth from freshly built comic book racks. The American comic book, scarcely eight years old, spurted toward its heady adolescence.

With sixty-four pages to fill each issue and a monthly publishing schedule, artists and writers worked around the clock and over weekends to meet the deadline demands of the rapidly growing industry. Editors searched for new stories, artists, titles, and ideas. Sometimes their research extended after office hours into the restaurants and bars of midtown Manhattan.

Charles Biro, the managing editor at Comic House, Inc., bought another round of drinks for Bob Wood, his associate editor. The two men had spent the day putting together the first issue of *Boy Comics*, a comic book with all-boy heroes. Biro and Wood, cartoonists and writers in their own right, had created the lead feature for the title, a teenage superhero called Crimebuster.

The two men first worked together in 1937 at the Harry "A" Chesler comic book shop. Biro was writing and drawing humorous western stories for *Star Ranger Comics* while Wood was knocking out one-page cartoon features such as "It's Really A Fact!" for *Funny Pages* ("The largest elephant tusk ever recorded weighed 232 pounds while the average tusk weighs only 55 pounds").

Biro was tall, ruddy, friendly, extroverted, and a voracious reader. Wood was short, pale, quiet, introverted, and an inveterate gambler. The two cartoonists got along well together in the Chesler studio. In 1940, Biro wrote and drew Steel Sterling, the Black Hood, and other superheroes for MLJ Publications. Meanwhile, Wood was writing the adventures of the Firefly and the Comet for the same publisher.

In 1941, publisher Lev Gleason of Comic House hired the two men as an editorial team for *Daredevil Comics* and *Silver Streak Comics*. Described by a contemporary as "a liberal, almost left-wing, politically committed kind of guy who lived by his philosophy," Gleason was enough of a socialist to offer Biro and Wood a share in the enormous profits afforded by the new comic book industry. Gleason reportedly told his new editors, "If you turn these books into some-

---

Facing Page: *Crime Does Not Pay #52* © *1947 Comic House.* Art by Charles Biro.

thing worthwhile, you will get as rich as I do."

Taking Gleason's words to heart, the two young men in the bar that night were looking for inspiration for a new best-selling comic book. As they talked and drank, Biro told Wood about an earlier encounter in a midtown bar. He had been approached by a nervous man who appeared to be a pimp and who offered to take Biro upstairs to "visit" a woman in his room. Biro declined. The next day, Biro saw the picture of the man in the newspapers underneath the headline: "Police Nab Oleomargarine Heir in Kidnapping." Biro discovered that the woman offered to him was the victim who had been kept bound and gagged over the barroom.

Biro shook his head in amazement.

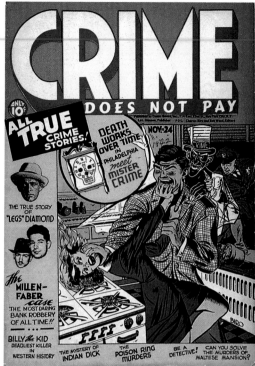

*Crime Does Not Pay #24 © 1942 Comic House.* Art by Charles Biro.

*Crime Does Not Pay #36 © 1944 Comic House.* Art by Charles Biro.

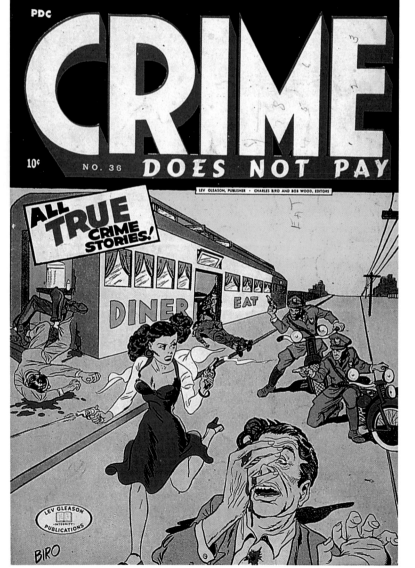

"Can you imagine a comic book about such weird doings—crimes and gangsters? You'd never run out of ideas for stories." Wood nodded vigorously and ordered another round. He reminded Biro that he had written and drawn a few crime features during their days at the Chesler studio, such as "Phoney Crime" and "How to Be an Amateur G-Man." So, why not do an entire comic book about criminals and bad guys?

"Crime," Biro told his partner, "has to be in the title."

The movie theaters in the Broadway area where the two men had their drinks ran newsreel documentaries along with the double features and cartoons. One of the most popular docudrama movie series at the time was Metro-Goldwyn-Mayer's highly successful *Crime Does Not Pay.* Begun in 1935, the short film series (one- and two-reelers) dealt with such topics as loan-sharking, shoplifting, slot-machine gambling, and the baby-barter racket. The series, endorsed by J. Edgar Hoover, won Academy Awards in 1936 and 1937. The two men already had their new comic book title lit up on the movie marquees.

"*Crime Does Not Pay*—I like it," Gleason

told his two editors. "We'll make it a continuation of *Silver Streak Comics*. Change the title and start it as No. 22 with the June issue."

The cover of the first issue of *Crime Does Not Pay* (June 1942) was packed with murder and mayhem in a bullet-shattered barroom. Real-life criminals, like "Killer" Lepke and the "Mad Dog" Esposito Brothers, peered out from photo mugshots down the side of the cover. The photographic reality of hardened criminals staring out from a comic book cover was highlighted by a blurb which promised that all the stories were "TRUE Crime Cases." It was a comic book based on real killers, desperate outlaws, and public enemies.

Like the true detective magazines of the 1930s, *Crime Does Not Pay* re-created stories of bizarre crimes and outrageous murders from newspaper, magazine, and historical accounts. The exploits of famous gangsters were adapted into comic book stories, and the early covers were edged with photographs of criminals like Pretty Boy Floyd, John Dillinger, Baby Face Nelson, and Legs Diamond. The comic book looked like a "true crime" magazine and it became popular with adults.

Thanks in part to the rapidly growing military audience, over one-third of the comic books sold in 1942 were read by adults. Biro and Wood hoped the graphic realism of *Crime Does Not Pay* would also attract the adult

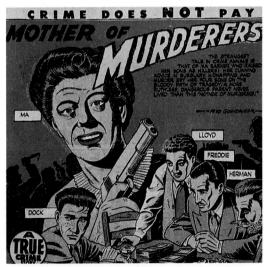

Ma Barker. *Crime Does Not Pay #49* © *1946 Comic House*. Art by Fred Guardineer.

Editors Charles Biro and Bob Wood appear in a comic book story. *Crime Does Not Pay #30* © *1943 Comic House*. Art by Dick Briefer.

readers of true detective magazines and hard-boiled pulp fiction. Billing itself as "The First Magazine of Its Kind," *Crime Does Not Pay* was the first comic book to target the adult audience. At the same time, however, its simply drawn stories of cartoon murderers and bad men were eagerly read by children.

Stories of brutality, sadism, and depravity could be published under the guise of moral docudramas ("Crime does not pay"). Since the crime stories were "all true," the violent lives of homicidal psychopaths could be excitingly detailed as long as they ended in punishment. It was like buying a ten-cent ticket to a public execution. Biro and Wood had created a cheap, bloody, and exciting comic book which lived up to its cover blurb: "The Magazine with the Widest Range of Appeal!"

The lead story in *Crime Does Not Pay* usually re-created the life of a famous gangster, such as John Dillinger, Baby Face Nelson, Machine-Gun Kelly, Pretty Boy Floyd, or Ma Barker. Among the dozens of other public enemies and mass murderers profiled in *Crime Does Not Pay* were Alvin Karpis, Wilbur Underhill, Joe Masseria, Two-Gun Crowley, and Vic Everhart ("The Kill-Crazy Scoundrel, who hated the law and proved it with every blast of his revolver!").

Many comic book biographies of the bad men began in childhood in order to show that the criminal was destined to be

# TRUE CRIME MAGAZINES

*Crime Does Not Pay* was a natural outgrowth from the true detective magazines of the 1930s and 1940s. Magazines devoted to true accounts of crimes and the apprehension of criminals were popular as early as 1845, when the *Police Gazette* was founded. The early stories on lynchings, murders, and civil riots were liberally illustrated with woodcut drawings. *The Illustrated Police News,* another nineteenth-century "true crime" magazine, loaded its pages with enough drawings (and later photo-

*True Detective Mysteries © 1930 Hillman Publications*

*Crime Detective © 1949 Hillman Publication*

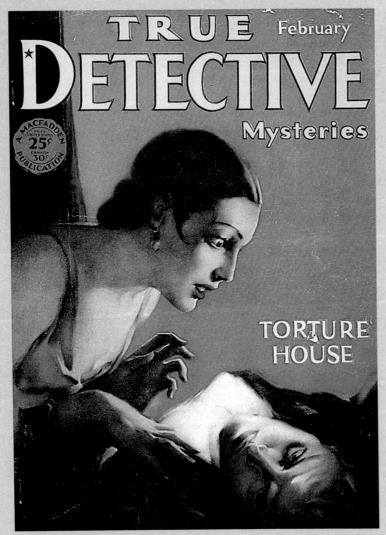

graphs) of murders to satisfy both the literate and illiterate.

With the use of more photographs in magazines during the 1920s, as well as the rising popularity of the detective hero in fiction, the "true crime" (or "true detective") magazine emerged as a distinctive newsstand genre. In 1924, *True Detective Mysteries* set the standard for photo-illustrated crime confessionals. It was followed by *Real Detective Tales* and then by dozens of more imitations all through the 1930s and early 1940s, such as *Inside Detective, Master Detective, Daring Detective, Famous Detective Cases, Official Detective, Crime Detective,* and *Front Page Detective.*

The lives and crimes of famous and nearly famous gangsters were often retold from the perspective of a law officer who was familiar with the case— ideally the arresting officer, but a country coroner would also do nicely (especially if he supplied photographs of the dead bodies). These true crime accounts, supplemented by police reports and press photos, were turned into stories by staff and freelance writers. For example, in the November 1934 issue of *The Master Detective,* the murderous exploits of Wilbur Underhill were related by Captain Thomas H. Jaycox ("Head of Identification and Records, Police Department, Wichita, Kansas") to Manly Wade Wellman, a science fiction and fantasy writer for *Weird Tales* magazine at the time. Wellman turned Jaycox's account into a story called "Hunting the Human Cougar of the Southwest." During the next decade, Wellman would turn his talents to writing comic books as well.

The "true detective" magazines led the way for crime comic books to fictionalize and glamorize the exploits of 1930s gangsters and bad men. Pretty Boy Floyd, John Dillinger, and Bonnie Parker and Clyde Barrow were the "stars" of dozens of recycled and rewritten true crime stories. The following excerpt from a story called "Capturing Ray Hamilton—Terror of the Southwest!" (*Inside Detective Magazine,* July 1935) was typical of the exploitive approach that would later show up in *Crime Does Not Pay* and other crime comic books of the 1940s:

> Slowly the white needle of the speedometer crept up from sixty to seventy. Ahead stretched the white ribbon of Texas road. Behind rushed another car, spitting fire. Outlaw Ray Hamilton, drunk with the excitement of the chase, gripped a sub-machine gun with one hand while with the other he gently caressed his sweetheart, Mary O'Dare.
>
> "Lay off the love-making Ray!" shouted Bonnie Parker, huddled in the front seat beside her companion in crime, Clyde Barrow. "They're gaining on us!"
>
> "Let 'em gain!" chortled Hamilton. "The closer they get the better chance I have of pluggin' 'em! Clyde, s'pose you slow up a bit."
>
> Bonnie Parker gasped at his audacity. Barrow crouched lower over the wheel and coaxed the machine to greater and still greater speed. The white needle moved to seventy-five . . . seventy-six . . . seventy-seven . . . No doubt about it, Clyde sure could handle a car.
>
> Forty miles back a deputy sheriff lay dying . . .

*Front Page Detective*
© *1939 Front Page Detective Publishing Co.*

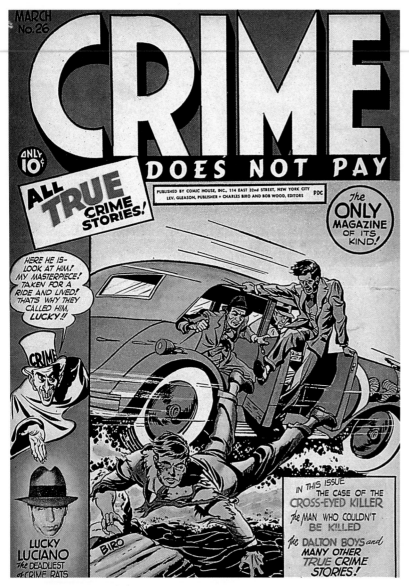

*Crime Does Not Pay #26 © 1943 Comic House.* Art by Charles Biro.

from the neighborhood drugstore. When he pretends to cry, the druggist drops the charges. The young punk thinks: "Gee, guess you can get away with anything if you know how!"

The failure to learn an early lesson—that crime does not pay—is the fatal character flaw in nearly every criminal. In the lead story from the May 1948 issue ("Felix Sloper—The Girl-Crazy Gunman"), the 13-year-old Felix threatens an elderly lady with a lead pipe: "Don't lie lady—I seen you change a big bill in the grocery store! Come across or you'll spend it on doctor bills!" When she screams for help, the young punk hits her in the head with a pipe: "Why don't you keep your big mouth shut? You think more of yer lousy dough than yer good health—you got it coming to ya!" After he is sent to reform school, only because he is too young for prison, he spits back: "Bunk! If I'd been older, I mighta' had a gun! Nobody woulda' come near me!"

Unrepentant and incapable of learning from their mistakes, the young criminals in *Crime Does Not Pay* begin their march to the gallows and grave by robbing candy stores,

*Crime Does Not Pay #26 © 1943 Comic House.* Art by Alan Mandel.

bad from birth. In "The Wild Spree of the Laughing Sadist—Herman Duker" (November 1947), the following scene takes place between the young killer-to-be and his boyhood friend: "What'cha bathin' the cat in *kerosene* for, Herman? Ain't ya gonna *drown* 'im like always?" Herman shakes his head as he pulls out a box of matches. "Naw, I got a better idea! Stick around, if you want to see somethin' hot! *Hee, hee!* A little light on the subject an' *zowie!* Look at that cat burn!" "MEEOWW!!"

In another story, a young boy starts his road to crime and ruination when he robs the purses of his mother's house guests: "Coast's clear! They're all busy guzzling coffee an' cake! Gives me a perfect chance at the pocketbooks!" A year later, he steals cash

*Crime Does Not Pay #53 © 1947 Comic House*

snatching purses, and extorting money from little kids: "Michael started like any average punk—first, lying and small thefts, then stickups! By the time he was twenty-one, he was bouncing in and out of the clink like a rubber ball—where he learned everything but how to go straight . . ."

The *Crime Does Not Pay* stories were careful not to blame a bad childhood environment as the cause for a criminal's future actions. Kids became juvenile delinquents and then hardened criminals because of a lack of character—not opportunity: "Chuck Danner was brought up in a slum environment and was always trying to act tough—but deep down inside, he was a frightened kid! But you can't blame his environment alone! If he had been any kind of man, he would have licked the poverty he was raised in . . ."

The emphasis on juvenile delinquency leading to a life of crime and punishment was part of the moral message which made *Crime Does Not Pay*, in the eyes of Biro and publisher Lev Gleason, "A Force for Good in the Community." On the other hand, young readers were probably secretly thrilled by stories which showed the boyhood exploits of tough gangsters. The juvenile delinquents in the stories may have voiced some young readers' own frustrations about growing up: "I hate school! Keep thinking of the money I can be getting while I waste my time learning stuff!"

By the third page of the lead story, the criminal is an adult and usually an alumnus of reform school or early prison term. He has not learned from his mistakes, however, and returns to a life of more desperate crime. He has a girlfriend or a gang and at least one murder under his belt. He grows cocky and believes that he can beat the law and escape punishment. Through pride, greed, stupidity, or misfortune, however, he is caught, killed, or punished. The last panel of the story, with the criminal dead or facing execution, reminds readers that "CRIME DOES NOT PAY!"

After the lead feature, which spotlighted a twentieth-century "big-name" criminal, *Crime Does Not Pay* sometimes reached back into history for its criminal sensationalism. The most outrageous crimes from the past 500 years were dredged up and retold in easy-to-read comic book stories. These historical accounts of infamous depravity were sometimes billed as "An Old Time TRUE Crime Story."

"The Case of the White-Eyed Butcher" (November 1944) begins: "In 1887 the white-eyed butcher of Boston began the most gruesome series of crimes that the state had ever known . . . mere words are far too weak to express such horror—but the facts speak for themselves." Jessie Pomeroy stalked the

*Crime Does Not Pay #58 © 1947 Comic House. Art by Fred Guardineer.*

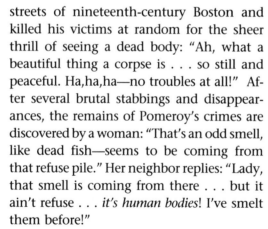

*Crime Does Not Pay #26*
*© 1943 Comic House*

*Crime Does Not Pay #24*
*© 1942 Comic House*

streets of nineteenth-century Boston and killed his victims at random for the sheer thrill of seeing a dead body: "Ah, what a beautiful thing a corpse is . . . so still and peaceful. Ha, ha, ha—no troubles at all!" After several brutal stabbings and disappearances, the remains of Pomeroy's crimes are discovered by a woman: "That's an odd smell, like dead fish—seems to be coming from that refuse pile." Her neighbor replies: "Lady, that smell is coming from there . . . but it ain't refuse . . . *it's human bodies*! I've smelt them before!"

The story unfolds in graphic detail until Pomeroy is captured ("Keep digging! From the smell we can't be far away . . . Ugh! A human arm!"). Although the last panel of the story shows the killer in prison, he expresses no guilt or remorse for his crimes: "Ha, ha . . . I'm on the side of right . . . those other fools are evil. They know I killed 38 people, but—ha, ha—what about those I didn't tell them about!"

The utter callousness of the crime was the primary qualification to be an "Old Time True Crime Story." The exploits of an 1880s Manhattan gang of mercenary killers (The Whyo Gang) were presented in a story called

"Cut Rate Murder" (January 1948). These nineteenth-century brigands advertised on their business cards that they would break an arm for $20, shoot someone in the leg for $25, or "do the big job (murder)" for $100. One gang member complains to his boss about a recent job: "I cut this dame's father into little pieces like she asked! But when I got to her hotel with the proof, they told me she'd checked out! There I was, left high and dry, with some cold fingers an' two ears!" Nonplussed, his boss replies: "Next time collect in advance."

Life and death were cheap in the resurrected crime tales from the nineteenth century. In "Yo-Ho-Ho and a Bottle of Blood" (November 1947), set in 1880, a captain sinks his ship and drowns his men for the insurance money: "Pull the plugs out—and hurry! We want to get off this rat trap before the crew knows what's happening!" In "Corpses for Sale" (November 1942), billed as "A True Crime Story of the Past Century," the murderous exploits of a pair who furnishes bodies (often still warm) to medical students are retold: "Never mind what happened to her. She's dead and I need a corpse. Here is your pay—good-night."

The old West of the nineteenth century also provided the writers and artists with the murderous exploits of Billy the Kid, Jesse James, and the Dalton Boys. Reaching back to the fourteenth century, *Crime Does Not Pay* acquainted readers with Francesco Ceni ("a monster of civilization so utterly ruthless that half a city trembled at his step") and the niceties of medieval homicide: "In those days it was the custom when committing murder to drive one nail through the victim's forehead and another through his throat."

With all the criminals and heinous crimes of history as grist for their comic book, editors Biro and Wood had no problem filling every issue. They soon discovered, however, that a comic book about true crime had a drawback. There could be no continuing characters since the criminal protagonists were either killed or imprisoned by the end of each story. Crime, after all, was not supposed to pay. Criminals could not escape and then return in the next issue.

What was needed was a narrator who could provide continuity and serve as a spokesperson for the comic book, much like the hosts of the mystery radio shows. By the November 1942 issue, they had a likely candidate:

"Ha—there you are! I see a question in your eyes! You wonder who I am! My name is on my hat—you can call me *Mr. Crime!!* Where do I come from? Everywhere and nowhere! I am everything that is bad and evil!! I am constantly on the lookout for new talent . . . say!!! You might be a good prospect for me—Naw, you're one of those honest, patriotic Americans! Now get comfy—dim the lights, draw the shades—for the tale I am about to tell is for your ears alone!"

Mr. Crime, with his vampire fangs and death's-head eyeballs, wore a top hat and carried a skull-crested walking cane. His spectral yet formal appearance made him look like a leering undertaker from hell. He was the Spirit of Crime—the patron "saint" of evildoers.

The ghostly Mr. Crime was the perfect narrator for Biro and Wood's true crime tales. Never seen or heard by the characters in the story, he usually appeared offstage as a sardonic commentator: "By any standards he

*Crime Does Not Pay #33* © *1944 Comic House.* Art by Charles Biro.

Mr. Crime. *Crime Does Not Pay #33* © *1944 Comic House.* Art by Rudy Palais.

was my number one boy—a vicious, heartless murderer, who was getting more so by the hour." He leaned over the shoulders of the criminals in the stories, like an evil conscience, and whispered in their ears: "Only one thing to do—shoot your way out! Kill him, kill him before it's too late!" Mr. Crime was an eager teacher searching for new pupils. "Just come along with me. I'll teach you everything you have to know! Yes, indeed, heh, heh!" He seduces the young and gullible ("Atta kid! Your mother's friend doesn't need money as much as you!") and encourages the desperate and dangerous ("Good! Good! Shoot some more of 'em! Make my old heart happy!").

Despite his unsavory appearance, Mr. Crime was also a moral sort who recognized

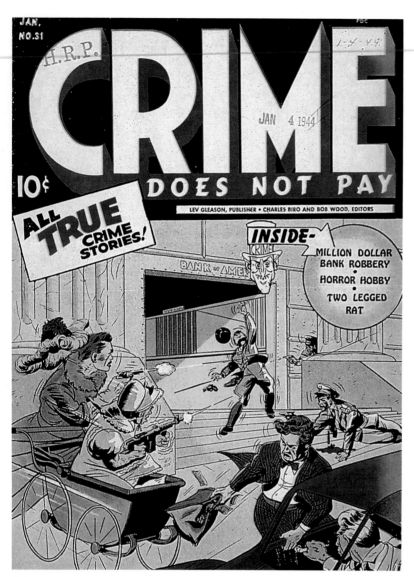

*Crime Does Not Pay #31*
© *1944 Comic House.*
Art by Charles Biro.

but whispered to his victims. When a man who drinks too much coffee expresses irritability over his neighbor's roaming chickens, Mr. Coffee Nerves hisses into his ear: "Why not settle this once and for all by wringing *his* neck right now!" With his handlebar moustache, top hat, and waistcoat, Mr. Coffee Nerves resembled the villain from a nineteenth-century melodrama ("Curses! I'm licked! Postum and I can't mix!"). The character was the product of newspaper strip artists Noel Sickels and Milt Caniff, who drew under the name of Paul Arthur.

In addition to the lead story narrated by Mr. Crime, another early feature was the "Who Did It Mystery" (soon shortened to "Who Dunnit?"). This solve-it-yourself mystery feature presented the clues to a crime and then challenged the readers to figure out the solution before the end of the story:

"Right now, if you have keen observation—very keen—you would see one clue that would tell you who killed Rodney Stark. But, this is not the end of the story! If you know the killer, congratulations! But hold on to your comic book and see the weird, startling, smashing finish of this tale!"

The solution to "whodunnit" was given

the futility of the lifestyle he endorsed: "So you're waiting to hear another story about one of my pupils—and you're thinking maybe this time it'll have a new twist—yeah, I know—all my stories have the same ending—the moral they teach is inescapable—you can't lick the law! Make sure you don't make my acquaintance! First my pupils start lying! Then stealing . . . and finally they all reach the same end—a horrible death!"

Mr. Crime was actually a reworking of a 1930s Sunday advertising comic strip character called Mr. Coffee Nerves, who appeared on behalf of Postum coffee substitute. Instead of would-be criminals, Mr. Coffee Nerves preyed upon middle class housewives and husbands who suffered from caffeine-induced jitters. Like Mr. Crime, he was an evil spectral figure who remained unseen

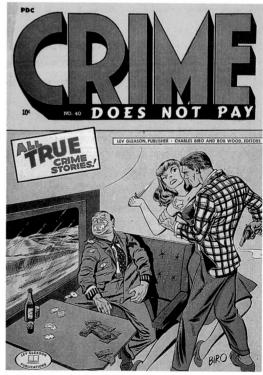

*Crime Does Not Pay #40* © *1945 Comic House.* Art by Charles Biro.

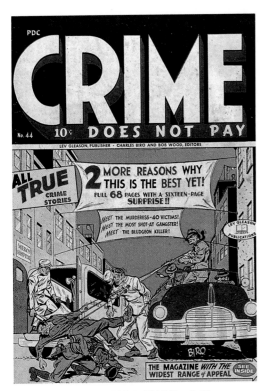

Crime Does Not Pay #44 © 1946 Comic House.
Art by Charles Biro.

on the last page: "Ruth sneaked into Rodney's study, stabbed him in the back. The clue she left was three pearls from her necklace. But what she really stabbed was a *dummy* that Rodney used in his fake daredevil scenes! Rodney took it out of the closet, sat it in the chair, and went to the garage. When he returned, he found the knife in the dummy, suspected it was meant for him. He went to the boathouse, called for Shaw, told him to conduct the seance. Rodney walked in on the group, appearing as his ghost, said he knew his murderer. Hysterical, Ruth dashed herself through the window to her death. Thus we close the story of the murder that was not a murder."

In late 1945, Biro and Wood began a readers' letters column called "What's On Your Mind?" Judging from the letters received, readers mostly had crime on their minds—at least until they read *Crime Does Not Pay*:

"I have a girlfriend who thought a life of crime would be profitable and exciting. One day she read a copy of *Crime Does Not Pay* and now she tells me that a life of crime is usually a short one as you can't win against

the law. Please, for her sake and others, don't ever stop publishing your wonderful, educational magazine."

Another letter stated: "I am a boy, thirteen years old. Until I read your book *Crime Does Not Pay*, I used to admire some criminals. But now that I have read all the facts in your swell magazine I have a different attitude toward them. Thanks for straightening me out."

One reader wrote: "A year and a half ago, I needed a brain operation and didn't have enough for it. I then foolishly decided that the one way I could get the necessary funds was to go into crime. I have your magazine to thank for my change of mind."

Not only did *Crime Does Not Pay* warn kids away from crime (as well as those in need of brain operations), it also prevented recidivism by hardened criminals: "I recently was released from the State Penitentiary. While I was there I had plenty of time to think of a 'job' to pull when I got out. While I was waiting for the day of the holdup, I read your magazine *Crime Does Not Pay*. I decided to play it straight. The others called me yellow but when they read your book, they agreed with me and we called the whole thing off. From now on it's the straight and narrow for me."

A boy confesses to Biro and Wood that "a nun caught me reading *Crime Does Not Pay* in the study hall of my school. She took it from me. Later on she returned it to me and said that this was one book she wouldn't mind having the boys and girls read. I asked her why. She replied, 'It is forceful in helping the young Americans of today in their future.' Thank you for publishing *Crime Does Not Pay*."

Almost every letter printed—from parents, police officers, and teachers—lavishly praised the comic book for its role in crime prevention. The letter column was Biro and Wood's way of deflecting criticism against the violence in a medium avidly read by children. The fact that each letter printed earned its writer two dollars might have inspired some testimonials.

Still, not every reader of *Crime Does Not Pay* took its moral message to heart. An August 1947 Atlanta, Georgia, newspaper story

Crime Does Not Pay #46
© 1946 Comic House.
Art by Charles Biro.

*Crime Does Not Pay #53 © 1947 Comic House.* Art by Charles Biro.

Biro introduced readers to the horrors of crime by drawing the front cover of every issue of *Crime Does Not Pay* during its first seven years. Biro knew that the front cover was the most important part in selling a comic book on the crowded 1940s newsstands. His background as cartoonist in the Chesler studio honed his talents for exaggeration and caricature, and his covers for *Crime Does Not Pay* carried an impact like no other comic book of the mid-1940s.

Some of the early *Crime Does Not Pay* covers were silent tableaus of cold brutality, like a bloody box surreptitiously dumped into a river, or a gagged and beaten corpse shoved from a speeding car. Later covers were often wordy psychodramas of human cruelty: "What'sa matter, Luciano. Don't ya like the kinda' medicine we dish out to squealers? We oughtta' punch a couple holes in ya mouth an' put a padlock through it!' "Don't Corky—don't give me the mark of the squealer! I swear I didn't squeal! May my mother drop dead if I did!" "What for? Yer old lady didn't do the yappin'? Hold 'im steady! I want a nice scar on that greasy cheek!"

Many of Biro's covers captured the terrifying moment *before* a brutality occurred—

reported that two men were recently imprisoned for writing extortion letters to a woman and threatening to blow up her house if she did not pay them $2,000. The men claimed that they had gotten the idea after reading an issue of *Crime Does Not Pay*.

Sensitive to charges about violence in a comic book that could be bought by children (and evidently, amoral imbeciles), Biro and Wood defended *Crime Does Not Pay* as early as the November 1943 issue in which they appear as characters in a "Who Dunnit" story. In their office, Wood asks Biro as they put together the latest issue: "Do you think this crime story is too bloody and gory, Charlie?" Biro replies: "It's bloody all right, but it's true! That's the important thing. We want our readers to see all the horror of the crooked path of crime!"

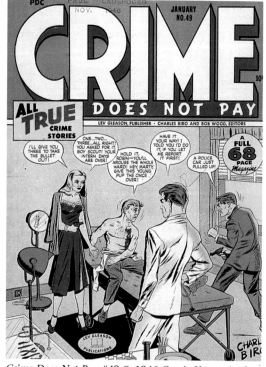

*Crime Does Not Pay #49 © 1946 Comic House.* Art by Charles Biro.

Crime Does Not Pay #57 © 1947 Comic House. Art by Fred Guardineer.

the final foreplay before the inevitable kidnapping, stabbing, or cement burial. At other times, Biro froze the moment of murder by painstakingly drawing the bloody red trail of the bullet as it entered and exited the body.

While Biro did not have time to draw interior stories for *Crime Does Not Pay*, his co-editor Bob Wood wrote and drew for the early issues. For awhile, however, the chief writer for the comic was Wood's brother Dick. He had been hired by Biro in late 1941 to write scripts for *Daredevil Comics* and *Boy Comics* on such series as Little Dynamite, Young Robin Hood, and Bombshell (a hero he helped create). Dick Wood's writing career eventually spanned over thirty years for a half dozen comic book companies. Both Bob and Dick were described by a colleague as "wild semi-literates who could bring a certain crude excitement to their stories." Dick Wood dished out brutal and bloody tales and his brother Bob drew them in his broad and cartoony style.

In a March 1943 story drawn by Bob Wood called "Death Gives a Lesson," a hillbilly couple (who look like characters from "Li'l Abner") methodically murder all the children in a family. The murder story was drawn almost like an animated cartoon, which made the violence all the more unsettling by contrast. For example, one scene shows the wife approaching a sleeping baby in its bassinet: "Bring me the copper hammer, John! Quickly while the other children

are out playing!" The next panel shows the woman bringing the hammer down on the baby's skull. The man and wife then lure the two older children in for cake so she can hammer in their heads as well.

Wood used other artists for *Crime Does Not Pay* who also had a cartoony style, such as Dick Briefer, who would later draw *Frankenstein* as a comedy feature, and Dick Hall, who would leave crime comics to draw Andy Panda and Woody Woodpecker for Dell Comics. Some of the murderers looked like slapstick comedians, especially when they laughed maniacally as they killed their victims.

Although not strictly cartoony, other artists who drew for *Crime Does Not Pay* during the early years had a similar exaggerated

*Crime Does Not Pay* #34 © 1944 Comic House. Art by Rudy Palais.

*Crime Does Not Pay #54 © 1947 Comic House. Art by George Tuska.*

since 1937, when he worked on "Speed Saunders, Ace Investigator" for the early issues of *Detective Comics*. An avid sportsman and hunter, Guardineer was thoroughly familiar with rifles and weapons and was one of the best "gun men" in comics. For *Crime Does Not Pay*, he accentuated and highlighted his characters so sharply and in such bold detail that you could actually see the brilliantine shining off the hair of a freshly coiffured gangster. Guardineer drew memorable faces, from steamy gun molls to pin-headed punks, and he was chosen for stories in which it was important to closely differentiate between the characters (such as in the "Who Dunnit?" series).

During the postwar years, the cartoony art in *Crime Does Not Pay* was phased out in favor of more realistic styles better suited for "true" crime stories. Biro also began writing more lead stories for *Crime Does Not Pay*, and his scripts were well-constructed, with a good balance of action and plot. Biro eschewed

*Crime Does Not Pay #62 © 1948 Comic House. Art by George Tuska.*

style. Artists like Jack Alderman, Al Mandel, and Bob Q. Siege could all effect an ugly manner well suited for tales about criminal degenerates. Rudy Palais delighted in filling his tortuously distorted panels with curling smoke that swirled from the cigarettes and gun barrels of sweating maniacs. His bad women were lanky, long-haired kittens who wore slinky gowns which barely restrained impossible breasts. A story by Palais was filled with rowdy people, tawdry surroundings, and an ever-present haze of alcoholic perspiration and cheap perfume.

Fred Guardineer, who had worked with Biro and Wood since the 1930s in the Harry "A" Chesler studio, was brought on board in 1945 and drew a story for nearly every issue until 1952. Guardineer had drawn stories of murder and mystery for the comic books

*Crime Does Not Pay #60*
*© 1948 Comic House.*
Art by George Tuska.

captions and preferred to let the dialogue carry the story. His characters talked—and talked and talked. While Biro's scripts were often wordy by comic book standards, they were also rich in color and characterization.

During the late 1940s, Biro began relying on artists like George Tuska, Bob Fujitani, and Dan Barry to portray the hard-edged and realistic violence that he wanted his stories to have. Tuska was one of Biro's favorites to illustrate his stories during the late 1940s, and it was his version of Mr. Crime which remains the most memorable.

Biro's background in both writing and art made him a knowledgeable and demanding editor when it came to working with his artists. Artist Alex Toth recalled that "Dan Barry and Biro were two monumental egos, clashing like thunderheads. Biro would reject something in Barry's artwork using black grease-pencil to mark his notations on the original art, or cross something out. Brutal.

And childish. But Barry did great work for Biro."

Biro was intent on crafting the postwar *Crime Does Not Pay* into the best-selling title of its kind. Alex Toth recalled that "Biro had all kinds of taboos, dos and don'ts. He hit me with things like, 'I don't want to see blacks (silhouetted figures). Blacks is cheating. Forget it. I want to see everything. I want people to *look* at each other when they're talking.' Everyone worked with nice, clean lines."

Biro's conscientious packaging of *Crime Does Not Pay* paid off. The first few issues in 1942 sold a little over 200,000 copies per issue. From 1943 to 1946, sales shot from 300,000 to over 800,000 copies. By 1948, sales were averaging nearly a million copies a month. In five years, *Crime Does Not Pay* went from a comic book that had been misshelved and lost among the true detective magazines to becoming one of the best-selling newsstand publications of all time.

# COMICS MAKE A KILLING

**W**ith the end of World War II, the American comic book industry was readjusting to the new opportunities of peace time. No longer limited by wartime paper allotments and shortages, both established and first-time comic book publishers launched new titles as artists and writers returned from the service.

By the end of 1946, the comic book industry was poised for its most rapid growth since before the war.

The only problem was that superhero characters, the impetus for much of the comic book's early growth, were sliding in popularity. No major costumed comic book hero had been introduced since 1942. The circulation of *Captain Marvel Adventures*, one of the most popular superhero comics of all time, peaked in 1944 and had been declining every year. The exodus of hundreds of superheroes from the comic books, which began in 1945 with the disappearance of Dr. Fate, the Hangman, and Steel Sterling, was nearly completed by the end of the 1940s. With the patriotism and heroism of the war years over, comic books were abandoning superheroes. Publishers looked at each other's best-selling comics and tried to discern the new postwar trends.

In late 1946, publisher Lev Gleason and editor Charles Biro ran a banner across the front cover of the March 1947 issue of *Crime Does Not Pay*, which made the incredible boast: "More than 5,000,000 Readers

Monthly." Given that the most popular comic books sold barely more than a million copies, Gleason was inflating his figures on the basis of surveys which showed that each issue of *Crime Does Not Pay* was read by several readers. Within a few months, Gleason had upped the cover blurb to over 6,000,000 regular readers. As far as the other comic book publishers were concerned, it was time to drop the heroics and turn to crime.

Beginning in 1947, crime comics became one of the best-selling genres of all time. During the next seven years, more than forty comic book publishers (nearly everyone in the industry) issued over 150 new crime comic titles. While the success of *Crime Does Not Pay* sparked the outpouring of similar titles, the wave of crime comic books was also a response to a postwar appetite for hard-edged and realistic popular entertainment. Crime and gangster movies, for example, made a comeback with films like *The Killers* (1946) and *Dillinger* (1945), which were done in a documentary true-crime style.

The crime comics also came to promi-

---

Facing Page: *Murderous Gangsters #4* © *1952 Realistic Comics.* Art by Everett Raymond Kinstler.

*Headline Comics #30 © 1948 Headline Publications.* Art by Joe Simon and Jack Kirby.

*Clue Comics,* which featured such minor costumed characters as Micro-Face and Iron Lady.

Simon and Kirby suggested that Cronin replace his superheroes with comic stories that would appeal to the new audience of ex-GIs and older readers—guys like themselves. To fill the need, Simon and Kirby created a crime story ("King of the Bank Robbers") for *Clue Comics* (March 1947). Cronin liked the approach so much that Simon and Kirby filled the next several issues of *Clue* with real crime stories like "Gang Doctor," "Case of the Superstitious Slayers," and "The Dummies Died Screaming." Besides comic books, Hillman Publications also published magazines, including a "true detective" title called *Crime Detective,* which had been around before the war. Cronin had little difficulty convincing the Hillman publishers to turn *Clue Comics* into an all-crime comic book called *Real Clue Crime Comics* (June 1947). A year later, Cronin launched a second crime comic book, *Crime Detective* (March 1948).

Simon and Kirby had also formed a partnership with the publishers of Prize Comics to package a new line of comics. Just as they had done with *Clue Comics,* the two men created a crime story for Prize's *Headline Comics* (March 1947), a title which had previously housed such superheroes as Atomic Man and Blue Streak. Their first crime story for Prize ("To My Valentine"), about the St. Valentine's Day Massacre, was touted as the

nence after American servicemen (nearly half of whom had been regular comic book readers) returned to civilian life. Older and no longer fascinated by the fantasies of patriotic superheroes, these ex-GIs were looking for a more mature type of comic book.

Jack Kirby and Joe Simon, two ex-GIs who not only read comic books but drew them as well, were looking for a job and a place to live in 1946. Before entering the service, Simon and Kirby had produced two of the most popular comic books of the war years, *Captain America* and the *Boy Commandos.* Now, the famous art team was struggling with other returning comic book artists to re-establish themselves in the comic book marketplace. In late 1946, Simon and Kirby called upon Ed Cronin at the office of Hillman Comics. Cronin was the editor of

*Real Clue Crime Stories Vol 2 #7 © 1947 Hillman Periodicals.* Art by Joe Simon and Jack Kirby.

Headline Comics #30 © 1948 Headline Publications.
Art by Joe Simon and Jack Kirby.

"first of a series of gun-blasting true stories—tales of guns, bullets, and thugs . . . When Crime Was King!" With its switch to true crime stories, *Headline Comics* gradually moved toward a circulation of a million copies.

The Simon and Kirby crime stories had an earnest realism to them, and for good reason. Jack Kirby grew up in an impoverished Bronx neighborhood during the Roaring Twenties. "There were gangs all over the place," Kirby recalled. "Gangsters were looked up to and feared. I'd see them in restaurants, and they'd hold all these conferences. They weren't the stereotypes you see in the movies. I knew the real ones, and the real ones were out for big money."

Joe Simon broke into the New York publishing field in 1937 when he landed a job drawing spot illustrations for the Macfadden line of magazines, which included *True Detective Mysteries*. Simon recalled that his "choice assignments" were the half-page illustrations for the "true detective" magazines, where he worked from photographs of professional models to capture the slick realism the editors demanded. His early true crime pen and ink illustrations prepared

Simon for his crime comic work a decade later.

Early Simon and Kirby crime stories, such as "I Was an Unwitting Accomplice to a Numbers Racket Combine!" (*Headline Comics*, June 1948), were sometimes told in a confessional style: "I considered myself extremely fortunate to escape that nightmarish experience with a shoulder wound from Curly's gun."

With *Headline Comics* under way and their studio in full force, Simon and Kirby created a new crime title for Prize Comics: *Justice Traps the Guilty* (October 1947). Joe Simon recalled that the first issue was a sellout, probably because the front cover showed a murderer being strapped into the electric

*Justice Traps the Guilty #2 © 1948 Headline Publications.* Art by Joe Simon and Jack Kirby.

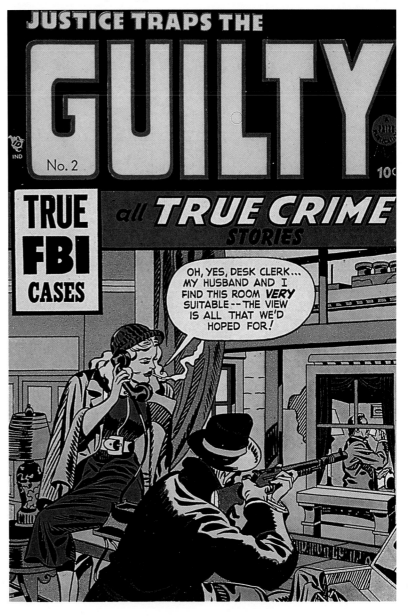

*True Crime Comics #2 © 1947 Magazine Village. Art by Jack Cole.*

the writing and artwork, he tapped his friend Alex Kotzky, who had assisted him on Plastic Man.

Before creating Plastic Man for *Police Comics* in 1941, Cole had drawn two crime series: "Manhunters" for *Top-Notch Comics* (December 1939) and "Crime on the Run" for *Blue Ribbon Comics* (November 1939). Around this time, the young artist was also drawing suitably brutal illustrations for *True Detective Magazine*. Cole was perfectly qualified to dish out stories of cartoon depravity and ultra-violence for *True Crime Comics*. Full of speeding cars, punctured bodies, slatternly women, hypodermic needles, and gratuitous torture, Cole's stories in *True Crime Comics* later became a favorite target for critics of crime comics.

Rae Herman, publisher, editor, and occasional writer of a line of teenage and humor comics from Orbit Publications, entered the crime comic book field with *Wanted Comics* (September 1947). Like Gleason's successful *Crime Does Not Pay*, Herman made *Wanted Comics* a true crime comic with stories "based on actual police files." She also copied the Mr. Crime character from *Crime Does Not Pay* to use as the host for *Wanted*. Dressed in top hat and funerary cape, the

chair. The comic, which professed to be based on "true FBI cases," eventually outlasted nearly every other 1940s crime comic book, including *Crime Does Not Pay*.

With the paper restrictions removed after the war, other publishers entered the crime comic book field. Magazine Village, which operated from the same office building as Lev Gleason's *Crime Does Not Pay*, began its career with *True Crime Comics* (May 1947). The publisher hired writer/editor/artist Jack Cole to package the title. Cole, best remembered as the creator of Plastic Man, had a reputation as a "wild mind" who filled his comic book stories with frenetic excitement and exaggerated action. To help with

*Wanted Comics #10 © 1947 Orbit Publishing. Art by Mort Leav.*

*Official True Crime Cases #24 © 1947 Marvel Entertainment Group. Art by Syd Shores.*

*Justice Comics #8 © 1948 Marvel Entertainment Group*

crime host for *Wanted Comics* acted somewhat like Mr. Crime, but he was actually Satan himself: "Most people are a great disappointment for me," he confides as he sits beside blazing brimstone. "No spirit. No guts. They abide by the law. They avoid trouble. They work hard. They live at peace with other people—it's enough to turn your stomach!"

As an added gimmick, Herman ran a "wanted" poster with a cartoon profile of a dangerous criminal on the cover of *Wanted Comics*. If you were lucky enough to identify a public enemy on the street from the comic book cover, you got a $100 reward. William Woolfolk, one of the most prolific comic book writers of the 1940s, recalled that for Rae Herman's *Wanted Comics*, "I was her chief and almost only writer. I worked for her because it was so easy since there was no editor there. There was no a*nything*. I could do anything I chose." Woolfolk later parlayed his comic book crime-writing skills into successful suspense novels (*The Naked Hunter*) and television series (*The Defenders; Arrest and Trial*).

When Marvel Comics publisher Martin Goodman saw the first issues of *True Crime Comics* and *Justice Traps the Guilty*, he smelled a trend. Besides comic books, Goodman was also publishing a line of magazines, including true detective titles such as *10 True Crime Cases*. He already knew the newsstand market for true crime publications was increasing, and the appearance of the new crime comics solidified his decision. In 1947, he temporarily suspended publication of *Sub-Mariner Comics*, one of his major superhero titles, and replaced it with *Official True Crime Cases* (Fall 1947). He also canceled *Wacky Duck* in favor of another crime title, *Justice Comics* (Fall 1947). Goodman's style was to ride a comic book trend and saturate the newsstands with similar titles. In 1948, Marvel Comics added *Crimefighters* (April 1948), *Crime Exposed* (April 1948), and *Lawbreakers Always Lose* (Spring 1948). By the end of 1949, Marvel published more crime comics than any other competitor. Carl Wessler, who scripted over 700 stories for Marvel Comics from 1945 to 1957, wrote many of the crime stories, sometimes from a

*Justice Comics #8*
*© 1948 Marvel*
*Entertainment Group*

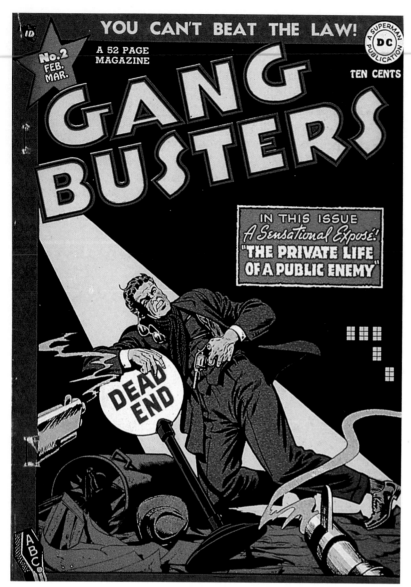

*Gang Busters #2 © 1948*
*DC Comics*

comic book, described as "punch-packed case-histories of men who tried to beat the law and of the lawmen who beat them to the final draw," ran several regular features, such as "Federal Agent," "A Perfect Crime Mystery," and "Special Crime Feature."

DC's second crime comic, *Mr. District Attorney*, was also a well-liked radio program (1939–53) that was later adapted as a 1951 television series. Its lead character, District Attorney Paul Garrett, was based on real-life crimebuster Thomas E. Dewey, who later became the governor of New York and a two-time presidential candidate. Both radio shows had previously been adapted for the comic books by Dell Publishing Company, another publisher careful with its reputation for producing wholesome comics. By adapting respected radio shows such as *Gang Busters*, *Mr. District Attorney*, and later, *Big Town* (January 1950) into comic books, DC Comics was able to attract fans familiar with the crime programs.

By late 1947, over a half dozen crime comics had sprung up to give *Crime Does Not Pay* competition. Publisher Lev Gleason and editor Charles Biro decided to alert readers to the proliferation of imitations with a page in

title suggested by editor Stan Lee.

In late 1947, DC Comics, the publisher of Superman and Batman, decided to enter the growing crime comic field. A prospering and somewhat conservative company, DC Comics was leery of the exploitive and sensationalistic approach used in *Crime Does Not Pay* and other true-crime comics. Instead, DC secured the rights to publish comic books based on the two most popular radio crime series at the time: *Gang Busters* (December 1947) and *Mr. District Attorney* (January 1948).

The *Gang Busters* radio show, created by producer Phillips H. Lord in 1936 as a spin-off from his *G-Men* radio series, ran for 22 years and inspired a short-lived but extremely popular NBC-TV series in 1952. The

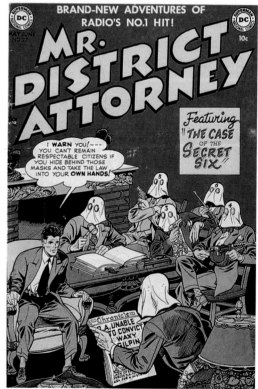

*Mr. District Attorney #27 © 1952 DC Comics, Inc.*

*Crime Does Not Pay* that spoofed the recent crime comics by giving them made-up titles like *Crime Doesn't Pay Enough, Crime Dares Not Pay, Crime Will Not Pay, Of Course Crime Doesn't Pay, Crime Ain't Payin' Off Lately, True Blue Crime Comics, Crime Never Wins,* and *Crime Just Can't Win*. (Ironically, Marvel Comics would actually release a comic three years later called *Crime Can't Win*).

Meanwhile, Gleason was preparing to jump on his own bandwagon. Under the editorship of Charles Biro and Bob Wood, he launched *Crime and Punishment* (April 1948) as a companion title to *Crime Does Not Pay.* The title followed the same successful format as *Crime Does Not Pay,* with its re-creation of "true criminal case histories." Instead of Mr. Crime, however, the host and narrator for *Crime and Punishment* was Officer Common Sense, a disembodied police officer (killed in the line of duty) who moralized over the cartoon lives of murderers and criminals: "Yes, I'm a dead cop, but I'm alive to the menace of the criminal. I know a million cases, and every one proves the futility of jealousy, greed, and hate—the ingredients of crime. I will reveal each terrible story before your astonished eyes! If everyone believes me, perhaps there will be no need for cops to die one day!"

Biro attempted to make *Crime and Punishment* stand out from the competition as a more literate and mature publication. By the end of 1948, he coined a new term to describe comic books, "Illustories," and he used it as the new subtitle for *Crime and Punishment.* This new medium of "illustories," Biro explained to readers, "now takes its place alongside the theater, movies, radio and television. It is not unlike the dramatic arts; its contact is both visual and literary. This new visual journalism is as American as hot-dogs and chewing gum. It is a development of our times, the beginning of a trend."

Biro was certainly correct when he termed it the beginning of a trend. Besides *Crime and Punishment,* there were over thirty more crime comics launched in 1948, including *Law Against Crime, Crime Reporter, Criminals on the Run, Guns Against Gangsters, Authentic Police Cases,* and *Crime Must Pay the Penalty.*

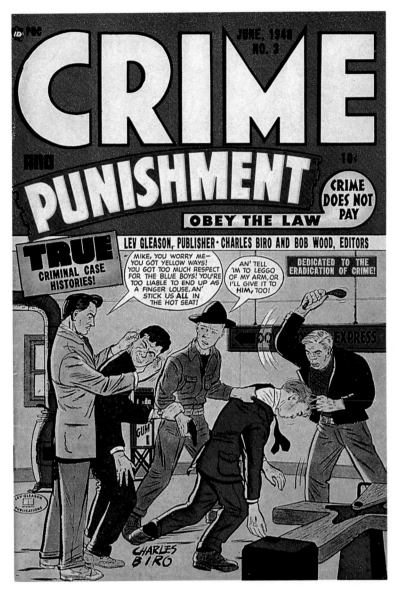

*Crime and Punishment #3 © 1948 Comic House. Art by Charles Biro.*

One publisher who entered the crime comic market in 1948 in a big way was Victor Fox, who began his publishing career in 1939 with an early imitation of Superman called Wonder Man. Promptly sued by the publishers of Superman, Fox returned with another line of costumed heroes. In 1948, Fox brought out the first titles of his future crime comic empire: *Murder, Incorporated* (January 1948), *Famous Crimes* (June 1948), and the infamous *Crimes by Women* (June 1948).

In an attempt to juice up the sales, Fox cynically stuck three words on the front cover of *Murder, Incorporated*: "For Adults Only." Until then, no comic book dared hint that its stories were not suitable for children; after all, there were no restrictions on selling comic

*Murder Incorporated #4*
*© 1948 Fox Features*
*Syndicate*

were a lot of one-shot artists who passed through his offices. Writers like Ken Fitch, who wrote true crime stories for several publishers, worked for Fox only when there were no other markets. Fox was so notorious, he was satirized in a story by the publishers of *Mad* comics as "Victor Wolf," whose company's motto was "Wolf Comics Makes 'Em Howl!" The Wolf line of comics contained such titles as *Crimes by Criminals* and *Crimes by Dogs* (a not so subtle dig at Fox's ultimate exploitive title, *Crimes by Women*).

Another publisher who entered the crime comic market in 1948 was Richard Davis of D. S. Publishing. Davis was a one-man crime wave who issued seven titles in seven months: *Gangsters Can't Win* (February 1948), *Underworld* (February 1948), *Exposed* (March 1948), *Public Enemies* (June 1948), *Pay-Off* (July 1948), *Whodunit* (August 1948), and *Select Detective* (August 1948). The comics from D. S. Publishing were uniformly well produced, with above-average lettering, coloring, and artwork. By the summer of 1948, Davis had published more crime comics than any other publisher, but he disbanded his company the following year.

Another modest-size publisher who saw possible fortunes in the 1947–48 crime comic boom was William Gaines, who had just inherited his father's funnybook business, Educational Comics (EC). The company consisted of kiddie comic books and wholesome fare like *Picture Stories from the Bible* and *Picture Stories from American History*. Gaines didn't know much about comics yet, but he knew that crime comics were selling better than bible stories. The company had already

books to minors. Readers, both young and old, who were looking for a little violence and sex on the newsstand could pick up a copy of *Murder Incorporated* and probably not be disappointed.

Fox's crime comics reflected his own publishing practices: cheap, mean spirited, and exploitive. There were plenty of senseless murders on every page. Criminals murdered helpless victims for pocket change, a tank of gas, or the chance to spit on their bodies. Bad women (and there were no other kind) tucked pistols in their stocking garters and wore brassieres pumped up like tractor tires.

The stories were often crudely drawn because Fox had a habit of not paying his artists unless threatened. As a result, there

*Crimes By Women #2 © 1948 Fox Features Syndicate*

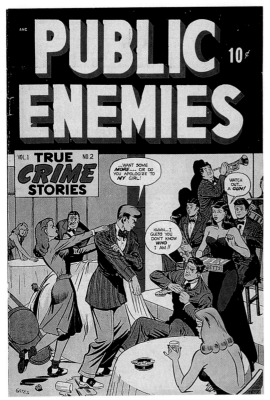

*Public Enemies #2 © 1948 D.S. Publishing Co.* Art by Art Gates.

*War Against Crime #7 © 1949 William M. Gaines.* Art by Johnny Craig.

*Crimes By Women #2 © 1948 Fox Features Syndicate*

and *Crime Patrol, Crime Suspenstories* was not about bank robbers, kidnappers, or famous gangsters. Instead, the stories usually took place in a domestic setting and were filled with jealous lovers, spurned spouses, and plotting business partners—in short, anyone who wanted to end a lousy relationship and make a few bucks off the insurance policy.

Like a James M. Cain novel or *film noir* movie, *Crime Suspenstories* existed in a peculiar moral vacuum where the perpetrator of the crime was rarely caught but often punished. As editor and writer Al Feldstein pointed out, "There was a kind of underlying morality. The formula was somebody had to get his just desserts, and whether he was a practical joker or a guy who screwed his partner, or who screwed his partner's wife, everyone had to get punished."

published an issue of *Blackstone the Magician Detective Fights Crime* (Fall 1947) under the Entertaining Comics (EC) imprint. For the spring of 1948, Gaines and his editor Al Feldstein launched *War Against Crime* and *International Crime Patrol* (which later became *Crime Patrol*).

Like *Crime Does Not Pay* and other early crime comics, the stories in *War Against Crime* and *Crime Patrol* were trumpeted as "true," or "real stories from police records." At the end of 1949, Feldstein and Gaines introduced EC's first horror comic stories in the two crime comics. By the beginning of 1950, Gaines turned *War Against Crime* and *Crime Patrol* into full-fledged horror comics with new titles: *Crypt of Terror* and *Vault of Horror.* Later that year, however, Gaines considered canceling *Vault* in favor of another crime comic. He finally decided to keep *Vault of Horror,* but he also came out with a new type of crime comic: *Crime Suspenstories* (October 1950).

With *Crime Suspenstories,* Gaines and Feldstein moved crime off the streets and into the bedroom. Unlike most crime comics, including the earlier *War Against Crime*

It wasn't the law or the justice system, however, that meted out punishment in *Crime Suspenstories*. Often it was the murderer's own "cleverness" or greed which was the final undoing. For example, in the story "Touch and Go" (*Crime Suspenstories*, June 1953), a murderer becomes so obsessed with erasing every possible fingerprint, he carefully polishes each object in the house of his victim over and over again—doorknobs, chandeliers, baseboards, even the soles of the victim's shoes. His intense paranoia causes a mental breakdown, and the police discover him wiping and rewiping nonexistent fingerprints.

To illustrate *Crime Suspenstories*, Gaines and Feldstein relied upon artists who had a

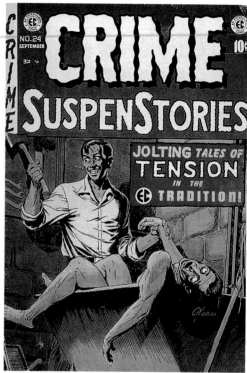

*Crime Suspenstories #24 © 1954 William M. Gaines. Art by George Evans.*

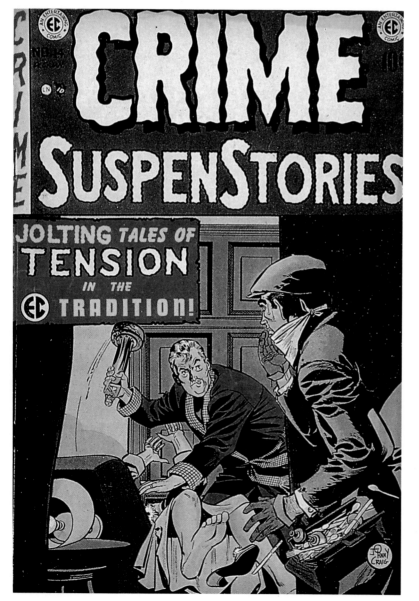

*Crime Suspenstories #14 © 1952 William M. Gaines. Art by Johnny Craig.*

clean and realistic style well suited for crime stories, including Reed Crandall, Jack Kamen, Bill Elder, and George Evans. EC's premier crime artist was Johnny Craig, who drew a story for nearly every issue of *Crime Patrol*, *War Against Crime*, and *Crime Suspenstories*, as well as the majority of their covers.

Craig's meticulous attention to detail, lighting, and natural composition yielded a realistic style of storytelling perfect for the crime comic genre. He was a slow and methodical worker ("I was supposed to do at least three stories a month. I was lucky if I did one") and he often wrote the stories he illustrated. "Since I had never been fortunate enough to have any extensive formal art school training," he recalled, "I was forced at a very early age to learn drawing by continually searching for flaws in my own work and then drawing it again and again to correct those flaws. I look upon each drawing as something to learn from and I work slowly so that I may search for knowledge as well as mistakes."

Craig began his work in comics in 1940 as a fourteen-year-old assistant to Harry Lampert, the artist for the Flash. While assisting Lampert, Craig met Max Gaines, publisher of the All-American Comics line. After the war, Craig worked in the art department for Gaines's new company, Educational Comics. Around the time that William Gaines took over the company from his father, Craig was beginning to freelance for other publishers, including Gleason of *Crime Does Not Pay* fame. When Gaines and his editor Al Feldstein decided to launch two crime titles in 1948, Craig was a natural and nearby choice.

Unlike most of the other EC artists, Craig often wrote the stories he illustrated. Most of the stories in *Crime Suspenstories*, however, were plotted by Gaines and Feldstein and subsequently scripted by Feldstein. Near the end of its run, other writers contributed scripts, including Otto Binder, Jack Oleck, and Carl Wessler.

From 1948 to 1949, roughly one out of every seven comic books sold was a crime title. Over 160,000,000 crime comics were bought by adults and children during those two years. Allowing for the industry average of four or more readers per copy, more than one *billion* crime comic books were read and reread in the United States from 1948 to 1950. By the end of 1950, over one hundred different crime comic titles had appeared on the newsstands. The majority of these crime comics were remarkably similar in their method and approach: They were often adult, usually sexy, always violent, and, as many of them claimed, sometimes even true.

*Crime Suspenstories #18 © 1953 William M. Gaines.*
Art by Johnny Craig.

*War Against Crime #7 © 1949 William M. Gaines.* Art by Johnny Craig.

# REALLY, TRULY BLOODY

Francis "Two-Gun" Crowley was holed up in a 90th Street apartment in New York City. He was a cop-killer who had finally been trapped. He hated all police officers with a passion and right now he had three hundred of them to use as targets.

Running from window to window, "Two-Gun" shot it out with the majority of the New York City police department as 15,000 spectators watched from the buildings and streets below. He wore two guns on his hips and two more strapped on his calves. He wasn't planning on leaving alive. As the police rushed the apartment building, "Two-Gun" snarled out a line he had learned from the movies: "Come and get me, coppers!"

This scene, which made national headlines in 1932, was brought back to life in a 1948 comic book, *War Against Crime*. The real-life exploits of criminals like "Two-Gun" Crowley and others provided ready-made stories for the dozens of crime comic books that flourished from 1947 to 1954.

Comic book writers resurrected infamous criminals and peppered their stories with "true crime facts" (dates, names, and locales) to capture a sense of hard realism. The crime comics, unlike the previously popular costumed superhero comics, were real stories about real people. *Justice Comics* promised its readers that "every case is taken from real life." *War Against Crime* featured "real stories from police records." *Trapped Comics* offered "true stories of real police records." *Justice Traps the Guilty* and *Headline Comics* insisted their stories were "adapted from TRUE Police and FBI Cases."

Some comic book stories were indeed based on materials supplied by the Crime Records Division of the FBI, which routinely fulfilled media requests for case histories. As early as 1936, the *War on Crime* comic strip, (the first "true" crime comic) was "based on the records of the Federal Bureau of Investigation—modified in the public interest."

The tabloids of New York City provided the raw material for the crime comic writers of the 1940s, as did the "true detective" magazines and the popular biographies of prohibition-era gangsters. The true-crime exploits of these murderers and robbers, which had also been made into movies, pulp magazines, and radio shows, were recycled as comic book stories. Occasionally, even the comic books themselves were the source material for writers working for other companies. After all, editors could hardly complain about similarities in stories based on truth.

Not all the crime comic books, how-

*True Crime Comics
Vol. 2 #1 © 1949
Magazine Village*

people's notice, a cover of *True Crime Comics* (September 1949) planted a seed of doubt in sharp-eyed readers' minds about the credibility of most true crime comics. The comic's front cover showed a photograph of a hand-cuffed and defiant criminal accompanied by a giant blurb: "This is a REAL PHOTOGRAPH of a criminal at bay! The sensational story of Phil Coppolla, the most vicious criminal in Massachusetts's crime history! See page 3 . . ." Next to the photograph of the vicious criminal, however, is a tiny line of type: "Character posed by professional model." So much for real photographs of real criminals.

Using a photograph on the front cover to make a crime comic seem "real" or "true" was first done by *Famous Funnies* (October 1936), with the first reprints of the "War On Crime" newspaper comic strip. The early issues of *Crime Does Not Pay* in 1942–43 ran black-and-white mugshots of famous criminals along the edges of its covers. Pretty Boy Floyd's face graced the front cover of the 1948 comic book *On the Spot*.

Beginning in 1949, several crime comics replaced the artwork on their front covers with a color photograph of a crime scene. As

ever, were strictly "true crime," although their titles might lead you to believe otherwise. *All-True Crime Cases*, for example, carried the disclaimer that "All names and places in these true-to-life stories are fictitious. Any similarity between actual persons or places and those used in these stories is purely coincidental." *Authentic Police Cases* had a circumspect waiver: "Although stories in this magazine are true stories, all names of persons and places are fictitious." Hillman's *Real Clue Crime Stories* took the diplomatic approach: "To avoid offending innocent parties or relatives, some names used in this magazine are fictitious, and are substituted for the real names of these otherwise true characters."

While these small disclaimers inside the crime comic book probably escaped most

*On the Spot #1 © 1948 Fawcett Publications*

*Crime Does Not Pay #46 © 1946 Comic House. Art by Bob Q. Siege.*

a result, front covers of crime comics like *Justice Traps the Guilty* (October 1949) and *All-True Crime* (September 1949) looked like the true detective magazines of the day. The crime comic book photo covers were generally supplied by the same agencies that furnished the photographs of professional models for the true detective magazines. For a couple of issues of *Headline Comics* and *Justice Traps the Guilty*, however, artists Jack Kirby and Joe Simon dressed up like cops and robbers and posed for the covers. By the end of 1950, the novelty of photo covers wore off and the half dozen crime comics that had used them changed back to traditional comic book cover art.

Besides photographs, crime comics also ran nonfiction features like "Science and the Criminal," "Crime Quiz," and most-wanted criminal lists, to add an element of reality. *Wanted Comics*, for example, furnished one-page descriptions of recently escaped murderers and parole breakers with cartoon mugshots and bounty-hunter information ("If located, notify State Prison, Raiford, Florida"). The editors even broke into a December 1952 story to give readers the latest in real-world crime events: "FLASH! As this issue of *Wanted* magazine was going to press, we received word that Leslie Stallings, last survivor of the bloody prison break at Death Row, was executed on June 10, 1952! The fate of Stallings and his companions in crime is one more proof that . . . CRIME CANNOT WIN!"

There were several reasons why crime comic books emphasized that their stories were "true" (even in cases where they were not). First, there was a huge audience familiar with big-time gangsters from newspaper and magazine stories. Notorious bad men like John Dillinger and Pretty Boy Floyd were almost better known than any U.S. president. The potential market for true crime comic books, with their stories of famous gangsters, was enormous.

The true crime comics also gave read-

*Artist Jack Kirby poses as a robber while his partner Joe Simon is "the long arm of the law." Headline Comics #37 © 1949 Headline Publications*

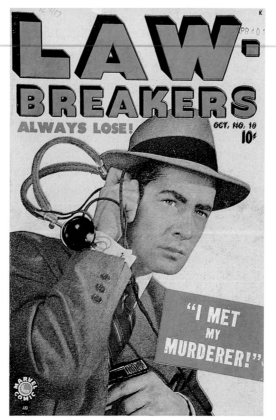

*Lawbreakers Always Lose! #10 © 1949 Marvel Entertainment Group*

*All-True Crime #37 © 1950 Marvel Entertainment Group*

ers a vicarious thrill of horror, violence, and retribution. Witnessing a true crime comic book murder based on fact seemed more exciting than some made-up killing. Real people were committing real crimes—spilling real blood. As *Justice Comics* put it: "It's thrilling because it's true!"

Another advantage true crime comics afforded writers and editors was that stories of depravity and sadism could be presented in the name of journalistic entertainment. Sure it's disgusting, but don't blame us. We didn't make this sickening stuff up—it's just the facts. Such was the case with "The Woman Who Wouldn't Die!" (*Crime Does Not Pay*, June 1947), a "true crime story" of two brothers who are cold-blooded murderers:

A cold February dusk was falling as Mr. and Mrs. Clifford Smith arrived at their farm near Ft. Collins, Colorado . . ."

"That's funny," Viola Smith tells her husband as they drive up, "There's no lights on . . . and

little Bobby said he'd watch the house for us!"

"I think something's wrong," her husband replies. "You stay here in the car while I look around."

As her husband enters the house, Mrs. Smith hears shooting. She runs to see what's wrong, but her way is blocked by two men whom she recognizes as migrant farm workers who had once worked for them:

"Dat's right, Miz Smith," says one of the men who points a pistol at her, "when we work for you couple months ago, my brudder an' me see you got lots of money so we come back now to take it! We shoot leetle boy! We shoot your husban'. . . now we shoot you!"

The two men force the woman to kneel and then shoot her in the back with both a rifle and a pistol. Thinking she is dead, they drag her into the house, drench her clothes with kerosene, toss a match on her soaked body, and sit back to watch her burn. The burning woman, however, is still alive but grits her teeth to keep from screaming and giving herself away.

After the two men leave their human barbecue, the woman drags herself across the floor and beats out the flames. She stumbles over the butchered bodies of her husband and little boy in their pools of blood and escapes to a neighbor's farm.

*Crime Does Not Pay #52 © 1947 Comic House*

A posse captures the two killers and we learn that "the Pacheco brothers were the second and third persons to die in Colorado's lethal gas chamber! Once more justice had triumphed—this time through the astounding will-power of a courageous woman! *Crime Does Not Pay*!" Perhaps not, but it sure provided a few moments of gruesome entertainment for true crime comic readers.

Entertainment and drama had to coexist with the facts in a true crime comic story, and writers sometimes had to play fast and loose with the truth to create a more enjoyable fiction. For example, in one comic book story about Los Angeles gangster "Bugsie" [sic] Siegel (*Colossal Features Magazine*, September 1950), the mobster is murdered in a violent fight over his partner's girlfriend. In reality, his death was quietly engineered by the mob, after he defied their authority during the construction of the Flamingo Hotel in Las Vegas. Still, the flamboyant comic book version of a spurned lover played better: "You outsmarted yourself Bugsie! While you were out joy-riding my girl around, I was here . . . Now here's yours!" Bang-Blam! "Agghh!"

The comic book lives of real-life criminals were often changed to make for a more satisfying ending, as was the case with Wilbur Underhill. Called the "Tri-State Terror" for his dozens of bank robberies carried out in Oklahoma, Kansas, and Arkansas in the late 1920s and early 1930s, Underhill was infamous for breaking out of prisons and gunning down anyone who got in his way. After a bank-robbing spree in the fall of 1933, Underhill married his childhood sweetheart and hid out in Shawnee, Oklahoma. On New Year's Day 1934, federal agents surrounded the couple's cottage and fired more than a thousand rounds of ammunition at Underhill, who fired back with a shotgun as he dashed from window to window in his underwear. Hit a dozen times, Underhill escaped the police cordon and ran into town. After crashing through a plate-glass window in a furniture store, he collapsed. Five days later, he died in a hospital.

Underhill's life of crime was the subject of at least four comic book stories, including "Killing Was His Business" (*All-True Crime*,

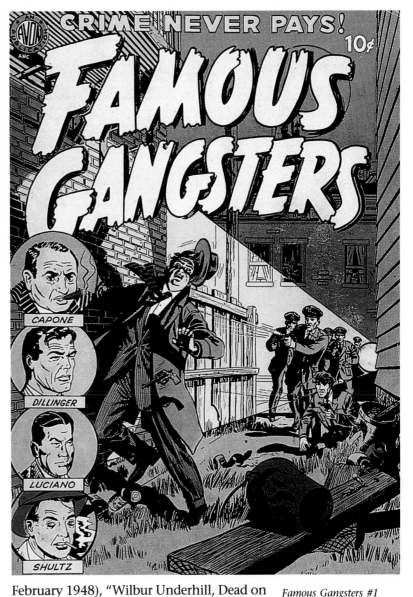

*Famous Gangsters #1*
© 1951 Avon Periodicals

February 1948), "Wilbur Underhill, Dead on Arrival" (*March of Crime*, September 1950), "Death of a Menace" (*Headline Comics*, September 1949), and the charmingly personal "I Broke Out of Oklahoma and Kansas State Pens, What's Different about This Dump?" (*Crime Does Not Pay*, May 1948). The four stories all claimed various degrees of accuracy, including actual dates and locales, and the climax of each story was Underhill's blazing New Year's Day gun battle. All the comic book stories ended with Underhill dying inside the furniture store at the feet of the policemen instead of later in a hospital room. Having Underhill die in a bed under medical attention was not a desirable end for stories that showed the bitterness of crime's evil fruit.

In another attempt to lessen sympathy

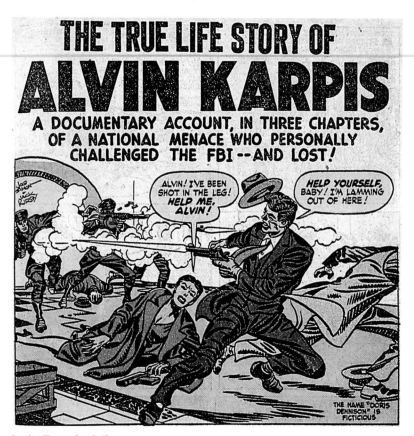

*Justice Traps the Guilty #2 © 1948 Headline Publications.* Art by Joe Simon and Jack Kirby.

for Underhill, none of the stories mentions his wife or the fact that the couple were on their honeymoon when law enforcement agents opened fire. Instead, in three of the stories, Underhill is shown hiding out with his gang when gunfire breaks out. In the fourth story, Underhill is portrayed as a loner who loves only his gun ("Sweetheart, you and I are going places!").

Criminals in the crime comics were usually cowardly and lacking in loyalty to even their fellow gang members. They were almost always cold-blooded killers. If for some reason the real-life criminal did not have all the requisite character flaws, he was ascribed those flaws in the comic book through invented scenes of betrayal, deceit, and gratuitous murders.

On the other hand, lawmen and G-Men were usually portrayed as fearless and self-sacrificing. For example, in "The True Life Story of Alvin Karpis" (*Justice Traps the Guilty*, January 1948), FBI chief J. Edgar Hoover was on hand to personally arrest Karpis, who was making headlines as public enemy number one. In the comic book story

by Joe Simon and Jack Kirby, Hoover disregards danger and pursues Karpis on foot until he finally knocks Karpis down with a roundhouse punch to the jaw: CRACK! "What's the hurry, Karpis? We had a date, remember?" In reality, however, Hoover hid behind a building until Karpis was subdued by other agents, and then made his well-publicized arrest.

Another case in which history was rewritten occurred in *Wanted Comics* (September 1950). The story "He Was Born to Hang" was about robber and murderer Thomas (Terrible Tommy) O'Connor, the last man to be sentenced to death by hanging in Illinois in 1921. The real-life O'Connor, however, escaped just days before he was to go to the gallows by overpowering three prison guards, scaling a twenty-foot wall, and commandeering three automobiles. He made good on a daring escape and was never seen again.

In the comic book, however, O'Connor jumps through a county jail window but becomes entangled in a clothesline. As he struggles to escape, the rope wraps around his neck and he strangles to death. "Look at that," says a policeman, "he hanged himself! He couldn't escape his sentence after all! Let's cut him down! The law wins another round!"

If the criminals were captured alive in a true crime comic story, they were expected to show remorse for their crimes or perhaps

*War Against Crime #2 © 1948 William M. Gaines.* Art by Lee Ames.

exhibit a streak of cowardice when faced with punishment and execution. Having the tough guy turn yellow at the end was one way to dispel the notion that crime comics promoted criminal bravado.

For example, in an adaptation of the life of Francis "Two-Gun" Crowley (*Crime Does Not Pay*, July 1946), the comic ends with a frightened Crowley strapped into the electric chair: "I don't want to die—not yet— I'm too young for that! Please, please—don't kill me! Please don't!"

In reality, Crowley was a publicity-hungry braggart and an unrepentant troublemaker all the time he was on death row. When he was finally strapped into the electric chair (after he insisted it be dusted off first), he loudly cursed the reporters and flicked his cigar butt into their faces.

Comic books were not the first to fictionalize the lives of famous badmen and real-life criminals in the name of entertainment. The movies, in particular, glamorized gangsters such as Al Capone in *Scarface* (1932) and *The Roaring Twenties* (1940). In 1945, however, the release of *Dillinger,* with Lawrence Tierney's cold-blooded portrayal of public enemy John Dillinger, caused a minor sensation and backlash in the film industry against the exploitive gangster movie.

In 1947, the Motion Picture Producers and Directors Association refused its MPAA Code Seal to a screenplay based on Westbrook Pegler's biography of Al Capone. A section was added to the MPAA Production Code, which read: "No picture shall be approved dealing with the life of a notorious criminal of current or recent times which uses the name, nickname or alias of such notorious criminal in the film, nor shall a picture be approved if based on the life of such notorious criminal unless the character shown in the film be punished for crimes shown in the film committed by him." After Dillinger (1945), no real-life criminals were portrayed in the movies until *Baby Face Nelson* (1957). The crime comic book of the late 1940s and early 1950s became the only visual medium to dramatize the lives of the following "notorious criminals" and hundreds of others:

*Famous Gangsters #1*
© 1951 Avon Periodicals

## GEORGE "MACHINE-GUN" KELLY

George R. Kelly was born in 1897 in Tennessee. By the mid-1920s, he was known in Memphis as a "society bootlegger" who dipped generously into his own wares. Running from local lawmen, Kelly moved his operations to New Mexico in 1925, where he was convicted and sentenced to three months in prison for bootlegging. Over the next six years, he peddled illegal liquor to small-town druggists in New Mexico, Oklahoma, and Texas. During Prohibition, Kelly liked to impersonate a tough-talking mobster, although he never carried a gun or hurt anyone in his penny-ante dealings.

His wife-to-be, Kathryn Shannon, however, had big plans for her husband. She told him he had to be tough so he could get respect from people. To help him out, she got him a machine gun. Kelly practiced blasting walnuts off fence posts at the Shannon Ranch in Texas until he became quite a marksman. Kathryn picked up the spent

HERE WAS A WOMAN, WHO CONCEIVED VICIOUS BANK ROBBERIES AND RUTHLESS, BRUTAL KIDNAPPINGS, WHICH SHE FORCED THROUGH TO A CONCLUSION, LARGELY THROUGH DOMINATION OF HER HUSBAND, WHO, IN SPITE OF HIS TERRORIZING NAME, WOULD ONLY BOW TO HER FURY! IF EVER THERE WAS A HENPECKED MAN, IT WAS GEORGE "MACHINE GUN" KELLY!

*Crime Does Not Pay #65*
*© 1948 Comic House*

machine gun cartridges and gave them to her underworld friends as souvenirs of "Machine-Gun" Kelly.

After Kelly was released from Leavenworth Federal Penitentiary in 1931 (where he had served a year for driving a truckload of whiskey onto an Indian reservation), he married Kathryn, who had been busy planning his future career as a bank robber. He brushed up with the machine gun and she got him a job with a gang who knocked off crackerbox banks in Tupelo, Mississippi, and Wilmer, Texas.

Determined to hit the big time, Kelly and his wife planned the kidnapping of a millionaire Oklahoma oilman in 1933. After collecting $200,000 ransom (in marked bills), the Kellys ran from the FBI until they were cornered in a Memphis flophouse. According to popular media reports, Kelly cowered before the FBI agent and pleaded: "Don't shoot G-Man!" (which, incidentally, began the popularizing of the term "G-Man"). In reality, Kelly made no resistance to his arrest and simply said with a smile: "I've been waiting for you."

"Machine-Gun" Kelly appeared in the June 1936 newspaper comic strip, "War on Crime." Since the comic strip was reviewed by FBI director J. Edgar Hoover, this account of the Kelly story (with emphasis on the kidnapping and FBI capture) was essentially true, although self-serving.

Kelly's story was told again in the July 1949 issue of *Murder Incorporated*, but with plenty of embellishments: "Machine-Gun Kelly was the swivel-hipped machine-gun-

ner who could toss hot, spitting lead in a wide arc . . . cutting down those who stood in the way of his climb to the top of the criminal heap. He was a ruthless killer when it served his pleasure . . ."

The comic book story tells us that "George Kelly was the sheriff of a small town . . . Lucher, Oklahoma." After this amazing rewrite of history, the comic tells us that Kelly began his descent into crime by posing as a masked bank robber who held up the banks he was hired to protect. After his arrest and exposure, Kelly enters the army to atone for his crimes and receives his training as a machine gunner: "In combat, Kelly earned the name of Machine-Gun Kelly and a reputation for merciless killing!!"

After his discharge, Kelly meets his future wife "Katherine," who is portrayed as an innocent waitress who knows nothing of Kelly's sordid past. When he is captured for bank robbery and sentenced to twenty years in Leavenworth, she tells her husband: "I'm your wife. I'll stick by you. If you go back into crime . . . I'll go with you. I'll wait for you."

In a continuing disregard for facts, the comic book Kelly pulls a daring jail break from prison and coldly tosses his hostage out of a speeding car. The kidnapping episode is next, and the FBI pursuit of Kelly and his wife ends with their surrender ("All right . . . all right . . . G-Man, don't shoot . . . I'll drop it!!!").

The June 1954 issue of *All-True Detective Cases* presented another account of Machine-Gun Kelly that was a little closer to the truth. The story opened with: "Kathy wanted George to be somebody! With her goading him on, his name became a blood-red synonym for murder! They don't call him George any longer . . . they knew him as . . . MACHINE-GUN KELLY!"

His wife was portrayed as the brains behind Kelly's bank robberies ("Get yourself a machine gun, darling! You can hit anything with your eyes closed!"). The comic also revealed that Kelly's mother-in-law was the "cold, ruthless" mastermind behind the famous kidnapping caper ("What could be better than to pull a snatch of say a rich oil man!"). For a dash of sex and violence, the comic book story also introduced the sub-plot of a jealous boyfriend named Bugsy Kiefer whom Kelly murders in a barroom. As the story ends with their capture, Kelly's wife tells him that they "should have bumped off" the kidnap victim so he couldn't have testified against them.

In these two comic book versions, Kelly was portrayed as a cold-blooded killer who represented a serious threat to society. In reality, no murder was ever attributed to him and he went quietly to prison—reportedly happy to be free of his domineering wife.

The July 1948 *Crime Does Not Pay* version of Machine-Gun Kelly was probably the most accurate comic book portrayal. His wife Kathy was shown to be the driving force behind his life of crime, buying him the machine gun and saving the spent cartridges as his calling card. During Kelly's bank-robbing spree, the comic showed him killing three police officers ("Will one of you guys keep count? I'd like Kathy to hear it from your lips how many bluecoats I'm poppin' off!"). In reality, Kelly was loath to fire his gun at anybody and preferred nonviolence whenever possible. The story ended with Kelly's shrewish wife trying to betray him to the police in order to save her own neck. As he is hauled away to court ("shaking all over"), he suffers the final indignity when a boy makes fun of him: "Look guys, there goes *Pop-Gun* Kelly! Hah, ha!"

*Crime Does Not Pay* #52
© 1947 Comic House.
Art by George Tuska.

## GEORGE "BABY FACE" NELSON

Lester Gillis, a short (5'4") graduate of the 1920s Chicago street gangs, wanted recognition any way he could get it, as a punk crook or public enemy. He adopted the name of "Big George Nelson" to get respect, but the media dubbed him "Baby Face," a name he hated. He robbed small-town banks in Iowa, Nebraska, and Wisconsin until he was able to worm his way into the John Dillinger gang in 1934. Unlike the methodical Dillinger, Nelson liked to roar into a town, shoot everybody in sight, and leave in a blaze of gunfire. Nelson, who left a string of dead FBI agents behind him, was the perfect murdering maniac for a crime comic book. Before he was finally killed in a running machine-gun battle, Nelson calmly walked through a hail of bullets, with seventeen slugs in his body, to kill his final two G-Men. "It was just like James Cagney," one eyewitness recalled.

In the *Crime Does Not Pay* (June 1947) treatment of Nelson's career of crime, several changes were made. Although no one in the underworld called the gangster "Baby Face" to his face, everyone in the comic book does, including his wife: "I never thought you had it in you! This shows you're big time, Baby Face!" During a robbery scene in the comic book, Dillinger tells Nelson: "Nice work, Baby

*Crime Does Not Pay #51*
© *1947 Comic House.* Art
by Fred Guardineer.

Face! You're a cool operator! I don't like nervous guys around me—now let's blow!" In reality, Dillinger considered Nelson a risky and uncontrollable psychopath. The comic book presented Nelson as perhaps a more competent and calculating criminal than he was.

At the end of the comic book, when Nelson is caught in a gun battle with federal agents, he shouts as he fires his machine gun: "Come and get it, you pesky boy scouts! Come and get it!" Allegedly, Nelson used stronger words than "pesky boy scouts" to describe the G-Men, with the mildest adjective being "yellow-belly." The comic book ends with Nelson's wife and partner coldly abandoning the bullet-riddled Nelson for the police. In reality, the pair managed to drag the wounded gangster into the car and escape from the police. "Baby Face" soon died, however, and his body was stripped naked of identification and dumped by the roadside.

## PRETTY BOY FLOYD

Charles Arthur Floyd was labeled "Pretty Boy" by a Kansas City brothel madam. He hated

the nickname, but it made for a good headline in the early 1930s when the press wrote about his string of bank robberies, murders, and prison escapes. He robbed so many banks in Oklahoma in one year, the insurance rates doubled. He sometimes knocked off two banks a day, and callously robbed his own hometown bank with a machine gun. Floyd was a cold-blooded murderer and public enemy number one when he was finally gunned down by FBI agents.

Pretty Boy Floyd was the only real-life criminal to have a complete comic book dedicated to his exploits. Fawcett Publications presented a forty-nine-page story about the "most ruthless killer ever to oppose law and order" in *On the Spot* (Fall 1948). The book was perhaps the best-researched of all the true crime comics and detailed the life of Floyd with accurate dates, correctly spelled names of even minor players, and actual locales. There are only a few discrepancies (such as underestimating his age by five years and his height by five inches) in what is otherwise a plausible biography. The ending, however, still played heavily to the moral that "crime does not pay," when Pretty Boy expresses a sense of relief at finally being

"How do you like bein' cut
in two by a stream of hot
lead, sheriff? Just like
having a knife slashed
across yer middle, ain't it?!
Well, ya asked for it,
ya rat!!!!"
—Pretty Boy Floyd (*Murder
Incorporated*, July 1949)

caught. His actual last words were a little more defiant: "I didn't do it . . . who the hell tipped you off?"

In "Pretty Boy Floyd—The Baby-Faced Killer" (*All-True Detective Cases*, April 1954), the killer's life story was dispensed with in seven pages, although nary a murder was omitted. The Kansas City brothel where Floyd holed up became a boarding house in the comic story and was run by Mother (not Madam) Ash.

The *Crime Does Not Pay* (May 1947) version of Pretty Boy Floyd ("The Two-Faced Terror") opens with the youth beginning his life of crime as a robber disguised as a dictionary salesman ("Look up the word sucker lady! It might come in handy next time someone rings your bell! Ha, ha!"). Another scene used to establish Floyd's character shows the young man shooting a dog to settle a grudge ("The face of an angel, the soul of a devil"). The story runs past most of the important events in Floyd's life, including his stretch of Oklahoma robberies, and concentrates chiefly on the Kansas City Massacre—an event for which Floyd was rumored to have been absent.

In "Pretty Boy Floyd" from *Murder Incorporated* (July 1949), the story begins with a fictionalized murder when a teenage Floyd stabs a friend in the back with an ice pick. The comic picks up in accuracy after Floyd grows up (this time including the whorehouse scene where he gets his nickname). Like all the other comic book adaptations, this one

Pretty Boy Floyd. *On the Spot #1* © 1948 Fawcett Publications

spotlights Pretty Boy's escape from a prison train. He kicks out the window, leaps from the speeding locomotive, and rolls down the embankment to disappear into the woods—a real-life scene perfectly staged for a comic book.

## JOHN DILLINGER

John Dillinger was America's most famous bank robber. He made more headlines and perpetuated more myths than any other gangster of the 1930s. He planned and executed dazzling holdups and getaways. He

*Crime Does Not Pay #49* © 1946 Comic House. Art by Bob Q. Siege.

*Famous Gangsters #1* © 1951 Avon Periodicals

*All-True Detective Cases #3 © 1954 Avon Periodicals.* Art by Mike Becker.

escaped time and again from jails and prisons. Even after he was supposedly killed in an FBI ambush, some people believe he escaped death, leaving another to die in his place. Dillinger's crime career was so well known and followed, even years after his alleged death, that there was a 1945 movie (*Dillinger*) about his life. Of course, he would make it into the comic books as well.

In "The TRUE Story of John Dillinger" (*Crime Does Not Pay*, May 1946), the gangster was described as "keen, clever, and diabolically daring" in his planning of bank robberies. He was also portrayed as a trigger-happy gunman who murdered an elderly bank clerk and bushwhacked a police officer with a machine gun in the middle of the street. From all accounts, however, Dillinger was never implicated in a murder and he preferred his robberies to go off without a violent hitch or fatal shooting.

In another Dillinger crime comic story, "A Date with Death" from *All-True Detective Cases* (June 1954), the bank robber is described as having "absolutely no mercy." For

over half the story, he guns down someone on every page: "I told you to shut up! RAT-TAT-TAT!!" Instead of a cold and methodical bank robber, Dillinger was drawn as an emotional basket case who was propelled by his desires for "banks and blondes."

The Dillinger myth was also deflated in the story "Case for the Morgue" (*Down with Crime*, September 1952), which referred to him as "Jack Dillon." The story opens with the editor lamenting the fact that some people still consider the bank robber a folk hero. He assigns his writer to get the real facts about the gangster: "He was far from a hero! Just a treacherous coward, with a too-quick finger, who found the violent death that his kind always merits!"

The comic promised its readers that it would bring them "the sensational story behind the headlines about Jack Dillon! Yes, you know his real name—although that name is not used in this true story! But do you know what his life was really like? From unimpeachable sources, the editors of *Down with Crime* bring you, for the first time, the sensational private life of a public enemy!"

A few details about Dillinger's life actually did find their way into the comic book, such as his early introduction to crime at a pool hall and his alleged death at a movie theater in an FBI ambush. Although he wasn't a homicidal maniac in this particular comic story, he was incorrectly portrayed as a coward who abandoned his friends and left them to die in order to save his own life.

While John Dillinger had the lion's share of glory in the nation's newspapers and magazines of the 1930s, he fared none too well in the crime comics of the 1940s and 1950s.

THUS...PENNILESS AND FRIENDLESS...ON A SMALL FARM ON SPRUCEDALE ROAD, SEVEN MILES NORTH OF EAST LIVERPOOL, OHIO...ON OCTOBER 22,1934, AT THE AGE OF 28, CHARLES "PRETTY BOY" FLOYD MET HIS UNTIMELY END.

*On the Spot #1 © 1948 Fawcett Publications*

# CHEAP SEX, HARD DRUGS, AND BAD GIRLS

"There's easier ways to get dough, even big dough, an' I'm goin' after it! If you weren't chicken-livered, you'd listen to me! First off, we're gonna hock everything we've got, except the rags on our backs! Then, we're gonna get us a couple of guns—an' lots of bullets!"—The Short But Furious Crime Career of Irene Dague and Her Yes-Man Husband (*Crime Does Not Pay*).

From 1947 to 1954, the principal years for the true crime comic genre, there were several thousand stories drawn by several hundred artists for dozens of publishers. Although there was a diversity in writing style, artistic quality, and production values, most crime comic stories shared common themes, attitudes, and values. The criminal in the true crime comic, for example, always came from the same mold. He or she was ruthless, brutal, immoral, greedy, vain, and ultimately stupid enough to attempt a life of crime. Characterization was established through choreographed scenes of rough action and hard dialogue.

Like gangsters in the movies or pulp fiction, crime comic characters spoke in bursts

of bravado peppered with gangland terms and underworld references: "OK, screw, stand back like nothin' was happenin' or I'll let you have it with my gat!" The tough talk and gang slang was used to distinguish the bad guys from the good guys. Hoodlums and punks spoke in a private language that was colorful, sassy, and brutal.

"Pipe all the ritzy ice," a robber says to his companion as they look at diamonds in a jewelry store window, "but those armed guards . . ." His buddy slaps his machine-gun case. "Forget 'em! My chatter-gun will take care of them!"

The crime comic gangsters had a rich vocabulary when it came to describing guns and law-enforcement officers—the yin and

---

Facing Page: *Famous Crimes #1* © 1948 Fox Features Syndicate

*Real Clue Crime Stories
Vol. 7 #1 © 1952
Hillman Periodicals*

While the crime comics were full of "#$*&!" and "&*@$+!", there were also scattered uses of "hell" and "damn"—something absolutely not done in other comic books about superheroes, funny animals, and cute teenagers. Even gangster movies of the time didn't have lines like: "So long suckers! I'll see you in hell!" Other expletives, like "Damn him!" and "Good God!", were used occasionally, although "darn," "gawddarn," "blasted," and "jeepers" were more common.

While crime comic criminals talked like bad guys, it was their actions which left no doubt that they lived a different life from decent, law-abiding folk. Gangsters in the crime comics worked their victims over with brass knuckles, shivs, saps, and lead pipes. Criminal maniacs shot off the ears of rivals, burned the bottom of their feet, and pressed hypodermic needles against their eyeballs.

Besides their brutal violence to their victims and rivals, crime comic criminals were noted for their cruelty to women, animals, children, the elderly, and even the blind. In *Crime and Punishment* (May 1948), a punk robs a corner newsstand. "You must need money pretty bad mister," the victim tells him, "if you're robbing blind war vets!" The gangster snarls: "Shut up, or I'll slit your throat! Two bucks in pennies! You can keep your lousy pennies! Go to blazes with 'em!" The blind man scrambles for his coins and mutters: "Thanks—you've got a kind heart mister—the *rotten* kind!"

yang of their violent existence. Police were "bulls," "coppers," and "flatfooters." A pistol was a "piece" or "rod" while a machine gun was a "chopper." When faced with the electric chair ("the hot seat"), an escaped killer pulls his gun and makes a vow: "I ain't gonna burn I tell ya! I ain't! Them coppers drive me off my nut. I hate their guts! I'll blast them with my rod!"

The criminals in crime comics had the dirtiest mouths in the medium. Cursing was the easiest way to show contempt for authority, public morals, and good manners: "You %*$# bulls won't queer me! I'll kill every last one o' you!" Cursing, however, wasn't restricted to life-or-death standoffs with the police. Cursing in casual conversation worked just as well to demonstrate bad upbringing: "$*?xx?%! It sure is cold!"

*Parole Breakers #3 © 1952 Realistic Comics*

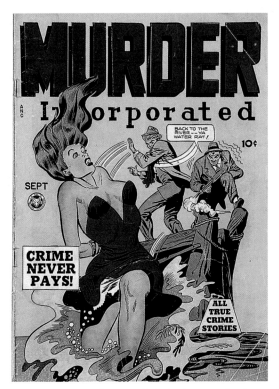

*Murder Incorporated #5 © 1948 Fox Features Syndicate*

The crime comic criminals were rotten to the core of their cowardly beings, and they were proud of it ("Don't ever call me 'cheap,' you punk! I'm big time, see? Big time!"). In the story "Big-Shot Killer" (*Fight Against Crime*, September 1951), a gangster brags that "the only time I raise my hands to a copper is when I'm shootin' at him!"

Murder, especially cold-blooded and senseless murder, was the defining act for the antihero of a crime comic. It was important to show the criminal killing someone—anyone—early in the story, be it a police officer, an innocent bystander, a bank guard, a spurned lover, or a disloyal gang member.

In the detective story, murder is a grim prerequisite usually addressed at the beginning, before the focus shifts to finding the killer. In the crime comic, however, the killer is the star. Murder is everything. It moves the plot, it establishes motive, it develops characterization, and it provides much of the action. Comic books with titles like *Murderous Gangsters*, *The Killers*, and *Murder Incorporated* left little doubt that most "crime" comics were about capital crimes.

When murder wasn't bad enough, torture was used: "Ha, ha, ha, ha! So we finally got our mitts on you sonny boy! Now we're gonna give you a little treatment for making us sweat! Vito—gimme the acetylene torch!" The two thugs slowly pass an acetylene torch back and forth over the face of the man who is tied, helpless, in the chair. His face is blistered and bloody as he pleads with them: "No more, please! I . . . I can't stand it! Kill me . . . ki . . ." One of the men steps back and pulls out his gun: "Sweet dreams, Robert—you get your wish!"

After death, there was still no honor. Bodies were pushed out of cars, tossed over cliffs, or weighted with rocks and dumped in the sea. Burial was but a means to hide the traces of the grisly deed, as in the "bump-

*Crime Smashers #6 © 1951 Trojan Publishing Corp.* Art by Newt Alfred.

**MY TRUE CRIME CONFESSION**

*Justice Traps the Guilty #2 © 1948 Headline Publications.* Art by Joe Simon and Jack Kirby.

tells a young gang member. "Killing is easy. I'll do it any time for money, see?"

In the story "Graduation for Murder" (*Public Enemies*, May 1948), a senior high school couple deliberately embark on a life of crime, and the girl kills an old man in cold blood. Her boyfriend greets her the following day on their way to school: "Hi, baby . . . how does a murderer feel the next morning?" The teenage girl smirks. "Swell . . . I slept like a log! I saw the papers . . . he died himself dead!"

The women in crime comics came in two flavors: the good girl who fell victim to bad company and the bad girl who laughed all the way to hell. The "good girl" tales were mostly cautionary confessions about how easy it is to sink into a life of crime because of misplaced trust or temporary lack of moral restraint. Far more popular were the bad-girl stories that sold a successful formula of mean-spirited violence and female degradation.

The popularity of such real-life figures as Ma Barker and Bonnie Parker lived on in the crime comics. Excited, leggy blondes with hot, smoking pistols blasted their way through titles like *Crimes by Women* (June 1948) and *Gangsters and Gun Molls* (Septem-

off" that took place in *Murder Incorporated* (September 1948): A sweating hoodlum tosses away a bloody axe and carries a corpse over to a pit he has dug in the ground. "I hacked his feet off wid da axe, boss," he tells another gangster as he points to a towel which covers two bloody ankles. "We'll dump 'em in the ocean so dey can't identify him by his crooked feet if dey find him before the lime rots his corpse!" His boss nods impatiently: "Speed it up, Andy! I've lined up a big job for tomorrow!"

Lack of remorse was important for a crime comic killer. There was no sympathy for victims, no trace of human decency, and no sense of sin. "Listen, in this business you can't have any regrets," a hardened gun moll

*Crime Does Not Pay #33 © 1944 Comic House.* Art by Dick Briefer.

Fight Against Crime #3 © 1951 Story Comics

ber 1951). The bad-girl gang leader was a popular role in stories like "The Gun Girl" (*Wanted Comics,* November 1947): "They say the female is the deadlier than the male! With a blazing gun, afraid of nothing, Irene Schroeder cut a swath of banditry and murder across the United States, egging on her male accomplices." The bad women in the stories were often cheerleaders for their male counterparts. In a story from *Crime Does Not Pay,* the woman boss holds up a glass of booze in a toast to her gang: "Well, boys—to hell and high water, diamonds and pearls, fur coats, and speedy cars!" The drooling gangsters quickly rejoin: "You said it, Blondie!"

In many cases, however, the bad woman was also an active participant in the robberies and the killings. In the story "Jean Torson—Satan's Daughter" (*Crimes by Women,* August 1948), the lead character is described as "cold, ruthless, and trigger-happy." She waves her pistol openly in public and taunts police officers: "Let 'em come. I'll blast the whole lot of 'em! As long as I've got a rod, they can't touch us!" When she robs a bank, she murders a woman who doesn't move fast enough ("Get down, sis-

ter! Get down or I'll kill ya! All right lady, you asked for it!" "EEEEEE!").

Besides the gang leader or gun moll, another role women played in crime comics was the scheming seductress who marries men for their money and then kills them. This popular *film noir* theme of a glamorous woman turned murderer is repeated in stories like "Sign Your Own Death Warrant" (*Thrilling Crime Cases,* January 1952):

"He's falling for me like a sack of potatoes . . . that's how I was able to finally get him out of here so I could peek into his safe! He's got plenty of dough stashed away in the safe . . . and a nice insurance policy which should net his widow a tidy sum of money when he kicks off! I'll have to go to work on him . . . bet I can get him to propose in less than a week if I really try! Have to get myself a new dress, a little perfume, a new hair-do, and. . . ."

In another story, called "The Female Blue Beard" (*Crime Does Not Pay,* May 1944), a woman poses before her vanity in a red robe that falls open over her nude body. She lifts her long hair over her bare shoulders and stares wistfully at her reflection in the mirror: "Marie, you are probably the most beautiful girl in all of France. Now what shall you do with your life—marry a rich man—or perhaps be a model? Bah! I would tire of a rich man—and modeling is a fool's business. Marie—you shall be a murderess—a queen of death!"

Another lady who also figured out what she wanted out of life was "Mrs. Bluebeard" (*Crime Does Not Pay,* March 1946), who married and buried a succession of hoodwinked husbands for their life insurance policies.

Justice Comics #8
© 1948 Marvel
Entertainment Group

Public Enemies #5
© 1948 D.S. Publishing
Co.

*Wanted Comics #46*
*© 1952 Orbit Publishing*

When the police begin to suspect her as a serial murderer, she kills her sleeping maid and burns down the house to disguise the corpse as her own. Before she slips away, she takes time to murder her own children in their beds: "No! Mamma! No—don't hurt me!" The woman grunts as she strangles her little girl: "This brat-killing is taking too long! It's good she's the last or the police'll be on my neck before I know it!"

Other women in crime comics preferred to have their husbands and boyfriends do the dirty work for them. In "I Married Murder!" (*All-True Crime*, June 1948), the woman tells her husband: "I'm telling you for the *last* time, Jimmy, if you can't buy me *nice* things, I'm going to find someone who *will*! I'm tired of slinging hash and wearing *cheap*

clothes! I want a *big shot*! If you were a *real* man, you'd buy yourself a gun and *take* what you wanted!"

In "Money Hungry" (*War Against Crime*, April 1949), a shrewish wife tells her spouse: "I'm sick and tired of our dates! Cheap restaurants, two-bit movies, riding around in that tin-can you call a car—I'm sick and *tired* of it. Why can't you take me out *swell*! Go to night clubs . . . buy me jewels . . . a fur coat . . . get a flashy car . . . *look* like something . . . *treat me right*!!" After robbing and killing for money, he has to run away and asks her to go away with him. "Don't be a fool," she snaps. "I never loved you. All I was interested in was money and a good time . . . and you were my ticket!"

The women in crime comics, especially the bad ones, were drawn with almost impossible feminine characteristics that were barely hidden by their sluttish costumes. Skirts rode over garter belts to expose derringers and derrieres. Exaggerated bustlines threatened to explode from flimsy blouses like so many torpedoes. As a 1940s comic book reader noted, the women in the crime comics were indeed a bunch of "wonderfully chesty girls."

Sex also became part of the crime in some comic stories. While rape was never directly shown, the abduction and aftermath figured prominently in stories like "Girl Trap" (*Wanted Comics*, March 1952): "To Marion Winters, time passed slowly as in a nightmare! Actually, her whole terrible adventure consumed no more than an hour, but it was lifetimes later when she found herself lying on the ground, watching with pain-blurred eyes as the car drove away and left her . . . "

In "Murder for Nothing" (*Lawbreakers*, October 1952), prostitution is the backdrop for a story which opens with two women lolling about in their underwear and wondering where they're going to make their next buck. "Let's get dressed and get out of here," one of the women says to her friend. "We'll visit Mike's tavern. He just opened up on Pine Street!" Her friend nods as she pulls up her slip. "Maybe we can find another sucker and bring him back here. I still got some of those knockout drops."

Knockout drops, alcohol, and even

drugs were all a part of the seedy crime comic milieu. As early as the 1930s, drug smuggling and drug taking were a way crime comics could add cheap sensationalism and a hint of the forbidden to a story. Steve Carson, in "Federal Men" (*Adventure Comics*, January 1939), breaks up a high school marijuana ring run by the school janitor. Carson, echoing the sentiments of the new cannabis prohibition era that had spawned such drug exploitation movies as *Reefer Madness* and *Assassin of Youth* the previous year, warns young readers that "marijuana is the drug that causes the smoker to lose all moral restraint!"

The warnings about drug use escalated in the late 1940s and early 1950s, labeling it a contributing cause of juvenile delinquency. In an editorial from *Perfect Crime* (April 1951), comic book readers were told that "there have been many bad things which have menaced the youth of our country but none so bad as one that has recently become the most prevalent. No one knows why there has been such a tremendous surge in the amount of drug addiction by youngsters. In comparison with this danger all other kinds

*Wanted Comics #52*
© 1952 Orbit Publishing.
Art by Mort Leav.

of juvenile delinquency pale into insignificance."

The growing concern over drug use among teenagers presented a perfect opportunity for exploitation by crime comic publishers. Harvey Comics reprinted a "Rex Morgan" newspaper comic strip sequence dealing with the treatment of juvenile drug offenders and packaged it as a ten-cent comic book called *Teen-Age Dope Slaves* (April 1952). Like pornographers masquerading as sex hygienists, the crime comic publishers passed off sensationalistic stories of moral degeneracy as public service messages to youngsters.

In most cases, however, the drug-related crime comic stories probably served only to increase morbid curiosity about such behavior: "You know what they say when a dope addict takes a dose of his favorite stuff? They say he has gone on—a *holiday*!" The story "Holiday of Horror" (*Wanted Comics*, December 1952) told the story of Larry Newson, "a hopeless drug addict" and his

*Harvey Comics Library #1* © 1952 Publishers Syndicate

*Wanted Comics #52*
*© 1952 Orbit Publishing.*
*Art by Mort Leav.*

Larry's friends back away nervously: "We shouldn't have given him that snifter! He isn't used to the stuff! *He's got hops on the brain!*" Larry quickly moved on from marijuana to heroin, as everyone dutifully did in the popularly perceived world of mid-twentieth-century drug culture.

Drug stories had to end with the addict suffering painful withdrawal symptoms or death or both. "It wasn't food that his tortured body craved! With every quivering muscle, every shrieking nerve ending, his body was desperately crying out for something else! The glare of the light from the street hurt his eyes! His head seemed ready to burst with the craving he was powerless to control! Larry was reaching the end of his rope . . . "

Without exception, the crime comic books condemned drug use as a destructive habit. The story "Horror Honey" (*Crime and Punishment*, June 1950), which was about "devil drugs that turn normal lives into nightmares of fear and violence," carried this warning for would-be drug users: "You'll dream nightmares for the rest of your life! You'll howl and scream like a maniac! You might even kill! And your life span will be shortened quicker than you can say 'narcotics'!"

For the most part, actual drug use was

"wild, disordered nightmare world to which drugs provide the final passport."

In most crime comic stories, greed or hate are the motivating forces for a criminal's actions and requisite killing spree. In the drug-related stories, however, it's the desire for a "fix" and a "high" which propels the addict into a life of crime: "For a brief moment, Larry Newson had felt the false confidence and sense of power that drugs gave him . . . and soon he needed to know that feeling again!"

Drug users in the crime comic stories underwent wild personality changes and experienced violent urges: "But the marijuana he'd smoked was working full blast on Larry Newson now! Exhilarated, half out of control, he waved his gun menacingly!"

*Wanted Comics #52 © 1952 Orbit Publishing.* Art by Mort Leav.

not so much portrayed as was drug smuggling and trafficking. The addict in the crime comic was often the victim and not the perpetrator of a crime. For example, the story "H is for Heroin" (*Down with Crime*, March 1952) describes dope smugglers as "human vultures preying on the lives and happiness of millions . . . and peddlers of misery and degradation and death." A hardened drug dealer tells her desperate customer in the story "Murder, Morphine, and Me!" (*True Crime Comics*, May 1947): "No cash, no dope. One needleful of joy-juice and you get so satisfied with the world you forget your obligations! No, we'll do it *my* way for a change!"

Drug addiction, prostitution, kidnapping, murder, violence by women, violence to women, infanticide, torture, whippings, bondage, mutilations, bloodletting, and bad attitudes ran throughout the crime comics. There were few good role models—the police were ineffectual or brutal, just like the criminals they killed. Children in crime comics were helpless victims or aspiring juvenile delinquents.

Adults comprised the major audience for the crime comics, a fact which probably accounted for the cynical, sexy, and violent themes which dominated the stories. According to a 1948 Dayton, Ohio, study, almost half of all young adults (ages 21–30) were regular comic book readers. During the late 1940s, readership surveys by publisher Lev Gleason determined that fifty-seven percent of the readers of *Crime Does Not Pay* were over twenty-one years of age. Although Gleason and his editor Charles Biro maintained throughout the 1940s that *Crime Does Not Pay* was beneficial reading for young people about the perils of crime, they put a disclaimer on the June 1950 front cover: "Not Intended For Children."

While crime comics may or may not have been intended for children, they were widely read by people of all ages. Younger brothers and sisters read their older siblings' copies, and kids in the neighborhood traded their *Batman* and *Archie* comics and got *Murderous Gangsters* and *Teen-Age Dope Slaves* in return. After all, comics were comics—at least in the eyes of most parents and newsstand

*Down With Crime #3
© 1952 Fawcett
Publications*

retailers—and there was no clear division between comics read by the youngest children and those read by adults. In the days before television's popularity, parents would often pick up and read their children's comics as well.

When Dad saw the story "Murder, Morphine and Me" in junior's comic, and Mom took a glance at Sis's *Crimes by Women*, eyebrows hit the ceiling. Donald Duck and Captain Marvel had been replaced by prostitutes and punks. While they shook their heads and wondered about their children's new reading material, a psychiatrist in New York City was peering at comic books, scribbling notes, and taking body counts.

# GUILTY, GUILTY, GUILTY: CRIME COMICS ON TRIAL

"**H**ere's the evidence,' I said and I showed them some comic books. And they were absolutely horrified. Here was blood all over, here was every kind of murder you can think of, here were men who were having their noses cut off and their eyes bloodied, and the judge said 'Doctor, where did you get this kind of . . .' and I said, 'The corner newsstand, your honor.'"

Dr. Fredric Wertham, senior psychiatrist for the New York Department of Hospitals from 1932 to 1952, recalled that "the first time I ever spoke about comic books at all was in 1947 when I was under oath in a court hearing in Washington in a case against censorship. I was testifying for the defense, defending publications that had nothing to do with comic books. Some of these were nudist magazines, which were completely harmless as far as I'm concerned. In the cross examination, I was asked if I think all publications are right and nothing is wrong. And I said, 'No, I don't think so at all. I have in my briefcase a lot of things that are wrong.'"

When Wertham pulled a stack of crime comics out of his briefcase that day in 1947, he began an eight-year crusade against comic books which, in his words, "contribute to

juvenile delinquency" and "impair the ethical development of children."

Wertham began his investigation into the effects of comic books on children in 1946, when he founded the Lafargue Clinic, a free psychiatric service in Harlem for disturbed and delinquent youth. He was bothered by the increasing brutality he was witnessing among his young patients and believed there must be contributing outside influences. He did not feel that violent impulses were an innate part of the human personality, but that they were stimulated by extenuating social conditions and the increasing amount of violence in the mass media.

Wertham recalled that as far as his young patients were concerned, "the easiest mass medium to study was comic books." During the postwar years, comic book read-

*Famous Gangsters #1 © 1951 Avon Periodicals*

ing was at an all-time high, with over 90 percent of children reading an average of eighteen comic books every week. Wertham explained that "if I see a child of nine or ten and we ask him what he does at home, and he says he has about fifty comic books that he reads over and over again, we can ask him to bring in the comic books for us to see. It's almost impossible to do that with movies, which we studied, and television hadn't begun yet—at least not widely."

Wertham began assembling and examining the comic books his patients had brought him, and what he discovered was unsettling. By his own calculations, the doctor determined that a sixteen-year-old comic book reader in 1948 had "absorbed a minimum of 18,000 pictorial beatings, shootings, stranglings, and blood puddles and torturing to death from comic books alone."

Nearly thirty years later, Wertham recalled that "at the time we had ample clinical proof that children under 13 are adversely affected by mass media—including comic books—which feature all these kinds of cruelty and brutality. They lose their sense of the dignity of human life and the suffering of other people. I felt that we should protect children until 13 or 14 so this kind of thing was not shown to them directly."

Wertham began his study of crime comic books in the late 1940s, when there was a growing public concern over such domestic problems as juvenile delinquency and postwar resettlement of the family. Faced with increasing teenage pregnancy, drug addiction and alcoholism, and violent crimes by youth, social scientists—as well as parents and teachers—looked for outside influences which might explain such aberrant behavior.

As early as 1940, children's author Sterling North had criticized comic books as "badly drawn, badly written, and badly printed . . . pulp-paper nightmares" with "hypodermic injections of sex and murder." More pointedly, North blamed "completely immoral publishers" for the "cultural slaughter of innocents." Children, he said, should be protected from the corrupting influence of comic books.

*All-True Crime #39 © 1950 Marvel Entertainment Group*

"All child drug addicts, and all children drawn into the narcotics trade as messengers, with whom we have had contact, were inveterate comic book readers."
—Dr. Fredric Wertham

In the February 1947 issue of the *New Republic*, Marya Maynes examined the American child's obsession with comic books in "Junior Has a Craving." The analogy between the "comic book habit" and the drug habit was not lost on parents. Perhaps there was something unnatural and harmful in their children's continual reading and swapping of comic books. Perhaps the comic books themselves were causing adolescent rebellion and lawlessness.

The Indianapolis police evidently thought so. In August 1947, they launched an anti-comic book crusade to bring community pressure on newsstand dealers to eliminate what they called "one of the contributing factors of the cause of juvenile delinquency." The following month, in Pittsburgh, a coroner's jury attributed the hanging suicide of a twelve-year-old boy to his "incessant" reading of comic books. The court concluded that the comic books may have caused him to hang himself while "re-enacting one scene."

The National Office for Decent Literature, established by the Catholic Bishops Council in 1938, was concerned primarily with magazines and paperback books. In 1947, it considered comic books for the first time and rated them as either "acceptable," "borderline," or "objectionable." Comic books rated "objectionable" were put on lists

and circulated to communities in an effort to pressure newsstands to remove them.

The March 1948 issue of *Collier's* first brought Fredric Wertham and his anti-comic book crusade to national attention. In an article by Judith Crist called "Horror in the Nursery," Dr. Wertham stated that his clinical studies showed that the effect comic books have upon children "is definitely and completely harmful." Along with the doctor's anecdotes about his disturbed juvenile patients and their comic book reading habits were photographs of children ("professional models") re-enacting crimes committed while supposedly under the influence of comic books. A boy and girl hold their playmate to the ground and stab him in the arm with a fountain pen, just "like a hypodermic." Another photograph, allegedly inspired by a comic book scene, shows a young girl gagged and bound in a chair while a group of boys decide "how to get rid of her." Such sensationalistic graphics and anecdotal research would typify much of the anti-comic book campaign of the late 1940s and early 1950s.

Wertham, author of *The Brain as an Organ* (1934) and *Dark Legend: A Study of Murder* (1941), published his first attack on crime comics in the May 29, 1948, issue of *Saturday Review of Literature*. In an article entitled "The Comics . . . Very Funny!", Wertham announced that "we are getting to the roots of the contributing causes of juve-

*All-True Crime #28*
*© 1948 Marvel Entertainment Group*

*War Against Crime #7 © 1949 William M. Gaines.* Art by H. C. Kiefer.

nile delinquency when we study the influence of comic books."

While Wertham and other early critics blamed the comic book for a variety of late 1940s ills, their criticism about crime comics in particular were fairly specific. Crime comics were harmful to children, critics maintained, because they made criminals and criminal acts attractive, suggested criminal or sexually abnormal ideas, inspired copycat crimes, stimulated unwholesome fantasies, desensitized children to brutality and cruelty, portrayed law enforcement officers in a bad light, and did not always adequately punish the criminal.

The charges against the mid-twentieth-century crime comic book had precedents one hundred years earlier. In 1850 London, there were a hundred different series of "Jack Sheppard" tales circulating in penny sheets that glorified for young readers the exploits of the infamous highwayman. The Report of the Select Committee on Criminal and Destitute Juveniles that year noted the widespread influence of Jack Sheppard, and other criminals such as Dick Turpin, on children through the penny press. A large number of the juvenile offenders were familiar with the stories and some confessed they had been influenced by them in their criminal acts.

Despite widespread criticism that children were made worse by their admiration for such criminals through the "Penny Dreadfuls," no action was taken.

In the United States in the nineteenth century, Anthony Comstock, a self-appointed moral guardian of youth, lobbied for early obscenity laws and successfully persecuted book dealers for selling criminal story papers and stories of bloodshed and crime. In his "Society for the Suppression of Vice's Sixth Annual Report," Comstock dealt in great length with the "Boy's Papers," which he attributed to making hardened criminals out of children, educating them in crime, and filling the courts with "baby felons."

Now, it was the crime comic books which were corrupting youth in 1948. It may have been an old message, but Dr. Fredric Wertham turned out to be the perfect messenger.

The Cincinnati Committee on the Evaluation of Comic Books was formed in May 1948 to develop criteria to rate comics as "no objection," "some objection," "objectionable," and "very objectionable." The results of the committee's first annual survey, which was widely distributed and published in *Parent's* magazine each year,

*Famous Gangsters #1 © 1951 Avon Periodicals*

listed 42 percent of all the comic books on sale in 1948 as being either "objectionable" or "very objectionable." The General Federation of Women's Clubs, which numbered four million members, appointed volunteers to police the newsstands and list objectionable titles.

Meanwhile, the 1948 news reports seemed to validate charges made by Wertham and other comic book critics. In April that year, a thirteen-year-old boy in Chicago, described as "an avid reader of crime comics," murdered a seven-year-old boy. In a case reported by *Time* (October 4, 1948), a four-teen-year-old boy poisoned a fifty-year-old woman after he got the idea and the poison recipe from a comic book. The magazine also added that "a ten-year-old boy's parents came home from the movies to find his body hanging in the garage. At his feet was a crime comic depicting a hanging body. Two boys, fourteen and fifteen, were caught committing a burglary. The crime comics they had with them had inspired the crime and shown them how to do it." In December that year, a Canadian case made the U.S. papers when two teenagers, described as "comic book addicts," went on a killing and robbing spree in Nova Scotia and the Yukon. The next year, Canada enacted legislation which made it a crime to publish or sell comic books depicting "any crime or containing obscene matter." The Minister of Justice of the Dominion of Canada singled out Lev Gleason's *Crime Does Not Pay* as "a shocking instance of abuse of freedom of the press."

In 1948, the City of Rochester, New York, forbade the sale of "lurid comic books" to anyone under the age of eighteen. Over fifty other cities that year sought action against the sale of comic books. By the following year, thirty-two bills or resolutions to curb the sale of comic books were introduced in state legislatures. By this time, Indianapolis had banned thirty-five comic books from sale in its city through voluntary cooperation with distributors, civic groups, and city officials. Likewise, Detroit banned thirty-six comic book titles, while in Chicago, parochial students of St. Cyril's Parish were building comic book bonfires.

In 1949, a censor was appointed in

*Crime Does Not Pay #53*
*© 1947 Comic House*

Boston to review comics sold at local newsstands. Connecticut made an attempt to regulate "objectionable comics" out of existence by requiring an approved application fee for each comic book. That same year, a sixteen-year-old in Philadelphia, "reportedly a crime comic book addict," slashed a twelve-year-old to death with a pair of scissors. A few weeks later, an Alabama man murdered his wife and her friend after studying an issue of *Crime Does Not Pay*. The growing hysteria over crime comic books was discussed by *Newsweek* in a February 1949 article which asked the question: "Are Comic Books a National Hazard?"

As the controversy over comic books, and crime comic books in particular, grew more heated, the comic book publishers had to address the problem out of self-interest and survival. Lev Gleason, publisher of *Crime Does Not Pay*, the most successful crime comic book of all time, had been using the letters column in his comic book as a forum for readers' endorsements of his efforts for teaching youth the perils of crime. In the May 1948 issue of *Crime Does Not Pay*, Gleason reproduced a letter which editor Charles Biro had sent to all writers and artists detailing the editorial standards.

The list of the twelve "do's and don'ts,"

published on the comic book's inside front cover, included such prohibitions as the following: Criminals must not be shown to enjoy a criminal act ("This means no laughter or glee during the commission of a crime"); gun molls and female criminals must not be made too attractive ("No scarcity of clothing will be accepted and no attempt to emphasize sex appeal will be permitted"); law officers must be pictured in a favorable light and criminals will not be made attractive either in appearance or character; stories dealing with sadism or torture of any form, or sex-motivated crimes, will not be accepted ("Blood must not be shown flowing from the face or mouth of a man and no blood to be shown flowing from women"); and all criminal acts or moral violations by characters in the stories must be accounted for by legal punishment—in other words, the punishment must fit the crime. Interestingly enough, there were several violations of Gleason's code in the same issue of his *Crime and Punishment* (June 1948), which also carried the list of standards.

This early attempt at self-policing was Gleason's damage-control response to the bad publicity the crime comics were engendering. By making his stories conform to

*Crime Smashers #8
© 1952 Ribage
Publishing Corp.*

"One day I was going to poison a lady. Then I picked up your wonderful book, *Crime Does Not Pay*. It was this, your magazine, that saved me."—G.R., Vallejo, California (letter from *Crime Does Not Pay*, July 1948)

standards that would placate his critics, Gleason hoped to escape newsstand boycotts. Gleason also made a plea to other comic book publishers "to make similar use of this list" in hopes that an industry-wide standard of good taste would prevail.

With nearly a million copies of *Crime Does Not Pay* selling every month, Gleason and his distributor, I. S. Manheimer, had a vested interest in seeing that Wertham and the other critics did not succeed in banning the sales of crime comic books. On July 1, 1948, the two men and a dozen other comic book publishers formed the Association of Comics Magazine Publishers (ACMP) in New York City. The purpose of the organization was to develop and adhere to an industry code of standards for comic books which would no longer make them objectionable to their critics.

The *New York Times* reported that the ACMP was an attempt at "self-policing, in an industry that has been meeting a growing criticism from educators' and parents' groups and marks only the first step in a plan for raising the moral tone of comic magazines." Phil Keenan, president of the ACMP, noted that "we are on trial in the court of public opinion. Our defense is this code of minimal

editorial standards designed to result in the production of comic magazines which are interesting, exciting, dramatic—and clean!"

The six-point code prohibited "scenes of sadistic torture," "vulgar and obscene language," and "ridicule or attack on any religious or racial group." In addition, no drawing could show a "female indecently or unduly exposed and in no event more nude than in a bathing suit commonly worn in the United States." In a nod to the power of the Catholic National Office for Decent Literature, one restriction specifically stated that "divorce should not be treated humorously nor represented as glamorous or alluring."

The most important part of the ACMP code, however, addressed the crime comic controversy: "Crime should not be presented in such a way as to throw sympathy against law and justice or to inspire others with the desire for imitation. No comics shall show the details and methods of a crime committed by a youth. Policemen, judges, Government officials, and respected institutions should not be portrayed as stupid or ineffective, or represented in such a way as to weaken respect for established authority."

The ACMP and its code, however, was doomed to failure. Only twelve of the thirty-five comic book publishers joined, and the standards were so loosely applied that there was no negligible change in the comic books produced. If the publishers had hoped the ACMP and its code would change the public's perception of the comic book industry and silence its critics, they were quickly disappointed.

Two months after the ACMP announced its code of standards, Dr. Wertham delivered a speech at the 1948 Annual Congress of Correction in which he stated that some of the worst comics he had seen were those very ones which had been labeled "Approved Reading" or "Wholesome Entertainment." Wertham stated that "just as we have ordinances against the pollution of water, so now we need ordinances against the pollution of children's minds." He called for both federal and state laws which would outlaw the sale of comic books to children under the age of fifteen. As a result, over one hundred local ordinances regulating or re-

*Justice Comics #8*
© *1948 Marvel Entertainment Group*

stricting crime comic books were enacted across the country.

Wertham's efforts also convinced the New York legislators to look into the threat that comic books posed to children. In 1950, Wertham testified before the New York State Joint Legislative Committee to Study the Publication of Comics that "the main bad effect of crime comic books on children is on their ethical development . . . juvenile delinquency is only one part of the crime comic book question. The greatest danger of crime comic books is to the normal child."

Earlier that same year, there had also been a special U.S. Senate subcommittee investigation on "organized crime in interstate commerce relative to the incidence of juvenile delinquency and the possible influence of so-called crime comic books during the five-year period 1945 to 1950."

The 1950 Senate subcommittee, under the chairmanship of Estes Kefauver, was established "because of frequently heard charges that juvenile delinquency has increased considerably during the past five years and that this increase has been stimulated by the publication of the so-called crime comic books." The subcommittee solicited letters from juvenile judges, probation officers, court psychiatrists, social workers, comic book publishers, cartoonists, and public officials about the relationship between juvenile crime and crime comic books. Wertham was also asked to contribute to the report, but declined because of short notice.

Among the hundreds of pages of letters and articles of exhibit received was a missive from J. Edgar Hoover, the nation's number-one crime-fighter. "A comic book," Hoover pointed out to the senators, "which is replete with the lurid and the macabre; which places the criminal in a unique position by making him a hero; which makes lawlessness attractive; which ridicules decency and honesty; which leaves the impression that graft and corruption are necessary evils of life; which depicts the life of the criminal as exciting and glamorous may influence the susceptible boy or girl who already possesses anti-social tendencies."

*Crime Does Not Pay #56* © 1947 Comic House. Art by George Tuska.

Publisher Lev Gleason, however, defended his crime comic books in a letter to Senator Kefauver by explaining that "our two magazines which deal with crime can better be called anticrime magazines. Our responsibility is to prove clearly to our reader that crime is unattractive and does not pay, to picture the law enforcement officer in a heroic and favorable light."

The comic book publishers made a convincing argument for their case with expert testimony, readership surveys, testimonials, and charts of criminal activity by age groups. No study was produced which linked crime comic book reading with juvenile crime; in fact, it appeared that juvenile delinquency actually declined during the years that crime comic books were increasing in popularity.

Newspaper headlines trumpeted the results of the 1950 Senate investigation: "Comics Don't Foster Crime" and "Study Finds Doubt Comics Spur Crime." An editorial in the New York Sunday *News* stated that "it's a pleasure to pass along the news that Senator Estes Kefauver's Senate Crime Investigating committee has now gone deeply into the subject of crime comic books and has brought up a mass of testimony which ought to spur the earnest souls to look around for something else to worry about . . . The Kefauver Committee took its testimony from largely unprejudiced sources . . . The verdict of the majority gave a clean bill of health to the comics. So we hope that the public has heard the last of this earnest soul-gripe."

One earnest soul, however, would continue to gripe. Dr. Wertham, stung by the committee's findings, pressed ahead with his campaign for the passage of state legislation regulating the sale of comic books to children. In 1951, he testified before the second hearing of the New York State Joint Legislative Committee to Study the Publication of Comics that crime comics "psychologically mutilate" children. Wertham again asked that the legislators consider his previous proposal to forbid the sale and display of crime comic books to children under the age of fifteen. In March 1952, New York State passed a law which made it a misdemeanor to publish or sell comic books dealing with "fictional crime, bloodshed, or lust that might incite minors to violence or immorality." Governor Thomas Dewey, however, vetoed the legislation because he considered it vague censorship.

Defeated at the state level, Wertham decided that the only way to effect a change in the comic book industry was to launch a national campaign through the media. In 1952, he began work on an anti-comic book manifesto, initially called *All Our Innocences,* that would document the harmful effects of comic books on children. Excerpts from his book, accompanied by examples of violent and sexy comic book art, first appeared in *The Ladies Home Journal* in a November 1953 article called "What Parents Don't Know about Comic Books." When the book was released in early 1954, it was retitled *Seduction of the Innocent.* In its 397 pages of lurid anecdotes and forensic arguments, Wertham managed to blame comics for the postwar rise in youth illiteracy, homosexuality, drug addiction, murder, teenage pregnancy, arson, truancy, vandalism, and a list of other assorted felonies and misdemeanors.

In the middle of the book were sixteen pages of the most gruesome illustrations Wertham could find in his comic book library of horrors assembled over the previous seven years. Presented in stark black and white, and out of context, the illustrations alone in *Seduction of the Innocent* probably convinced some parents to toss out Junior's comic book collection that very weekend.

The book condemned all types of comic books, from romance to funny animals to westerns and even to educational comics, as having detrimental effects on children. Wertham, however, singled out the crime comics as the most injurious of all the comic books. "The atmosphere of crime comic books," he wrote, "is unparalleled in the history of children's literature of any time or any nation. It is the distillation of viciousness. The world of the comic book is the world of the strong, the ruthless, the bluffer, the shrewd deceiver, the torturer, and the thief. Force and violence in any conceivable form are romanticized. Trust, loyalty, confidence, solidarity, sympathy, charity, compassion are ridiculed. Hostility and hate set the pace of almost every story. In comic

*Public Enemies #2*
© 1948 D.S. Publishing Co.

books life is worth nothing; there is no dignity of a human being."

Wertham's main objection to crime comic books was that they create a "moral and ethical confusion" in young readers. He explained that "children seek a figure to emulate and follow. Crime comics undermine this necessary ingredient of ethical development. They play up the good times had by those who do the wrong thing. Those who at the tail end of the story mete out punishment use the same violence and same lingo as those whom they punish. Everybody is selfish and force and violence are depicted as the most successful methods."

The message of the crime comics, Wertham maintained, was that "crime usually does pay, and pay very well, until the last picture or two. The crimes are glamor-

*Pity was the keynote when Homer described a dead body dragged behind a war chariot. Dragging living people to death is described without pity in children's comics.*

*What comic-book America stands for.*　　*A sample of the injury-to-the-eye motif.*

*One of the illustrated pages from Fredric Wertham's* Seduction of the Innocent. *Published in black and white, these illustrations have been recolored to approximate their original comic book appearance.*

ous; the ending is dull." He offered as evidence the fact that a typical crime comic story "has ninety-seven pictures where the criminal is winning and one for the apotheosis of his suicide . . . My clinical findings leave no room for doubt that children learn from crime comics that the real guilt is getting caught."

Much of Wertham's research for *Seduction of the Innocent* was conducted through interviews with his young, disturbed patients at the Lafargue Clinic in Harlem during the late 1940s. In talking with them, the doctor discovered what he thought was a link between comic book reading and their delinquent behavior. A boy who was arrested for burglary explained to Wertham: "I read the

comic books to learn how you can get money. I read about thirty a week. There was this one case in the back of a factory with pretty rich receipts. It showed how you get in through the back door. I thought the side door was the best way. I carried it out the same way as the comic book did it, only I had to open two drawers to do it. I didn't do every crime book, some of them were difficult. Some of them I just imitated. I had to think the rest out myself. I know other boys who learned how to do such jobs from comics books."

Besides encouraging delinquent behavior and copycat crimes, Wertham claimed, the comic books also desensitized children to violence and caused an increase in brutal crimes by the same age group. "Many children are so sheltered that they have not come in contact with real brutality," Wertham wrote. "They learn it from comic books. If they have a subconscious liking for it, comic books will reinforce it, give it form by teaching appropriate methods and furnish the rationalization that it is what every 'big shot' does."

Wertham related the accounts of two of his teenage patients, who told him: "I learned from crime comic books that when you want to hit a man, don't get face to face—hit him in the back." His companion helpfully added that "in some comic books they also hit them in the eye!"

Wertham noted that "in many comics there is nothing but violence. It is violence for violence's sake. The plot: killing. The motive: to kill. The characterization: killer. The end: killed."

Along with the violence, Wertham deplored the sexual messages that crime comics gave young readers. He related the experience of the eleven-year-old boy who told him that "the girls in the crime stories are always on the gangsters' side. The gangsters pick them up. They just roam around with the gangsters. They are always dressed in new clothes. The dresses have a V-shape in the front. When they do something bad, a man slaps them and beats them up."

Wertham told parents that "comic books stimulate children sexually. That is an elementary fact of my research. In comic books over and over again, in pictures and text, attention is drawn to sexual characteristics and to sexual actions."

Wertham, however, hastened to conclude that "legal control of comic books for children is necessary not so much on account of the question of sex, although their sexual abnormality is bad enough, but on account of their glorification of violence and crime."

Wertham also used the book to renew his call for comic book legislation. He was still upset with the veto by Governor Dewey of the New York legislation and the relatively clean bill which the 1950 Kefauver committee had given the comic book industry. "Forgotten are the announcements of self-control and self-regulation," Wertham wrote about the publishers. "Anything goes. And all of this is possible because many well-meaning adults live under the skillfully induced illusion that comic books have been getting better and better."

Wertham warned his readers that the comic book publishers and editors won't stop in their attempt to "seduce" the innocent with their violent fairy tales of crime and criminals. He incredulously repeated one publisher's defense that "I don't think comics hurt children because they grow out of it." Another publisher reportedly defended his comics from sexual salaciousness with this comment: "I don't see a child getting sexual stimulation out of it. Looking at those large mammary glands he'd remember that not long ago he was nursing at his mother's breasts."

To further illustrate the moral bankruptcy of the comic book industry, Wertham

*Justice Traps the Guilty #2 © 1948 Headline Publications.* Art by Joe Simon and Jack Kirby.

attributed another quote to a crime comic book editor, who said: "Naturally after the kid has identified with the crook in the beginning, and after he's followed him through various adventures, he's going to be a little sorry when the crook gets shot. Sure he'll resent the officer who does the shooting. Maybe he'll resent all cops. But what the hell they sell. Kids like them."

*Seduction of the Innocent* was a Book-of-the-Month Club selection and received widespread attention in newspapers and magazine reviews. The book's strident anti-comic book message gained greater exposure when

*Police Line-Up #3 © 1952 Realistic Publications.* Art by Joe Kubert.

*Crime Must Pay the Penalty #3 © 1948 Ace Magazines*

an excerpt appeared in *Reader's Digest* under the title, "Comic Books, Blue Prints for Delinquency." Wertham's media campaign had its desired effect. Shortly after the book was published, another Senate committee was established to investigate the relationship between comic books and juvenile delinquency.

The Senate Committee of the Judiciary to Investigate Juvenile Delinquency began hearings in New York City on April 21, 1954, under the chairmanship of Robert Hendrickson and with the aid of fellow senators Kefauver and Thomas Hennings. The hearings began with Hendrickson's announcement that "authorities agree that the majority of comic books are as harmless as soda pop. But hundreds of thousands of horror and crime comics are peddled to young people of impressionable age." The committee was concerned, Hendrickson said, with "effects of crime and horror comics on young minds."

On the first day of the hearings, the senators were shown slides of examples of violence and sadism from crime and horror comic books. The plots from seven typical crime and horror comics were then summarized, along with the number of murders and deaths which occurred in each story. The plot summary of a crime story called "Frisco Mary" (*Crime Must Pay the Penalty*, August 1948) was given as follows:

"This story concerns an attractive and glamorous young woman, Mary, who gains control of a California underworld gang. Under her leadership the gang embarks on a series of holdups marked for their ruthlessness and violence. One of these escapades involves the robbery of a bank. A police officer sounds the alarm. The next scene shows Mary poised over the wounded police officer, as he lies on the pavement, pouring bullets into his back from her submachine-gun. The agonies of the stricken officer are clearly depicted on his face. Mary, who in this particular scene looks like an average American girl wearing a sweater and skirt with her hair in bangs, in response to a plea from one of her gang members to stop shooting and flee, states: 'We could have got twice as much if it wasn't for this frog-headed rat!! I'll show him!'"

Testifying in defense of the industry was Henry Schultz, general counsel for the Association of Comics Magazine Publishers (ACMP), who presented the 1948 ACMP code of editorial standards as evidence of the industry's attempt at self-regulation. Schultz, however, acknowledged that the ACMP was largely ineffectual by 1954, with its membership now accounting for only about one-fourth of the comic book publishers.

The star witness for the prosecution, Dr. Fredric Wertham, appeared that afternoon. Wertham told the senators that his research into comic books and their effects on children convinced him that they were a contributing cause to juvenile delinquency. "If it were my task, Mr. Chairman," Wertham testified, "to teach children delinquency, to tell them how to hurt people, how to break into stores, how to cheat, how to forge, how to do any known crime—if it were my task to teach that, I would have to enlist the crime comic book industry."

Wertham's impressive arguments, the

weak defense fostered by the comic book industry, and the damning evidence of the cartoon images of twisted, tortured, and bloodied bodies all had their effect on the subcommittee members. Chairman Hennings, at a conference on juvenile delinquency held after the hearings, denounced crime comics for being "packed with every form of vice, sadism, and violence conceivable."

In their report, the senators concluded that "this country cannot afford the calculated risk involved in feeding its children, through comic books, a concentrated diet of crime, horror, and violence. There was substantial, although not unanimous, agreement among the experts that there may be detrimental and delinquency-producing effects upon both the emotionally disturbed and the emotionally normal delinquent. Children of either type may gain suggestion, support, and sanction from reading crime and horror comics."

The verdict had been handed down. Crime comics were guilty, guilty, guilty. Sentencing was about to begin.

*Justice Comics #8 © 1948 Marvel Entertainment Group*

# A CODE TO LIVE AND DIE BY

"The chair!! YEEEAHHH!! N. . .NO! I don't want to die!!"—*Crime Does Not Pay*

By summer's end, 1954, the comic book industry was thoroughly shaken by the Senate hearings and dismayed by the growing number of proposed state regulations regarding the sale of crime comic books. Every comic book publisher had suffered from the crime comic controversy and a few were out of business.

To avoid further public censure and government regulation, the Senate subcommittee urged the comic book publishers to develop their own "clear and explicit" code of standards, educate the public about the meaning of the code, make sure the code's standards are adhered to through some enforcement mechanism, and get the entire industry to participate in the self-regulation process.

On September 16, 1954, twenty-four of the nation's twenty-seven comic book publishers announced the formation of the Comics Magazine Association of America (CMAA), which would develop a voluntary plan and code to eliminate horror comics and to screen crime comics. They announced the appointment of New York Magistrate Charles F. Murphy to enforce a set of standards which Murphy promised would be "one of the strongest codes ever adopted by a communica-tions medium...a code with teeth in it." Comic books which adhered to the code would bear the seal "Approved by the Comics Code Authority."

The Code of the Comics Magazine Association of America, prepared in cooperation with Roman Catholic, Protestant, and Jewish leaders, was adopted on October 26, 1954. A newspaper article reported that "the new code has 31 specific prohibitions and bars everything from adultery to sex perversion. Suggestive poses, exaggerated feminine qualities, walking dead, ghouls, torture, vampires, cannibalism, and werewolves are not permitted. A companion code ends advertisements in comic books that sell nude pictures, salacious pinups, knives, close facsimiles of dangerous weapons, questionable toilet preparations, and fireworks."

One section of the Comics Code (Editorial Matter, General Standards, Part A) was devoted to regulating crime comics to make sure they did not glorify criminals, make crime attractive, or give details on how to commit a crime. The new Code did what no G-Man could ever have done: it eliminated crime overnight—at least as far as comic books were concerned. During the first two months of the Comics Code, 440 issues of

---

Facing Page: *Real Clue Crime Stories Vol. 5 #7 © 1950 Hillman Periodicals*

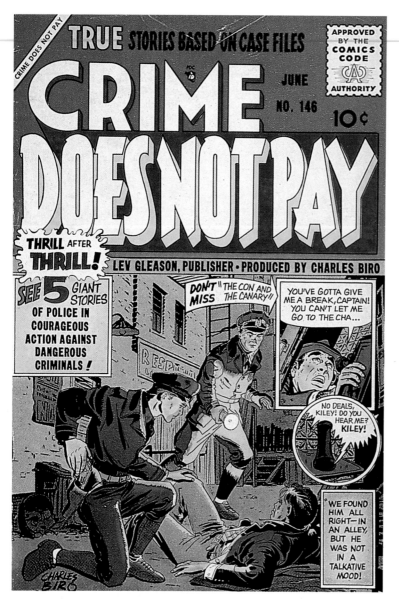

*Crime Does Not Pay
#146 © 1955
Comic House.* Art
by Charles Biro.

its ensuing Code, made sure that the word "crime" was allowed to remain in a comics title under the new Code restrictions. Thanks to this provision, two of Gleason's best-selling titles, *Crime Does Not Pay* and *Crime and Punishment*, were allowed to appear with the CMAA Seal of Approval. Two other comic books with the word "crime" in their title, *Crime Must Pay the Penalty* and *Police Against Crime*, also continued publishing under regulation by the Comics Code.

With the explicit restrictions placed on crime comics by the Code, however, the Code-approved issues of *Crime Does Not Pay* and the other surviving crime titles became tame "cops and robbers" tales with no gun-play, no murders, no blood, no guts. Even with the Code seal of approval, the crime comic books of late 1954 and 1955 were often undisplayed or returned by newsstand dealers who still remembered community boycotts.

While the Senate subcommittee had not proposed legislation to restrict the comic book industry, in part because of the publishers' willingness to regulate themselves, there were other comic book hearings and laws proposed in state legislatures around the country in 1954. Even with the Comics Code in operation, eighteen states were still investigating the comic book problem and considering regulatory measures. Colorado, Kansas, New Hampshire, Missouri, and South Dakota had comic book control legislation pending for their 1955 sessions.

In early 1955, a bill was introduced in the California House Assembly which prohibited the giveaway or sale of any crime comic book to persons under 18 years of age. The California Senate introduced a bill at the same time which made the sale and distribution of crime comics a misdemeanor. Among the criteria for defining a crime comic, the bill listed "pictorially depicted accounts . . . reasonably calculated to terrify and produce unreasonable fears in children." The restrictions in the California definition were even more restrictive than the Comics Code and would prohibit a comic book from depicting even minor crimes of burglary, theft, or malicious mischief.

The death knell for the crime comic

285 different titles were reviewed. Of these, 126 stories were completely rejected as unsuitable while 5,656 individual drawings were blue-penciled and replaced with panels to conform to the code. Despite Dr. Wertham's criticism in April 1955 that the new Code had a "hypocritical aura of good taste" and that its "overall effect was that murder looked more like a game under this new seal of approval," the Comics Code was successful in eliminating what most of the public found objectionable about comic books.

Contrary to popular belief, however, the 1954 Comics Code did not cause the immediate end of the crime comic book. Publisher Lev Gleason, who helped form the Comics Magazine Association of America and book came in May 1955 when a law took effect in New York State which made it illegal to sell "obscene and objectionable comics" to minors and use such words as "crime, sex, horror, terror" in the titles. (While the Comics Code had also prohibited the use of "horror" and "terror" in a title, the New York restriction against "sex" seemed like inflammatory overkill since no newsstand comic book had ever used a word stronger than "lust" in its logo.)

Burdened by New York State's explicit prohibition of the word "crime" in a comic book title, Lev Gleason's *Crime and Punishment* and *Crime Does Not Pay* could no longer be sold in a major marketplace. The last issues of these two titles, as well as *Police Against Crime* and *Crime Must Pay the Penalty*,

went on the newsstands in April and May of 1955 and then either vanished or changed names. The crime comic was now gone in name as well as spirit.

Some "crime" comics made it past the Comics Code and the ensuing states' legislation by becoming police or mystery detective comics. Prize Comics's long-running *Justice Traps the Guilty* survived until 1958, and DC Comics's *Gang Busters* and *Mr. District Attorney* continued until nearly the end of the decade. For the most part, however, there was a washout of crime comics from late 1954 through 1955, with over twenty titles publishing their last issues.

Smaller publishers, like William Gaines of EC Comics, who relied heavily on crime and horror, were nearly forced out of busi-

## CODE OF THE COMICS MAGAZINE ASSOCIATION OF AMERICA, CODE FOR EDITORIAL MATTER, GENERAL STANDARDS, PART A

1) Crimes shall never be presented in such a way as to create sympathy for the criminal, to promote distrust of the forces of law and justice, or to inspire others with a desire to imitate criminals.

2) No comics shall explicitly present the unique details and methods of a crime.

3) Policemen, judges, government officials and respected institutions shall never be presented in such a way to create disrespect for established authority.

4) If a crime is depicted it shall be as a sordid and unpleasant activity.

5) Criminals shall not be presented so as to be rendered glamorous or to occupy a position which creates a desire for emulation.

6) In every instance good shall triumph over evil and the criminal shall be punished for his misdeeds.

7) Scenes of excessive violence shall be prohibited. Scenes of brutal torture, excessive and unnecessary knife and gun play, physical agony, gory and gruesome crime shall be eliminated.

8) No unique or unusual methods of concealing weapons shall be shown.

9) Instances of law enforcement officers dying as a result of a criminal's activities should be discouraged.

10) The crime of kidnapping shall never be portrayed in any detail, nor shall any profit accrue to the abductor or kidnapper. The criminal or kidnapper must be punished in every case.

11) The letters of the word "crime" on a comics magazine cover shall never be appreciably greater in dimension than other words contained in the title. The word "crime" shall never appear alone on a cover.

12) Restraint in the use of the word "crime" in titles or sub-titles shall be exercised.

## THE COMICS CODE

The Comics Code placed severe editorial and artistic restrictions on what could take place in a crime comic story. One way to see the changes the Code brought about is to compare a crime comic story drawn before the Comics Code with the same story reprinted after the Comics Code.

In order to save money, Ace Publishing reprinted a story from its May 1948 issue of *Super-Mystery Comics* in the code-approved January 1956 issue of *Penalty Comics*. To meet the new Code standards, the original story had to be redrawn and rewritten in several places.

Notice how in these "Before" and "After" pictures, the story was cleaned up to meet Code approval by filling in the cleavage on dresses, erasing bullets and sound effects, and rewriting dialogue to make it less threatening.

*Super Mystery Vol. 7 #5 © 1948 Ace Magazines*
*Penalty #48 © 1956 Ace Magazines*
*Super Mystery Vol. 7 #5 © 1948 Ace Magazines*
*Penalty #48 © 1956 Ace Magazines*

ness. Gaines was one of three publishers who initially refused to join the Comics Magazine Association of America (the others being Dell Publishing and the publishers of *Classics Illustrated*). He changed his mind, however, when newsstands refused to handle his comics without the Comics Code Seal of Approval. Gaines replaced his horror and crime titles with comics which conformed to the Comics Code, but canceled these as well after becoming frustrated by the Code's restrictions.

In late 1955, he made a decision to bypass the Comic Code by publishing a line of comic *magazines* which he termed "Picto-Fiction: A New Form of ADULT ENTERTAINMENT." Gaines and editor Al Feldstein wrote: "We deliberately label Picto-Fiction 'adult entertainment' because it is designed to be just that . . . entertainment for the more mature fiction reader."

The EC "picto-fiction" magazines, which included *Shock Illustrated*, *Terror Illustrated*, and *Crime Illustrated*, were printed in black and white, with text typeset separate from the comic art to create an illustrated story effect. The magazines, subtitled "Adult Suspense Stories," dealt with such issues as wife-swapping, drugs, prostitution, and rape-stranglings. Gaines hoped that the higher price and magazine format of the "Picto-Fiction" line would attract an older audience looking for non-code comic stories. Many of the artists from the pre-code EC crime and horror comics worked on the "picto-fiction" magazines as well.

Johnny Craig, who drew more crime stories for EC than anyone else, worked on both issues of *Crime Illustrated* (November 1955–Spring 1956). "I enjoyed it very much," Craig recalled. "I think most of the artists did. It was a great challenge in that we were allowed a greater freedom in depicting the story—it required a greater ability to do the job right. It made us feel we were advancing and doing a better grade of artwork—a more illustrative type of artwork. I'm sorry it didn't go over better than it did."

While Gaines's attempt at a crime comic magazine for adults failed (primarily because of continued distribution problems), he succeeded beyond his wildest dreams in capturing the adolescent market with another comic magazine. Formerly published as a 10-cent color comic book, Gaines had turned *Mad* into a black-and-white 25-cent magazine several months before launching his "picto-fiction" line.

By 1957, there were only a half dozen crime or police comics among the more than 450 comic book titles. In ten years, the crime comic genre had gone from birth to boom to bust. After the number of crime comic titles hit bottom in 1959, however, a renewed interest in detective comics came with the growing popularity of crime and detective television shows in the early 1960s.

Beginning in the 1950s, Dell Publishing Company adapted such popular television shows as *I Love Lucy*, *Leave It to Beaver*, and *Gunsmoke* into comic book format. Similarly, in 1962, Gold Key Comics also began adapting TV shows into comic book series. Among the early 1960s detective- and crime-related television shows adapted into comic books were *77 Sunset Strip* (January 1960), *Peter Gun* (April 1960), *The Detectives* (March 1961), *The Untouchables* (October 1961),

*Danger Man* (November 1961), *Mike Shayne, Private Eye* (November 1961), *87th Precinct* (April 1962), *Target: The Corrupters* (May 1962), *Cain's Hundred* (July 1962), *Checkmate* (October 1962), *The Defenders* (September 1962), *Hawaiian Eye* (July 1963), and *Burke's Law* (March 1964). Almost all the comic book covers featured photographs of the TV stars and the stories were drawn with the actors' likenesses.

The Code's restrictions against the portrayal of crime in comic books were far stricter than what was allowed by network censors on the TV screen. A TV series like *The Untouchables*, for example, was more in the tradition of the pre-Code 1940s crime comics, with its rampant machine-gunnings and cold-blooded murders. Dell Publishing

*Crime Illustrated #1 © 1955 William M. Gaines.* Art by Joe Orlando.

*Detectives, The #1168 © 1961 Four-Star Hastings*

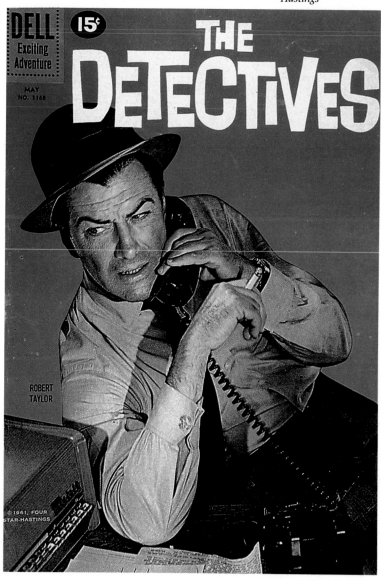

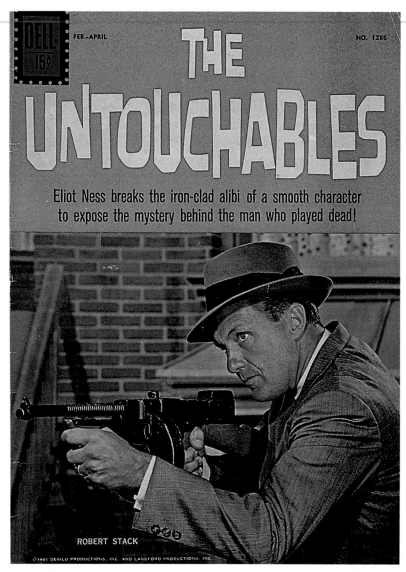

*Untouchables, The #1286 © 1961 Desilu Productions, Inc.*

*77 Sunset Strip #1291 © 1962 Warner Bros. Pictures, Inc.*

James Bond movies in 1963 and 1964, however, television shifted from detectives to secret agents and super-spies and the comic books followed suit. From the mid- to late 1960s, the following spy TV shows were turned into comic book series: *Espionage* (May 1964), *The Man from UNCLE* (February 1965), *I Spy* (August 1966), *Secret Agent* (November 1966), *Honey West* (September 1966), *The Girl from UNCLE* (January 1967), *Mission: Impossible* (May 1967), *The Avengers* (November 1968), and *Mod Squad* (January 1969).

In 1964, the first issue of *Creepy*, a black-and-white horror comic magazine, appeared on the newsstands. It was full of vampires, werewolves, blood, and ghouls. Not surprisingly, it did not sport a Comics Code Seal of Approval. Like Gaines's "Picto-Fiction" series, *Creepy* and later black-and-white horror comic magazines of the 1960s, such as *Eerie*, *Horror Tales*, and *Terror Tales*, bypassed the Comics Code. In 1970, the first black-and-white crime comic magazines appeared when *Murder Tales* (November 1970) and *Tales of the Killers* (December 1970) reprinted stories from 1940s issues of *Crime Does Not Pay*. The

*Hawaiian Eye #1 © 1963 Warner Bros. Pictures, Inc.*

adopted the violent TV series as a comic book in 1961 without the restrictions of the Comics Code. Since Dell (and later Gold Key) maintained a set of editorial standards supposedly stricter than the Comics Code, it never submitted its comics for review or approval. As a result, Dell could publish detective- and crime-related TV comics which might otherwise be severely regulated by the Comics Code. The level of violence in the Dell and Gold Key comics, however, was still considerably toned down from that in the television shows.

The stars of the early 1960s television series (and their comic book adaptations) were generally glamorous private-eyes, such as in *77 Sunset Strip*, *Peter Gun*, *Hawaiian Eye*, and *Burke's Law*. After the popularity of the

*Avengers, The #1 © 1968 Gold Key*

pollution, and drug addiction. Just as television and movies had changed over the previous two decades, comic book publishers felt the need to grow beyond restrictions imposed by a frightened industry in 1954.

In January 1971, the Comics Code was revised by agreement of its members to allow editors, writers, and artists to create stories which addressed drug abuse issues. A new article added to Part B of the Code's General Standards for Editorial Matter decreed that "Narcotics or Drug addiction shall not be presented except as a vicious habit." Such presentation in a comic book story was still strictly limited by eight conditions. Narcotics, illegal drug use, or drug production and trafficking could not be shown as attractive, justifiable, or alluringly profitable and

following year, two other black-and-white crime comic magazines appeared without the Comics Code Seal of Approval: *Crime Machine* (February 1971) and *In the Days of the Mob* (Fall 1971).

Jack Kirby, who had drawn stories twenty-five years earlier for *Justice Traps the Guilty* and *Real Clue Crime Comics*, was the editor, writer, and artist for *In the Days of the Mob*: "Goons, hoods, punks, torpedoes! They fought for the control of the rackets—lived quickly—died suddenly! And those left branched out—enveloped cities—became the evil entity called—THE MOB!" Kirby's *In the Days of the Mob*, the first original true-crime comic in seventeen years, was set in the 1930s with stories of Ma Barker, Al Capone, and Pretty Boy Floyd. The black-and-white magazine had more gunplay, violence, and murders than the Comics Code permitted in regular color comic books.

In late 1970, the comic book publishers re-evaluated the Comics Code in order to keep up with the changing times. Writers and editors were introducing a new realism into comic books which addressed such problems as racial discrimination, environmental

*Man From UNCLE, The #9 © 1966 Metro-Goldwyn-Mayer, Inc.*

*Murder Tales #10 © 1970 World Famous Periodicals. Art by Bill Alexander.*

price." Additionally, law enforcement officers could be killed as a result of a criminal's activities when the "guilty, because of their crime, live a sordid existence and are brought to justice because of the particular crime." Finally, criminals could now be presented in "glamorous circumstances" if an "unhappy end results from their ill-gotten gains, and creates no desire for emulation."

The revisions in the 1971 Code, however, had little effect on crime comics—or more properly, their continued absence. There were few crime comics published in the 1970s except for short-lived police comics, including the quintessential crime comic title of that decade, *Lady Cop* (July 1975, *First Issue Special*).

In the 1980s, the growth of specialty comic book stores provided a new market and distribution network independent of the newsstands and their requirements for Code-approved comics. As a result, many new publishers who entered the industry in the 1980s and 1990s produced comic books outside of the Comics Code purview. These "independent" publishers were also distinguished by their willingness to produce comic book titles outside the superhero field, the

comic books could not show the details of drug use or procurement, nor could they portray the use of narcotics in a casual manner or in such a way that implies the drug habit could be quickly or easily broken.

The revised code also allowed the use of such classical horror characters as vampires and werewolves in comic books for the first time since 1954. As a result, there was a horror comic boom from 1971 to 1974.

There were also changes made to the code which specifically applied to crime comics. For example, in order to show the evil of corruption, it was now permitted to show "policemen, judges, government officials, and respected institutions" committing an illegal act, provided that it was "declared an exceptional case and that the culprit pay the legal

*In the Days of the Mob #1 © 1971 Hampshire Dist. Ltd. Art by Jack Kirby.*

*Justice Comics #37
© 1953 Marvel
Entertainment Group*

dominant genre of the industry throughout the 1980s.

As a result, the 1980s and 1990s saw new opportunities for the crime and detective comic book genre. Max Allan Collins, writer for the "Dick Tracy" comic strip, and artist Terry Beatty created the most successful comic book detective of the decade with their woman private-eye, Ms. Tree. Originally published by Eclipse Comics as *Ms. Tree's Thrilling Detective Adventures* (February 1983), the character survived and grew into the 1990s with a new title (*Ms. Tree Quarterly*) and publisher (DC Comics). *The MAZE Agency* (December 1988), another successful 1980s detective series, was created by comic book and mystery writer Mike Barr. Featuring a female-male detective duo, *The MAZE Agency* was described by Barr as a "love story about detectives, a detective story about love."

Although comics are able to depict violence more freely in the 1990s, it is often the "whodunnit" detective comic and not the "shoot-to-kill" crime comic which enjoys the greatest popularity. Even one hundred years later, the world's greatest fictional detective, Sherlock Holmes, continues to appear and reappear in new comic book series—a fitting testimonial to the eternal appeal of the crime, the crime-solver, and the crime comic.

*Ms. Tree Quarterly #2
© 1990 DC Comics,
Inc.* Art by Denys
Cowan.

# COMIC BOOK DICKS AND PRIVATE EYE WISE GUYS

"I came on them at the end of the corridor. I didn't talk, but let the rod in my hand speak for me. I let it go and didn't stop pulling the trigger, watching the rats drop like flies hitting an electric screen." —Johnny Dynamite (*Dynamite Comics*)

The detective heroes in the American comic book were borrowed from movies, radio, television, pulp magazines, best-selling mystery novels, and comic strips. The comic book counterparts of popular detectives like Sherlock Holmes, Charlie Chan, and Perry Mason ran through action-packed stories that were resolved with less than a thousand words of dialogue. Deduction, character analysis, and psychological probing were gladly sacrificed for car chases and brass knuckles. At the same time, however, the sparse dialogue and fist-in-the-face action were perfectly suited for the hard-boiled private eyes of the early 1950s comic books.

The first detectives in the comic books came from the newspaper comic strips. Norman Marsh's comic strip G-Man "Dan Dunn" was reprinted in *Famous Funnies* (February 1935) while the "Dick Tracy" strips were collected and published in *Popular Comics* (February 1936) and other titles. Since the comic book story usually only serialized four to eight pages of the newspaper strips, the adventure was continued over several issues. Dick Tracy was soon popular enough, however, to rate an entire comic book that reprinted a "complete" (although usually edited) newspaper strip adventure. Almost all of the "Dick Tracy" newspaper strips from the mid-1930s to the late 1950s have found their way into one of the more than four hundred Dick Tracy comic books published over the past fifty years.

The only other comic strip detective to remotely rival Dick Tracy in the comic books was Kerry Drake, a white-haired private investigator created in 1943 by writer Allen Saunders and artist Alfred Andriola. The "Kerry Drake" newspaper strip lasted until 1983, although it became a police soap opera in its final years. The 1940s and 1950s

---

Facing Page: *Jeff Jordan, U.S. Agent #1* © 1947 D.S. Publishing Co.

adventures of Kerry Drake, however, were anything but tame. Like Dick Tracy, Kerry faced an awesome array of grotesque villains whose names matched their physical and psychic deformities: Bottleneck, No Face, Stitches, Dr. Prey, Shuteye, Torso, Fingers, Vixen Vargo, Ecstasy, Meatball, Bullseye, Mother Whistler, Kid Gloves, Mossy Green, and Angel-Puss. A man of action in his early years, Kerry was assisted by Sandy Burns, his perky brunette secretary. The "Kerry Drake" newspaper strip was reprinted in comic book format from 1944 to 1956 by three publishers. Although Alfred Andriola, the artist for "Kerry Drake," also helped create a comic book superhero called Captain Triumph (*Crack Comics*, January 1943), he never drew

*Saint, The #12 © 1952 Avon Periodicals*

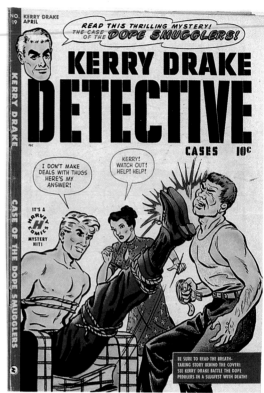

*Kerry Drake Detective Cases #19 © 1950 Publishers Syndicate*

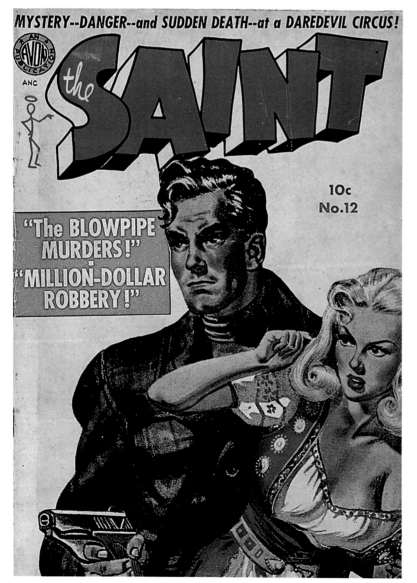

any original Drake stories for the comic books.

There were several other comic strip detectives whose adventures wound up as reprints in comic books. Alex Raymond's "Secret Agent X-9," as well as the later adventures of his sophisticated detective "Rip Kirby," appeared in several one-issue comic books. Vic Flint, a blond private eye with a permanent cigarette fixed to his lip, had a newspaper strip (1946–67) which was reprinted in various comic books of the 1950s.

While comic strip detectives like Dick Tracy and Kerry Drake enjoyed a healthy life in the comic books as reprints, the most widely recognized comic book detectives came from the movies and best-selling mysteries of the time. Charlie Chan, the star of dozens of movies, hundreds of radio shows, and a line of novels, not only had his own comic strip, he also had a series of comic books from several publishers. Sherlock Holmes, Ellery Queen, Perry Mason, and Mike Shayne were a few of the other popular fictional detectives who appeared in original comic book series.

## THE SAINT

The Saint, Leslie Charteris's sophisticated and dashing detective, enjoyed a life that spanned both the comic strips and the comic books. Created in 1928 for the novel *Meet the Tiger*, Simon Templar (aka, the Saint) was a self-styled, modern-day Robin Hood who used his cunning to help the unfortunate. He often left his calling card (a stick figure with a halo) at the scene. After starring in a series of novels, movies, and radio shows through the 1930s and 1940s, the Saint appeared in the February 1942 issue of *Silver Streak Comics*. Charteris wrote the scripts for the four comic book stories, which were illustrated by Edd Ashe. The novelist broke into comics a few years earlier when he wrote the continuities for the "Secret Agent X-9" comic strip after Dashiell Hammett left the feature. As befitting the time, Charteris had the comic book version of his character fighting Nazi spies and saboteurs.

The *Saint* comic book, which lasted five years, began in August 1947 with original stories. The following year, Charteris brought his detective to the newspapers in a daily comic strip drawn by Mike Roy. Roy, who began his comic book career at the Funnies, Incorporated studio before the war, had drawn for Lev Gleason's *Crime Does Not Pay* a few months prior to working on the "Saint" daily newspaper strip. By the time the strip began, Charteris was a wealthy man who enjoyed traveling around the world on his boat. Roy recalled he often had to chase Charteris from port to port to get the next script installment of the Saint. Some of the newspaper strips were later reprinted in the last issues of the comic book. Although the newspaper strip lasted into the 1960s and the character was featured in a 1967–69 television series starring Roger Moore, the Saint made no other original comic book appearances after 1950.

## NICK CARTER

Nick Carter, who has appeared in well over one thousand adventures and more than five hundred novels, is the longest running American detective series. Only England's Sexton Blake has solved more mysteries than Carter. Created in 1886 by writer John Russell Coryell and Ormond G. Smith, the son of one of the founders of Street & Smith Publishing, this premiere "action detective" was one of the most popular fictional characters of the late nineteenth century, starring in a long-running weekly series of boys' "dime detective novels" known as the *Nick Carter Library*.

Nick Carter was written by a number of people under Street & Smith house names for novels, short stories, and pulp magazines such as *Detective Story*. He matured from a nineteenth-century boyhood hero into a modern private investigator. From 1939 to 1940, there were three Nick Carter movies starring Walter Pidgeon.

When Street & Smith Publishing began a line of comic books in 1940 which featured its popular pulp magazine heroes (such as the Shadow, Doc Savage, and Frank Merriwell), Nick Carter was added to the lineup in *Shadow Comics* (March 1940). In 1943, a long-running radio show "Nick Carter, Master

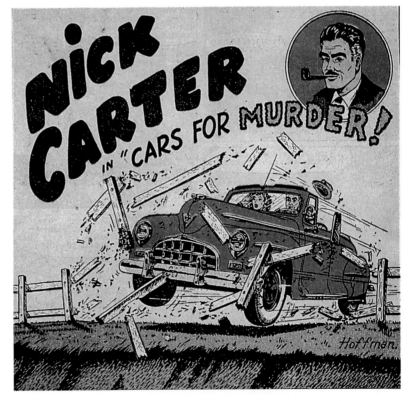

*Shadow Comics Vol. 8 #8 © 1948 Street & Smith Publications.* Art by Harry Hoffman.

*Charlie Chan #3 © 1948 Prize Publications.* Art by Carmine Infantino and Charles Raab.

Detective" began, and the detective was also added that year to *Doc Savage Comics* (one cover featured radio actor Lon Clark in his role as Nick). The detective's seventy-two comic book adventures ran from 1940 to 1949 and were drawn by several artists, including Jack Binder, Joe Meditz, Kurt Menczer, Owen Middleton, Harry Hoffman, Bob Powell, and Joe Maneely.

In the comic books, Carter was often accompanied by Patsy, a comely blonde sidekick who was originally a *boy* bootblack (Patsy Garvan) in the Nick Carter dime detective novels. Carter was a good deal taller in the comics than he was in the original novels (in which he was often referred to as "The Little Giant"), and older as well. The comic book Nick Carter was drawn with a moustache and with his hair graying at the sides—a fitting concession perhaps to his longevity as one of the most popular detectives of both the nineteenth and twentieth centuries.

## CHARLIE CHAN

Charlie Chan, a Chinese-born detective from Honolulu, first appeared in Earl Derr Biggers's 1925 novel *The House without a Key*. Biggers wrote five more novels over the next seven

years starring his quick-witted detective who spouted memorable Oriental aphorisms in every chapter ("Tongue often hang man quicker than rope" and "Time only wasted when sprinkling perfume on goat farm").

While the novels were popular enough, it was the movies (over fifty produced!) which made Charlie Chan one of the most recognizable detectives of all time—only Sherlock Holmes appeared in more films. Several actors portrayed the detective throughout the lengthy series, including Sidney Toler and Roland Winters. The definitive Charlie Chan of the movies for many, however, was Warner Oland, who starred as the Hawaiian sleuth in sixteen films from 1931 to 1937.

The popularity of the Oland movies, along with the growing success of Dick Tracy, prompted the McNaught Syndicate to offer a Charlie Chan comic strip to newspapers in October 1938. The strip was drawn and written by Alfred Andriola, an artist who previously assisted Milt Caniff on "Terry and the Pirates." Andriola read the Charlie Chan novels in preparation for the strip, but he based his portrayal of the detective from the movies and on Oland's likeness.

"I write the dialogue like a movie con-

*Charlie Chan #3 © 1948 Prize Publications.* Art by Joe Simon and Jack Kirby.

tinuity," Andriola explained, "plotting it weeks in advance of the actual drawing. Then I transcribe it to the strips and my assistant does the lettering. After that, I fill in what's left with pictures because in the adventure strip the story is the important thing and you may as well get that down first."

Andriola took a free hand with the character and introduced a second detective—Kirk Barrow—into the strip in 1939. Barrow did the footwork and took the pratfalls for the dignified and portly Chan. The role of the Hawaiian detective's "number one son," or Son Lee, was downplayed as the strip progressed—a change more in keeping with the spirit of the original novels than the movies.

The Charlie Chan newspaper strips were reprinted in the comic books first in *Feature Comics* (August 1939) and later in *Big Shot Comics* (May 1940). Although the newspaper strip ended in 1942, the reprints continued in the comic books until 1947. In 1948, a new and original Charlie Chan comic book series was created for Prize Comics under the direction of Joe Simon and Jack Kirby. Simon and Kirby, who were also putting together crime comics for Prize such as *Justice Traps the Guilty* and *Headline Comics*, made "Charlie Chan" an interesting mix of humor, adventure, and detective work.

Taking a cue from some of the later Charlie Chan movies, the Prize Comics series played up the role of the detective's Number One Son and made him the hapless foil for his father's wit: "Like bargain counter alarm clock, Number One son is wrong again!" In fact, most of the stories were filled with Chan's lamentations over being saddled with his son as his helper: "Truly written: children great gamble, never know how turn out. Chances against parent being proud of offspring most slight."

More so than the earlier comic strip, the Prize comic book series delighted in filling the panels with Chan's pithy observations: "Wisely said, man who laughs last still alive" and "Even bull in china shop sometimes manages to do more good than damage." The comic book ended in 1949 and was briefly revived by Charlton Comics for another year in 1955. Chan was a little denser

*Charlie Chan #2 © 1966 Dell Publishing Co.* Art by Frank Springer.

in this run, muttering things like "Trouble appears in strange places!" and "Bold thief in daylight needs no stealth."

With the syndication of the 1957 television show, "The New Adventures of Charlie Chan," DC Comics brought out a comic book series of the same name (1958–59), with Chan resembling the TV series star, J. Carrol Naish. Charlie Chan's next comic book series from Dell Comics in 1965 reflected the growing popularity of comic book superheroes. The March 1966 issue had Chan fighting the Cat, a costumed villain who flies through the air with a jet-propulsion pack. Charlie Chan, however, still remained nonplussed: "Confucius say empty barrel make most noise."

*Perry Mason Feature Book #49 © 1946 David McKay.*

## PERRY MASON

Perry Mason is the best-known lawyer/detective in the world, thanks to over eighty best-selling books and a television/movie series which has spanned four decades. Erle Stanley Gardner wrote *The Case of the Velvet Claws*, his first Perry Mason novel, in 1933, and followed it with a new "Case" almost every six months for the rest of his life. Warner Bros. Studio produced six Perry Mason movies from 1934 to 1937, and a CBS radio show premiered in 1943.

In 1946, King Features Syndicate obtained the rights to produce comic strip adaptations of two Gardner novels. The following year, David McKay Publications issued "a picturization of the best-seller" *The Case*

of *The Lucky Legs* (originally published in 1934) and *The Case of the Shoplifter's Shoes* (1938). Vernon Greene, the artist on the "Shadow" newspaper comic strip, drew *Lucky Legs,* while artist/writer Paul Norris adapted *Shoplifter's Shoes.*

The comic book Perry Mason of the 1940s was much like Gardner's hero of the early days. Described in the first novel as "reasonably young . . . good condition" and poised "like a man getting ready to slug someone," Mason makes his comic book cover debut by punching out a suspect. Unlike the slower-moving and more cerebral character of the later novels and popular television series, the comic book Perry Mason thrives on personal confrontation and imminent danger: "I'm deciding what happens next . . . Open that door without a search warrant and I'll break your jaw!"

In 1964, another comic book version of Gardner's detective/lawyer appeared. The comic book, which owed its existence and inspiration to the enormously popular *Perry Mason* television show starring Raymond Burr, played up the roles of Della Street and Paul Drake, and used photos of Burr for its front covers.

## ELLERY QUEEN

Ellery Queen, an absentminded mystery writer and amateur sleuth, regularly helps his father, who is an inspector with the New York Police Department. The mild-mannered

*Perry Mason Feature Book #49 © 1946 David McKay. Art by Vernon Greene.*

detective unravels crimes and names their perpetrators by noticing the clues others overlook.

Ellery Queen first appeared in 1929 as the hero of *The Roman Hat Mystery*. Written by Frederic Dannay and Manfred Lee, under the pen name of Ellery Queen, the novel was the first of forty Ellery Queen mysteries that appeared over the next forty-two years. Their detective was so popular, Dannay and Lee soon found themselves writing screenplays for a series of Ellery Queen movies that began in 1935, as well as the scripts for a radio show that ran from 1939 to 1948. The Ellery Queen trademark was to stop the story before the culprit was revealed and then "challenge the reader" (who by now had all the necessary clues) to solve the mystery before continuing.

In early 1940, following a successful radio series and a series of movies starring Ralph Bellamy, Ellery Queen's next medium to conquer was the comic books. *Crackajack Comics* (May 1940) introduced the amateur detective in "The Adventure of the Coffin Clue," the first of twenty episodes. Although Dannay and Lee did not contribute to the comic book series (other than to review it), some of their radio scripts were recycled into the stories.

Queen's secretary Nikki Porter, created originally for the radio show, played a prominent role in the comic book series as well (although she appeared as a brunette despite the original description of her as a "small, slim miss with nice red hair"). Bill Ely was one of the first artists to adapt Ellery Queen to the comics and his rendition of the detective failed to include glasses—a mistake usually made in the movies as well.

The comic book Ellery Queen was also more action-oriented than the cerebral detective of the novels. In a six-page story from *Crackajack Comics* (June 1941), Queen leaps from a flaming airplane, slugs a fifth-column spy, dodges a blowtorch to his face, jumps out of a speeding car, takes a bullet graze to the head, and ends up in a hospital bed. His secretary Nikki is no shrinking violet either: "If he didn't have a gun El, I'd scratch his eyes out!"

Like the novels, the comic book stories

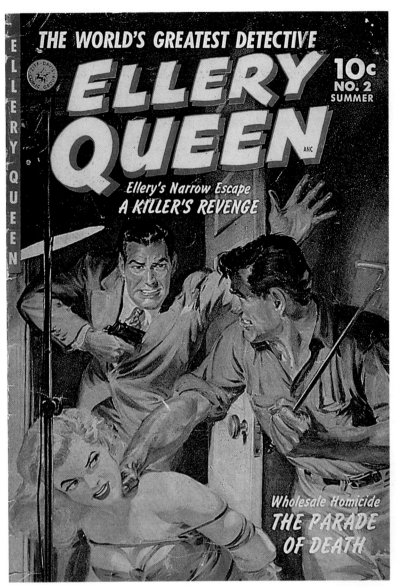

*Ellery Queen #2 © 1952 Ziff-Davis Publishing Company*

were also halted right before Ellery named the suspect in the crime: "STOP! Again at this seemingly innocent point, Ellery Queen has deduced the identity of the culprit. It's a simple solution and hinges on two clues. The first was pointed out several times. The *second*? Ah—that requires use of your deductive powers!"

After disappearing from the comics in 1942, Ellery Queen returned in 1949 for four issues of his own comic book from Superior Comics. The stories for *Ellery Queen* (May 1949) were supplied by Jerry Iger's art studio in New York. The stories, like many in the Superior comic book lineup, were lurid little ditties with a liberal dose of horror and flesh. Ellery Queen stumbles into opium dens and the open arms of willing women ("A roman-

*Ellery Queen #1243 © 1961 Ellery Queen*

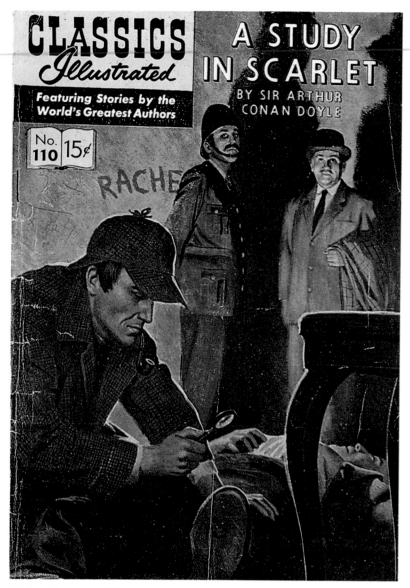

*Classics Illustrated #110*
*© 1953 Gilberton*
*Publications*

1961 to 1962, were more true to the original novels than the other comic book adaptations. Ellery was correctly portrayed as wearing glasses and his dad, Inspector Richard Queen, was in every story. Nikki the secretary, however, was nowhere to be seen. Each story, of course, was still interrupted so the reader had a chance to guess the suspect: "I've told you all I found out, so you should be able to add up the clues! Do YOU know who murdered the missing man—and can YOU prove it?"

## SHERLOCK HOLMES

The world's greatest fictional detective, whose original sixty cases were recorded by Arthur Conan Doyle, achieved even greater recognition as the star of countless stage, radio, television, and movie productions. Sherlock Holmes and his companion Dr. Watson appeared in over two hundred films (the first in 1903), making the British sleuth one of the most popular movie heroes of all time. Both the movies and the original stories by Doyle would greatly influence the various comic book incarnations of Sherlock Holmes.

tic weekend was drawing to a close but high adventure was just around the corner of The Crooked Mile . . ."). The character was certainly not the one Dannay and Lee had envisioned.

The next Ellery Queen comic book series, which appeared in 1952 from Ziff-Davis Publishing, coincided with the release of the 1951–52 ABC television series, "The Adventures of Ellery Queen." The comic also made Ellery more of a fist-throwing detective than the novels. Both the TV show and comic book disappeared at about the same time.

Ten years later, Dell Publishing (the original publisher of *Crackajack Comics*) brought Ellery Queen back for his fourth comic book series. The three issues, from

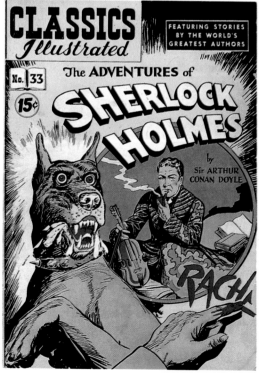

*Classics Illustrated #33 © 1947 Gilberton Publications.*
Art by H. C. Kiefer.

The first appearance of Sherlock Holmes in the comics occurred in 1930, one year after the release of the first "talkie" Holmes movie (*The Return of Sherlock Holmes*), starring Clive Brook. For the Bell Newspaper Syndicate, artist Leo O'Mealia drew the daily comic strip adventures of Sherlock Holmes, who bore a passing resemblance to Brook's film character. The comic strip was copyrighted by Arthur Conan Doyle and featured straightforward illustrations for his accompanying text from "The Silver Blaze," "The Musgrave Ritual," and other stories. The comic strip, which lasted until 1932, was reprinted in comic book format over fifty years later.

Sherlock Holmes made his first comic book appearance in the July 1944 issue of Classic Comics's *Famous Mysteries,* which featured an adaptation of Doyle's "Sign of the Four." This first comic book adventure of the master detective and Dr. Watson was drawn by Louis Zansky, who had warmed up for the job by adapting *Moby Dick* and *Huckleberry Finn* for Classic Comics as well. For Classic Comics (later known as Classics Illustrated), Zansky also drew *The Adventures of Sherlock Holmes* (January 1947), which adapted "The Hound of the Baskervilles" and "A Study in Scarlet." Classic Comics marked the only 1940s comic book appearance of Sherlock Holmes, despite the enormous popularity of the movie series with Basil Rathbone and Nigel Bruce as Holmes and Watson. Like the movies, the 1940s comic book version of Holmes invariably had him wearing the deerstalker cap and holding a calabash pipe in almost every scene—instantly identifiable yet a caricature of the literary Holmes.

The last "classic" treatment given Doyle's detective was in the August 1953 issue of *Classics Illustrated,* which featured adaptations of "A Study in Scarlet" and "The Speckled Band." Kenneth Fitch, who had written dozens of true-crime comic stories in the late 1940s, adapted the script for artist Seymour Moskowitz.

Sherlock Holmes returned as a newspaper comic strip in 1954 for the New York Herald Tribune, with art by Mike Sekowsky and Frank Giacoia. Holmes never looked

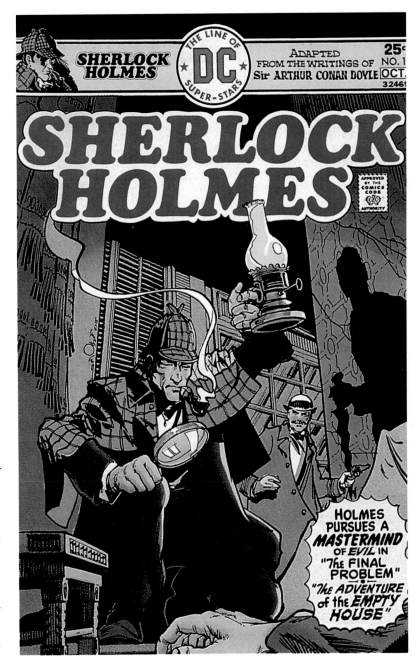

*Sherlock Holmes #1*
© 1975 DC Comics, Inc.
Art by Walt Simonson.

younger and, although he sucked on a pipe in every panel, he had ditched his hat. Edith Meiser, who had adapted Sherlock Holmes for the radio, supplied the scripts, which alternated between the traditional (Professor Moriarty) and the esoteric (vampires from Sussex). The daily and Sunday strip, authorized by the Doyle estate, lasted until 1956 and was reprinted in a 1988 comic book series.

In October 1955, Charlton Comics released the *All New Baffling Adventures of Sherlock Holmes.* Unauthorized and bearing

Marvel Preview #6
© 1976 Marvel
Entertainment Group.
Art by Ken Barr.

From 1975 to 1976, Sherlock Holmes experienced a popularity boom when a best-selling novel based on the detective by Nicholas Meyer (*The Seven Percent Solution*) was also made into a movie. At the same time, there was the debut of a Sherlock Holmes play on Broadway, a TV movie (*Sherlock Holmes in New York*), a movie spoof (*The Adventures of Sherlock Holmes' Smarter Brother*), and a couple of comic books.

For DC Comics, writer Dennis O'Neil and artist E. R. Cruz adapted Arthur Conan Doyle's "The Final Problem" for the first and only issue of *Sherlock Holmes* (September 1975). It was the first comic book adaptation of a Doyle story in over twenty years and was fairly faithful to the Victorian settings, but Holmes seemed out of character with a pronounced fondness for fisticuffs and melodramatics.

A more cerebral Holmes appeared in Marvel Comics's adaptation of the *Hound of the Baskervilles* in *Marvel Preview* (April 1976) by writer Doug Moench and artist Val Mayerik. The story, faithfully told from the viewpoint of Dr. Watson, allowed a dozen pages to show Holmes's deductive abilities at work in his Baker Street study—a luxury in a medium that thrives on physical action. Unlike other adaptations that made Watson a comic sidekick and foil, this version gave the good doctor his due. Originally conceived as a three-part series, the story had to be condensed into two issues, with some liber-

little resemblance to the Doyle creation, Sherlock Holmes in this version was based in New York and worked on cases with Sergeant Flaherty. Instead of Watson, this Holmes had an assistant (still with the requisite white moustache and doctorly bearing) who went by the name of Frothingham. Not surprisingly, the series lasted only two issues ("Elementary, my dear Frothingham??").

The next comic book featuring Sherlock Holmes also departed from the Doyle canon. Dell Comics issued two issues of the *New Adventures of Sherlock Holmes* (1961–62), with art by Bob Fujitani and the team of Mike Sekowsky and Frank Giacoia, which had worked on the 1954–56 newspaper strip. While stories like "Derelict Ship" and "The Cunning Assassin" were not Doyle, they were faithful to the original concept.

*Classics Illustrated* #33 © 1947 Gilberton Publications.
Art by Louis Zansky.

ties taken to make the ending a little more visually exciting than the original *Hound of the Baskervilles.*

Perhaps the most faithful comic book adaptation of the world's greatest detective was the *Cases of Sherlock Holmes*, a fifteen-issue series from 1986 to 1988. Employing a turn-of-the-century style, artist Dan Day illustrated the unabridged text by Arthur Conan Doyle from such stories as "The Adventure of the Beryl Coronet," "The Adventure of Silver Blaze," and the "Adventure of the Naval Treaty."

Along with the "serious" comic book and comic strip appearances of Sherlock Holmes, there were also many parodies. One of the earliest was "Sherlocko the Monk," a 1910 newspaper strip by Gus Mager which portrayed Doyle's detective as a simian sleuth who is assisted by Dr. Watso. Doyle threatened a lawsuit in 1913 and Mager renamed and redrew Sherlocko and Dr. Watso into the more humanized Hawkshaw the Detective and his assistant, the Colonel.

"Spurlock and Watkins," the first original comic book parody of Sherlock Holmes, entertained readers in the December 1936 issue of Detective Picture Stories—the first issue of the first detective comic book. The best-remembered Holmes parody, however, occurred years later in the *Mad* comic book stories "Shermlock Shomes" (October 1953) and "Shermlock Shomes in The Hound of the Basketballs!" (October 1954) as drawn by Bill Elder. When Holmes examines an ordinary umbrella, he deduces the following facts about its owner: "Well, Whatsit, I would say it belongs to a young lady . . . a handsome brunette . . . 24 . . . 5-4 . . . 36-22-34!! 36-22-34? 23 . . . Skidooo! Furthermore, her fingernail on her left forefinger has a 1/32nd inch chipped off the edge. She has a tiny beauty mark 1/16th of an inch in diameter under her right arm-pit and a tattoo on her right bicep of a simulated dagger piercing the flesh and inscribed with the word . . . Mother!"

Although Sherlock Holmes appeared in barely more than two dozen comic books, his shadow falls on all the comic book and comic strip detectives from Dick Tracy everlastingly onward.

## THE PRIVATE EYES

Although the best-known comic book detectives originally came from comic strips, popular fiction, movies, or television, there was a memorable outpouring in the early 1950s of private eyes created especially for the comic books. Most of the comic book private eyes played a role like Humphrey Bogart's Sam Spade from *The Maltese Falcon*. Chip Gardner, the hard-boiled detective from *Crime Does Not Pay*, parrots a line that Bogart could have delivered: "For twenty-five bucks a day, I'm anybody's servant." Like Sam Spade, comic book private eyes ran modest two-room de-

*Johnny Danger #1*
© 1954 Toby Press

*Crime Detector #3*
*© 1954 Timor*
*Publications*

(1950), *My Gun Is Quick* (1950), *The Big Kill* (1951), *One Lonely Night* (1951), and *Kiss Me, Deadly* (1952). By 1953, there were over fifteen million Mike Hammer paperback books, and all seven of Spillane's novels (*The Long Wait*, 1951, was not a Hammer book) ranked in the top ten of the all-time best-selling American fiction.

Spillane's Mike Hammer was tough, intimidating, and out for his own brand of bloody justice: "I lived only to kill the scum and the lice that wanted to kill themselves. I lived to kill so others could live. I lived to kill because my soul was a hardened thing that reveled in the thought of taking the blood of the bastards who make murder their business."

During his days of writing comic books at the Funnies, Incorporated studio in New York City before the war, Spillane was remembered by artist Dan Barry as a "handsome cocky Irishman who seemed to be out most of the time. Search parties were always out looking for him at the great bars around 45th street." During the war, Spillane served with the Ski Troopers while stationed in Alaska. After the war years, he decided to get back into comic books, but this time as a publisher. He contacted artists and writers he had known from the Funnies, Incorporated studio, such as Harry Sahle, Joe Gill, and Mike Roy, to help with his publishing venture which would include a ski magazine as well as a comic book.

In 1946, Spillane wrote the script for a new comic book detective he called *Mike Danger* and gave it to Mike Roy and others to draw. Roy, who first worked with Spillane in 1941, recalled that the *Mike Danger* comic book was drawn but never published. "One of the business partners disappeared with about $25,000 in cash," Roy remembered, "and that sunk the ski magazine and comic book. I don't know what became of the artwork."

In 1947, Spillane wrote a "Mike Danger" comic strip for the newspapers. Drawn by Mike Roy and offered by Jerry Iger's syndicate, the comic strip appeared briefly in New York area newspapers and disappeared. Spillane decided to leave the world of comics to become a mystery writer.

tective agencies fronted by a girl Friday who stalled bill collectors and occasionally helped crack a case.

While creators of the comic book private eyes followed in the footsteps of Dashiell Hammett and Raymond Chandler, their biggest influence was a former comic book writer who had just created the most popular private eye of twentieth-century fiction. Mickey Spillane, who wrote the *Human Torch, Blue Bolt Comics,* and other comics before World War II, knocked out a 1947 novel called *I, the Jury,* which introduced his tough-guy detective, Mike Hammer.

Spillane's book, panned by critics and loved by lowbrows, became a runaway bestseller and was followed by five more Mike Hammer novels: *Vengeance Is Mine!*

Spillane took his concept for the ill-fated Mike Danger comic book and turned it into *I, The Jury* (1947). Mike Danger became Mike Hammer and got a little more violent, sexy, and adult.

Several years later in 1954, the missing *Mike Danger* stories from Spillane's original comic book somehow appeared in two issues of *Crime Detector* (May, July 1954), a comic book published by one of the smallest outfits in the business.

"Meet Mike Danger, private detective! He's rough . . . he's tough . . . he's terrific!" Like Mike Hammer, Mike Danger was about six feet tall and 190 pounds. Like Hammer, he constantly wore a felt hat and packed a .45 in his arm holster. Like Hammer, Danger had his two-room office in the Hackard Building in New York. Like Hammer, he also had a secretary called Velda who wore her hair in a long page boy style and had "million dollar legs." When Danger speaks in "Murder at the Burlesque" (*Crime Detector* July 1954), it is Hammer's voice who is heard:

I brought my knee up and dug it into his stomach. Grunting, he dropped me. I let go a wild right and felt the pain hit my knuckles as I connected. I'm known to have a pretty good kick in my fist, but this guy just smiled and let one go against my head.

I went back and he followed, smashing another deep in my stomach. I went over the coffee table and landed on my back. Rolling away, I started to get up when I saw a size thirteen leather coming at me. I tried to get out of the way and felt it smack a rib. I grabbed for my side and a mule kicked me in the head.

I woke up later . . . much later. The big guy was gone . . . thank God. My stomach was holding a private revolution and my head felt like a cold draft in a shower. For a few minutes I lay there trying to go back to sleep until the pain disappeared. It wouldn't and I couldn't.

I got up trying not to disturb the revolutionists inside of me and at the same time favoring a bruised rib that was beginning to show signs of life. I went into the bedroom and hit the sack without trying to undress.

It was a a good, deep sleep. I didn't know any of the reasons yet, but I wouldn't have gotten this working over if Babs' death was accidental. I had somebody really worried.

And by the time I got through they'd be really dead.

Spillane's style of writing influenced the speech patterns of a dozen comic book private eyes of the early 1950s, such as Rocky Jorden, Sam Hill, Ken Shannon, and Johnny Dynamite.

Like Hammer and Danger, Rocky Jorden of *Private Eye* comics (March 1951) addressed his readers in a terse, first-person point of view: "Things began to happen fast! Shots went off and I felt a searing pain in my left arm! Vaguely, I saw the punk collapse with

*Private Eye #4 © 1951 Marvel Entertainment Group.* Art by Vernon Henkel.

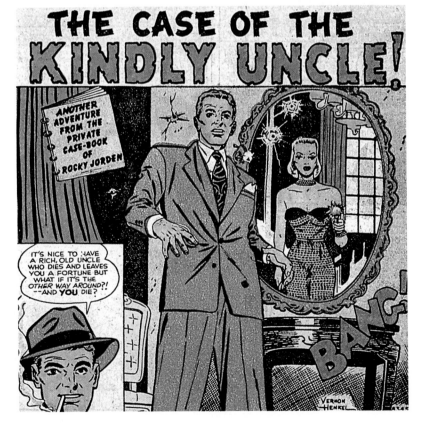

**107**

*Private Eye #2 © 1951 Marvel Entertainment Group.* Art by George Tuska.

wise-cracking detective for the "spicy" adult mystery pulps of the 1930s. In the 1940s, he wrote several Dan Turner, Hollywood Detective comic strip stories and he preserved the same racy dialogue that characterized the original pulp character.

When the Hollywood detective finds a woman with her head split open, he remarks: "Somebody bashed her on the conk! She's defunct!" After he finds a woman who has been killed when a blowgun dart strikes her in the eye, Turner quips: "She's defunct! And with a poisoned barb in her peeper!" And when he runs across another dead body, he snorts: "Unconscious, my adenoids! He's defunct!" The breezy detective refers to beautiful women as "she-males" and to his gun as "roscoe." He has a one-line throwaway for every outrageous murder: "He's deader than a Jap's honor!"

Like Mike Hammer and his secretary Velda, the comic book private eyes were usually paired up with their girl Fridays. Ken Shannon, the hard-hitting Irish private eye from *Police Comics* (December 1950), had a redhead companion named Dee Dee Dawson who scheduled his appointments and accompanied him in his investigations. She was plucky, loyal, sexy, and brave: "Not that I scare easy, Kenny, but at this moment even my goose-pimples have goose-pimples!"

Sex and booze, the bread and potatoes of hard-boiled detectives everywhere, showed up in the lives of the comic book private eyes—although with more discretion than

a death rattle in his throat." Similarly, Steve Duncan, "famous Licensed Investigator" from *Perfect Crime* (December 1950), shares his innermost thoughts as he stumbles across a bullet-riddled body: "This was one hot potato I didn't want to hold. I started to put a call in to Lieutenant M. R. Grimshaw of homicide . . ."

Private eye Sam Hill, "America's Hard-Boiled, Wise-Cracking Sleuth," also speaks the tough-guy talk of his profession: "Folsom had already cooled two people in a week and I knew he wouldn't hesitate making it three of a kind. When they fry you, you don't cook any longer for three than you do for two."

One of the best practitioners of the tough-guy patter was Dan Turner, Hollywood Detective from *Crime Smashers* comics. Writer Robert Leslie Bellem originally created the

Dan Turner. *Crime Smashers #8* © 1952 Trojan Publishing Corp.

Ken Shannon. *Police Comics #127* © 1953 Quality Comics.

the paperbacks exhibited. Chip Gardner (*Crime Does Not Pay*, May 1950) nods approvingly over the contents of his client's liquor cabinet: "There's enough alcohol here to keep me in anti-freeze for life." Sam Hill also knew when he needed a drink as well: "I started driving home to sleep it off, but I couldn't forget her! I was half afraid she'd be waiting to haunt my dreams . . . if that's what they were. I felt a need to see people . . . to talk . . . so I walked into my favorite pub!" Sam finally did get home to bed, but it didn't stop there: "They say if you eat too much before going to bed, you'll have crazy dreams, but I never expected to see that third piece of angel cake come walking right into my bedroom! Her body was beautiful, and the voice was like black velvet topped with whipped cream, but the story sounded strictly ninety proof . . ."

The comic book writers were trying to capture the gritty and violent realism of the best-selling paperback novels by Spillane and others. There were shootings, fist fights, deceitful women, and gratuitous torture scenes. After delivering a deserved beating to a suspect, private eye Chip Gardner from *Crime Does Not Pay* tells us: "Vingo went out like a

light. I revived him by dipping his greasy locks into the sink . . ."

Sam Hill also wasn't afraid to get his hands dirty if it meant solving a murder: "There was a light shining under the door but no bell. I spent a few minutes cracking the lock. Inside Roy Magg was slumped in a chair staring wistfully at a drink . . . a drink he couldn't use . . . because there was a bullet hole in his pretty white shirt and he was very dead!"

It was not all raw action, however. The comic book private eyes usually solved a case only after perseverance, observation, and deduction. Although not as refined as Sherlock Holmes, Chip Gardner knew a body when he saw one—and all of its nasty implications: "One look put the nix on suicide . . . dead men do tell tales when they sit that way. If the impact of the bullet doesn't topple a man when he shoots himself in the head, the recoil of the gun will, so it was about two chances out of two that a trigger man had tagged him and set the scene as suicide! But where did that leave me? A dead client is no client at all, I thought, and there would be a

*Sam Hill Private Eye #4* © *1951 Close-Up Publications.* Art by Harry Lucey.

*Dynamite #7 © 1954 Comic Media.* Art by Pete Morisi.

"The four of them worked me over good. They laughed as I lay there coughing up my guts. Somehow I got hold of a gun. They stopped laughing . . . fast!"

Perhaps more than any other comic book private eye, Johnny Dynamite was cast in the mold of Mickey Spillane's Mike Hammer. Like Hammer, Dynamite distinguished himself by his eager willingness to inflict pain and suffering on his enemies: "I was boiling when I struck. I was sore at Rocky for mauling Ginger. But I was most sore at the gorilla for the kick in the face so I gave it to him where it would hurt the worst!" The accompanying drawing left no doubt where it "hurt the worst" as Dynamite's heel ground in at the crotch line ("OWWW—OWWW OH, JEEZ!").

In the story "An Eye for an Eye" (*Dynamite*, November 1953), Dynamite becomes known as "the one-eyed private eye" after he loses an eye when a woman shoots him with a gun disguised as a camera. He lets his anger over the incident turn him into an even more explosive character. Donning an eyepatch, Dynamite tracks down the gang who set him up for the shooting and then takes his revenge slowly and sweetly: "I grabbed

lot of official questions—and I didn't know a single answer."

The best realized of the private eyes created for the 1950s comic books was Johnny Dynamite, "the wild man from Chicago." Described as "solid, 35, medium-height, and handsome in an ugly way," Dynamite lived up to his explosive name as a "rough, tough private eye who packs knock-out drops in both brawny fists . . . an old experienced hand at rough and tumble, who makes one hell of a sidekick in a rough-house brawl . . . a rip-roaring holy terror."

Johnny Dynamite's first story (*Dynamite*, September 1953) opens quickly enough:

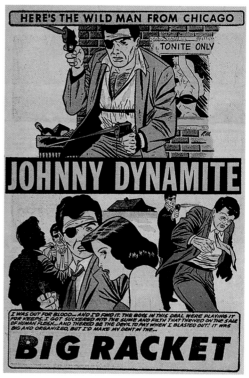

*Dynamite #4 © 1953 Comic Media.* Art by Pete Morisi.

the sap and headed for the little guy who was still trying to get off a shot at me. I let him look at the sap a split second before I brought it down full force across his blubbering face. He moaned as the flesh was laid open to the bone, and fell into a stupor as his teeth crumpled under the impact."

Besides aping the ultra-violence of the Mike Hammer novels, Johnny Dynamite also took after Spillane's shamus in the sex department as well. Like Hammer, Dynamite is described as a "guy who can love a dame or leave her alone, a guy who can take a lady in his arms or break her arms."

Dynamite runs into plenty of women who run into his arms, but often with strings attached: "My love is dead, Johnny. But I'm still alive. And gratitude can take the place of love. If you find the killer I'll be yours whenever you want me." Dynamite takes a split second to decide. "There was promise in her eyes and she didn't resist when I found her lips . . ."

For a comic book detective, Johnny Dynamite got plenty of action. With scenes like the following, it was little wonder that later issues of *Dynamite* were labeled as "Exciting Adult Reading":

"I was on my second butt when she entered the room. She stood there, motionless, and let me drink in her beauty. Her jet black hair fell to her shoulders and played havoc with the milk white flesh at its base. Her eyes told me our thoughts were one. I reached out for her and crushed her ripe pouting lips to mine. She kissed back with a savage embrace that made her body grow taut and shudder. She was loosening every mad desire she had suppressed . . . and she was mine."

Johnny Dynamite was the creation of artist Pete Morisi and writer Ken Fitch. Morisi honed his skills for drawing a comic book detective by working as an assistant on the "Saint" newspaper strip, doing the inking and the backgrounds. He kept his backgrounds dark while highlighting the faces and figures of his characters in the foreground. The resulting sharp black-and-white contrast created a *film noir* look in a four-color medium.

Ken Fitch was perhaps the most expe-

*Dynamite #3 © 1953 Comic Media.* Art by Pete Morisi.

rienced crime comic writer in the business when he tackled Johnny Dynamite. Beginning his comic book career in 1936 as a writer for the Harry "A" Chesler comic book studio, Fitch wrote for thirty-one comic book publishers over a thirty-five-year period. His first crime comic work was for *Keen Detective Funnies* in 1939, and he wrote stories for dozens of the crime comics during the late 1940s and early 1950s, including *Crime Does Not Pay*, *Gangsters Can't Win*, and *Women Outlaws*. With Johnny Dynamite, Fitch took advantage of the first-person point of view to write a direct and hard-hitting comic book. From the first lines in "Big Racket" (*Dynamite*, November 1953), Fitch put the reader right in the middle of the action:

"The slug that tore into my ribs made me buckle with pain. But I kept the .45 working until I heard the scream that told me my slugs had found their target. Now it was over. The whole filthy mess. I let the empty .45 drop from my hand as I staggered across the room. The pain at my side made me want to vomit, but nothing came. I reached for the phone. That's as far as I got. The hole in my side throbbed with a burning fury. As I crumpled up, I tried to claw for support, but the room was a hazy void that wavered before me. All I could do was lay there and think back to the beginning of the dirty deal . . . "

The hard-hitting violence and sex of Chicago's one-eyed private eye could not last beyond the arrival of the Comics Code in late 1954. The last issue of *Dynamite* with Johnny Dynamite was published in September 1954. The character continued after the Comics Code in his own comic book from another publisher (*Johnny Dynamite*, June 1955) but in a much more mellow mode. With the restrictions of the code, Dynamite dropped his shadowy private eye role to become a respectable government agent. Eventually, his comic book became a cold war spy title called *Foreign Intrigues* (March 1956) with Johnny fighting behind the Iron Curtain.

Although both comic book heroes and

*Dynamite #7 © 1954 Comic Media. Art by Pete Morisi.*

*Johnny Dynamite #11 © 1955 Charlton Comics*

fictional detectives have been predominantly male, there are several memorable female comic book private eyes. One of the first was "Sally the Sleuth" who began in November 1934 as a comic strip in the back pages of a mystery pulp magazine called *Spicy Detective*. As may be guessed by its title, *Spicy Detective* peddled formula mystery stories heavily spiked with suggestive sex scenes. The magazine's lurid covers of bondage, breasts, and blood earned it a spot "behind the counter" where it was generally sold only to adults.

The illustrations that accompanied the stories in *Spicy Detective* (which invariably pictured women in various stages of undress) were supplied by Majestic Studios, a tiny art shop run by Adolphe Barreaux. Readers who wanted more pictures of lightly clad ladies were probably tempted by advertisements in the magazine which offered "adult" comic strip booklets for sale. Realizing that there was a healthy market for nearly naked cartoon characters, Barreaux created a two-page comic strip for *Spicy Detective* called "Sally the Sleuth," which featured a beautiful blonde detective who always lost her clothes but got her man.

In Sally's first appearance ("A Narrow Escape"), she decides to wear a disguise to track down a gang of "dope" smugglers. "I'll just slip out of these feminine things," she says as she unrolls her stockings and models her unmentionables. Before she can get dressed, however, she is kidnapped and winds up in bra and bondage until she is rescued by "the Chief," her boss at the detective agency. For the next ten years, Sally spent much of her time nearly naked. She gamely pursued (and was pursued by) kidnappers, killers, and counterfeiters. Printed in black and white, the "Sally the Sleuth" comic strips (along with the rest of the magazine contents) were deemed "off-color" by various moral guardians.

Bowing to community pressures, *Spicy Detective* was turned into *Speed Detective* in the January 1943 issue, with milder content and covers. Sally kept more of her clothes on and her adventures expanded to four-page installments. In 1949 and 1950, Sally appeared in the back pages of *Private Detective* pulp magazine in a series of eight-page comic

Toni Gayle. *Young King Cole Vol. 3 #11* © 1948 *Novelty Press*

*Crime Smashers #13* © 1951 Trojan Publishing. Art by Pierre Charpentier.

*Spicy Detective (January 1935)* © 1935 Trojan Publishing. Art by Adolphe Barreaux.

stories drawn by Gerald Altman. By this time, her publisher Frank Armer, who had been around since the *Spicy Detective* days, was also making plans to enter the booming comic book field. With Sally's original artist and writer Adolphe Barreaux as his comic book editor, Armer began Trojan Magazines with an early lineup of *Crime Smashers* (October 1950) and *Western Crime Busters* (September 1950).

Barreaux brought back his underdressed sleuth in full color to *Crime Smashers* both in reprinted strips from the pulps and in original stories drawn by Keats Petree and Pierre Charpentier. Sally also appeared later in *Crime*

*Ms. Tree's Thrilling Detective Adventures #1 © 1983 Max Allan Collins and Terry Beatty. Art by Terry Beatty.*

professional model," is also a freewheeling detective and crime buster: "Stop interrupting me," Toni snaps to a would-be boyfriend. "While you murmur sweet nothings, the killer will escape!" In the *Charlie Chan* comic book series from the late 1940s, the secondary feature starred Keri Krane, a woman who begins a private detective agency after her sister, a police officer, is killed in the line of duty. When a killer pulls a knife on one of her detectives and tells her not to make too much "disturbance," Keri replies: "Disturbance is the thing we want most right now," and shoots him in the face.

The most successful woman private eye in comics—in fact, the longest-running *original* private eye in a comic book series—was created by writer Max Allan Collins and artist Terry Beatty for the May 1981 issue of *Eclipse Magazine*. Ms. Michael Tree follows in her late husband's footsteps and becomes a private investigator in order to solve his murder.

Collins, a mystery novelist and writer of the "Dick Tracy" newspaper strip since 1977, said that he and Beatty wanted to do

*Mysteries* from the same publisher. The comic book Sally was much more demure than her pulp magazine counterpart. She wore a tight red dress but she did keep it on. She was also less likely to remain helplessly tied up in underwear until she was rescued by her "Chief." Sally packed a gun and she knew how to use it: "Get started," she says to a suspect as she prods him in the gut with her pistol. "You're under arrest for the murder of Jason—and maybe other murders! I'm *walking* you to town!"

The scattering of women private eyes in the comic books almost all shared Sally's toughness and readiness to go "man to man" while still preserving their femininity. In *Young King Cole* comics, Toni Gayle, "famous

*Original Dick Tracy #4 © 1991 Tribune Media Services*

"a straight, tough mystery story in a rather adult fashion" with "no talking down" to the reader. "The Ms. Tree character springs from a specific source," Collins noted, "the Mike Hammer novels of Mickey Spillane and specifically Hammer's relationship with his secretary Velda—who is a licensed private eye, too, a pistol-packing mama who stands near six feet herself and is damn near tough as Hammer. She is, in fact, essentially the female Mike Hammer. So it occurred to me— what if Hammer ever really did marry Velda, and what if Hammer were then murdered on their wedding night? Why, Velda would quite naturally step into her late husband's shoes— taking over the detective business, and solving his murder. . . ."

Collins and Beatty made the decision that the Ms. Tree character would grow and evolve throughout the story line which first began in *Ms. Tree's Thrilling Detective Adventures* (February 1983). Over the next ten years, Ms. Tree would come to terms with her husband's death, fall in and out of love, and eventually have a child. She became the first breast-feeding private eye in the comics or perhaps anywhere else. While she may have been a female Mike Hammer, it's hard to imagine Spillane's character showing the depth of emotion experienced by Ms. Michael Tree during the first moments of motherhood.

Despite the careful attention to showing the feminine side of Ms. Tree, Collins is quick to point out that the character "is not, as some critics have mistakenly labeled her, a 'feminist'—at least not in some political, activist sense. Ms. Tree is a feminist only in the way that any modern, intelligent working woman is likely to be."

The last decade of the twentieth century saw the comic book detective returning to its origins. With the 1990 *Dick Tracy* movie, Chester Gould's square-jawed detective regained his public prominence and appeared in several comic book series for a new generation of readers. From the 1930s to the world of tomorrow, the action detective in the comics will surely be one of our favorite heroes—or, at least, as long as there is that need for someone who (in the words of Dick Tracy's creator) "could toss the hot iron right back at them along with a smack on the jaw thrown in for good measure."

# CRIME AND DETECTIVE COMICS

## A Guide and Checklist

The following checklist is a title-by-title guide to comic books devoted primarily to crime, detective, or spy stories. Over three hundred comic book titles are listed (beginning in 1933), with more than 3,100 issues noted.

The peak years for crime comics occurred from 1948 to 1950, when nearly one-fourth of all the crime comics ever published appeared. After the advent of the Comics Code in late 1954, the true crime comics disappeared. The 1960s and 1970s saw new titles appear that were based on police and detective TV shows, as well as those inspired by the James Bond and The Man from UNCLE spy craze. The 1980s and 1990s experienced a growth in crime and detective comics resulting from a number of small and independent publishers who issued comic books that bypassed the Comics Code.

All the major (and most minor) crime and detective comic books published in the United States are listed as of publication time. Some titles, particularly low-circulation black-and-white comics of the 1980s and 1990s, may have been overlooked due to limited distribution. Comic books with only an occasional crime, detective, or spy story are usually not included unless the title is of special note.

For each title, the publisher and the dates and numbers of the first and last issues are listed. Not all titles start with issue #1 since they may have picked up the numbering from a previously published or canceled title. In some cases, issue numbers out of sequence reflect a publisher's esoteric numbering system, while other issue numbers may be omitted because they did not contain crime or detective stories.

When known, the artists who worked on the title are listed along with the writers. The term "black and white" means that the comic was published in black and white instead of color. "Magazine" refers to comics published in a magazine-size format (about 1½" wider and longer than a comic book).

---

Facing Page: *Trapped! #4* © *1955 Ace Magazines*

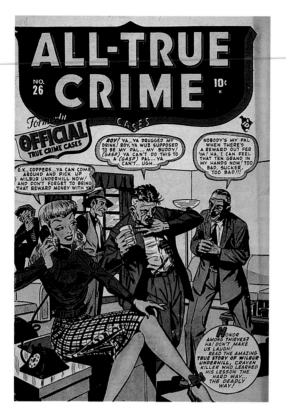

*All-True Crime #26
© 1947 Marvel Entertainment Group. Art by Syd Shores.*

## ADAM-12

Gold Key
1973 December–1976 February
1–10

Comic book adaptation of the 1968 NBC television series that centered on the routine work of Los Angeles police patrolmen, Officer Pete Malloy (played by Martin Milner) and Officer Jim Reed (Kent McCord). The comic book began during the TV show's fifth season and was published for several months after the program was canceled. Paul Newman and John Warner scripted the series.

## ADVENTURES OF THE DETECTIVE

Humor Publishing Co.
1933
1

Early black-and-white comic magazine featuring the adventures of detective Ace King as drawn by Martin Nadle.

## AFTER DARK

Sterling Comics
1955 April–1955 September
6–8

Detective Sergeant Mark Fabian (from *The Informer* comics) continues his career in stories drawn by Mike Sekowsky.

*All-Famous Crime #5
© 1952 Star Publications. Art by L. B. Cole.*

## ALL TRUE ALL PICTURE POLICE CASES

St. John Publications
1952 October–1952 November
1, 2

Three assorted crime comics were rebound and sold as a giant comic book for 25 cents.

## ALL-FAMOUS CRIME

Star Publications
1951 May–1952 June
8–10, 4, 5

Original stories and reprints from Fox crime comics make up these "True Cases from Police Files." Ma Barker and her boys appear in issue #10.

## ALL-FAMOUS POLICE CASES

Star Publications
1952 February–1954 September
6–16

These "True Cases from Crime Files" were drawn by Joe Kubert, L. B. Cole, Al Hollingsworth, and others.

## ALL-TRUE CRIME

Marvel Comics
1948 February–1952 September
26–52

Formerly published as *Official True Crime Cases*, artists included Jerry Robinson, Syd Shores, George Tuska, Bernard Krigstein, Vern Henkel, Myron Fass, Werner Roth, Mike Sekowsky, and Chu Hing. Real-life criminals included Wilbur Underhill (#26) and Lucrezia Borgia (#39).

## ALL-TRUE DETECTIVE CASES

Avon Periodicals
1954 February–1954 August
1–4

Famous gangsters who passed through these pages included Pretty Boy Floyd (#2), Frankie Yale (#2), Waxie Gordon (#3), John Dillinger (#3), Jack "Legs" Diamond (#2), Machine-Gun Kelly (#3), and Bonnie Parker and Clyde Barrow (#4). Artists included Wally Wood, Mike Becker, Rocco Mastroserio, Edward Goldfarb, and Moe Marcus.

## AMAZING DETECTIVE CASES

Marvel Comics
1950 November–1952 September
3–14

Artists included Bill Everett, Bernard Krigstein, Gene Colan, Mike Sekowsky, Joe Sinnot, Bill Walton, Fred Kida, Robert Q. Sale, and George Tuska. With issue #11, the title changed to a horror-crime format.

## AMAZING MYSTERIES

Marvel Comics
1949 October–1950 January
34, 35

Previously a horror title, the format was changed to "true crime stories" with issue #34.

## ATOMIC SPY CASES

Avon Periodicals
1950 March
1

Based on "true stories," the comic featured such espionage cases as "Devil in Petticoats" and "Donovan of Central Intelligence." Art by Myron Fass and others.

## AUTHENTIC POLICE CASES

St. John Publications
1948 February–1955 March
1–38

Nearly three-fourths of the covers featured glamorous blondes (usually drawn by Matt Baker). Also appearing were reprinted stories by Jack Cole and the newspaper strip adventures of detective Vic Flint.

## AVENGERS, THE

Gold Key
1968 November
1

Although based on the British television series from ABC, the comic book adaptation was referred to as *John Steed & Emma Peel* on the front cover so as not to infringe on Marvel Comics's superhero title, *The Avengers*. While the likenesses of Patrick Macnee (John Steed) and Diana Rigg (Emma Peel) were used in the comic book, Rigg had already been replaced on the televison series by Linda Thorson as Tara King.

## BADGE OF JUSTICE

Charlton Comics
1955 January–1955 October
22, 23, 1–4

The first two issues (#s 22, 23) appeared before the Comics Code took effect. Artists include Mike Sekowsky, Rocco Mastroserio, Bill Fraccio, and Charles Nicholas.

## BEHIND PRISON BARS

Realistic Publications
1952
1

Bad boys, bad times, and bad food. Convicts got revenge on their guards at Newgate Prison.

## BIG TOWN

DC Comics
1951 Janury–1958 March
1–50

Steve Wilson, crusading editor of *The Illustrated Press,* fights organized crime, political corruption, and social injustice in the thriving metropolis of Big Town. Originally a radio melodrama (1937–52), *Big Town* became a television show in 1950 and was made into a comic book at about the same time. The comic book adaptation paralleled the television show so that when Lorelei Kilbourne (Steve's star reporter and romantic interest) was dropped from the TV series in 1955, she also disappeared from the comic book. Similarly, city editor Charlie Anderson and cub reporter Rush Martin became part of the comic book cast after being introduced in the 1954–55 TV season. *Big Town*'s other features included "Johnny Law, Headquarters Detective" and "Casebook of Unsolved Mysteries," with Steve Wilson as the host of an

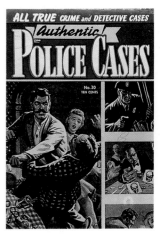

*Authentic Police Cases #30 © 1953 St. John Publications*

*Big Town #9 © 1951 DC Comics, Inc.*

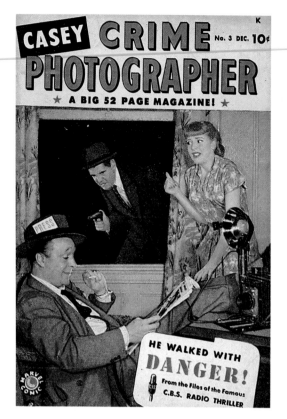

*Casey, Crime Photographer #3 © 1949 Marvel Entertainment Group*

investigative television show. John Broome wrote several scripts, with art by Dan Barry, Howard Nostrand, Ed Robbins, Manny Stallman, John Prentice, Gil Kane, Howard Purcell, and others.

## BOLD STORIES

Kirby Publishing Co.
1950 March–1950 July
1, 2

This 144-page, digest-size comic book featured "humor, crime, and gorgeous dames" and was aimed at the adult reader. Typical stories included a Sherlock Holmes parody and a nudist camp mystery featuring a female private eye who goes "undercover." The real crime in the comic came from the adventures of hard-boiled detective Pete Webb. The stories borrowed heavily from Raymond Chandler novels and *film noir*, lifting plots and actual lines of dialogue. Graham Ingels, of EC horror comics fame, drew the Webb yarn ("The Cobra Kiss") for the second issue.

## BOY DETECTIVE

Avon Periodicals
1951 May–1952 May
1–4

Young Dan Tayler ("boy mastermind") fights vice-lords, spies, and laughing killers.

*Caught #2 © 1956 Marvel Entertainment Group. Art by John Severin.*

Artists included Tex Blaisdell, Everett Kinstler, and Michael Becker.

## BURKE'S LAW

Dell Publishing Co.
1964 March–1965 May
1–3

Based on the 1963 ABC-TV series starring Gene Barry as Captain Amos Burke, Los Angeles Chief of Detectives. The comic book adventures of the Rolls-Royce-riding investigator were drawn by Gene Colan.

## CAIN'S HUNDRED

Dell Publishing Co.
1962 July–1962 November
207, 2

Based on the 1961–62 NBC-TV series, the comic book adaptation of *Cain's Hundred* presented the adventures of ex-gangland lawyer Nick Cain, who becomes a special agent for the federal government. With the help of a G-Man squad, Cain's mission was to bring the one hundred men who controlled organized crime in America to trial.

## CASE OF THE WINKING BUDDHA

St. John Publications
1950
1

This unusual digest-size comic book (132 pages for 25 cents) attempted to appeal to the adult paperback buyer. This "original, all-picture mystery" was drawn by Charles Raab, who had worked on the *Charlie Chan* comic book two years earlier.

## CASES OF SHERLOCK HOLMES

Renegade Press
1986–1988 August
1–15

Employing a turn-of-the-century style, artist Dan Day illustrated the unabridged text by Arthur Conan Doyle from "The Adventure of the Beryl Coronet," "The Adventure of Silver Blaze," "The Adventure of the Naval Treaty," and other Sherlock Holmes stories. Black and white.

## CASEY, CRIME PHOTOGRAPHER

Marvel Comics
1949 August–1950 February
1–4

Flashgun Casey, ace photographer for *The*

*Morning Express,* was the hero in a series of novels by mystery writer George Harmon Coxe. The jazz-loving photographer and investigator later became the star of a popular CBS radio series (1943–50) and was portrayed by Staats Cotsworth. When the show was adapted into a comic book, photographs of Cotsworth were used for the front covers. Vern Henkel, who drew his first crime comic stories for *Crime Does Not Pay* in 1946, drew some stories.

## CAUGHT

Marvel Comics
1956 August–1957 April
1–5

The "Guilty Never Escape" in this comic with stories by artists Joe Maneely, Mac Pakula, Angelo Torres, Reed Crandall, Bernard Krigstein, Vic Carrabotta, Mort Drucker, Don Heck, and Syd Shores.

## CHAMBER OF CLUES

Harvey Publications
1955 February–1955 April
27, 28

Formerly *Chamber of Chills,* the book was renamed during the crackdown on horror comics. Stories of decapitation and torture were replaced with reprints of the "Kerry Drake" newspaper strip.

## CHARLIE CHAN

Prize Publications
1948 June–1949 February
1–5

The first original comic book series to feature Earl Derr Bigger's Honolulu detective was drawn by Charles Raab and Carmine Infantino, with covers by Joe Simon and Jack Kirby. Kerri Kane, a hyperkinetic female private eye drawn by Dick Briefer, appeared as a backup feature.

## CHARLIE CHAN

Charlton Comics
1955 June–1956 March
6–9

This second original Charlie Chan comic book series featured art by Charles Nicholas and scripts by Ken Fitch.

## CHARLIE CHAN

Dell Publishing Co.
1965 October–1966 March
1, 2

Charlie Chan returned to the comic books in the 1960s at about the same time he was enjoying a revival in the paperbacks and movie houses. Frank Springer handled the art chores.

## CHECKMATE

Gold Key
1962 October–1962 December
1, 2

Based on the 1960–62 CBS-TV sophisticated detective drama starring Anthony George as private investigator Don Corey and Doug McClure as his partner Jed Sills. Corey and Sills operated a San Francisco detective agency which specialized in preventing crimes and thwarting would-be murderers. The pair was aided by an Oxford professor of criminology, Carl Hyatt, played by Sebastian Cabot. Ironically, the first issue of the comic book appeared the month before the television show was canceled.

## CLASSIC COMICS/CLASSICS ILLUSTRATED

Gilberton Publications
1944 July–1953 August
21, 30, 33, 40, 61, 110

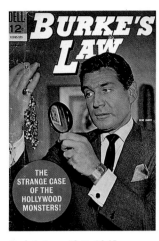

*Burke's Law #3 © 1965
Four Star-Barbety*

*Charlie Chan #8 © 1956
Charlton Comics*

*Clue Comics #11
© 1946 Hillman
Periodicals*

This series, which adapted classical works of literature into comic book format, included the following mystery novels and short story collections: *Famous Mysteries* (#21, July 1944, with "The Sign of the Four" drawn by Louis Zansky; "The Flayed Hand" drawn by Allen Simon; and "Murders in Rue Morgue" drawn by Arnold Hicks); *The Moonstone* (#30, September 1946, with art by Don Rico); *Adventures of Sherlock Holmes* (#33, January 1947, with art by H. C. Kiefer and Louis Zansky); *Mysteries by Poe* (#40, August 1947, with "Pit and the Pendulum" drawn by A. M. Froehlich; "Adventures of Hans Pfall," drawn by H. C. Kiefer; and "Fall of the House of Usher," drawn by H. M. Griffiths); *The Woman in White* (#61, July 1949, drawn by Alex Blum); and *A Study in Scarlet* (#110, August 1953, with art by Seymour Moskowitz and script by Ken Fitch).

## CLIMAX!

Gilmor Magazines
1955 July–1955 September
1, 2

This early code-approved comic promised "suspense, mystery, and intrigue," with some stories drawn by Fred Bell.

*Colossal Features Magazine #3 © 1950 Fox Features Syndicate. Art by Wally Wood and Harry Harrison.*

## CLOAK AND DAGGER

Ziff-Davis Publishing Company
1952 Fall
1

Al Kennedy of the Secret Service blazed away at foreigners in stories like "Kismet" and "The Krosno Butcher."

## CLUE COMICS

Hillman Periodicals
1947 March–1947 May
Vol. 2 #1–Vol. 2 #3

The first volume of *Clue Comics* (January 1943–February 1947) featured costumed crime fighters like Zippo, Twilight, Micro-Face, and Nightmare. The superheroes were phased out in favor of crime stories by early 1947, and Joe Simon and Jack Kirby's "King of the Bank Robbers" in the first issue set the tone for the new series. Other artists included Carmine Infantino and Dan Barry. After three issues, the comic book was retitled *Real Clue Crime Stories* (June 1947).

## COLOSSAL FEATURES MAGAZINE

Fox Features Syndicate
1950 September
3

This anthology of "true crime stories" featured the exploits of notorious Hollywood gangster Bugsy Siegel and other lesser luminaries like Gene Simpson, "the mad Houdini of crime."

## COMPLETE BOOK OF TRUE CRIME COMICS

William Wise
1945
1

Reprints from 1942 issues of *Crime Does Not Pay*.

## COMPLETE MYSTERY

Marvel Comics
1948 August–1949 October
1–8

The first four issues contained "book-length" novels with such titles as "Jigsaw of Doom!" and "A Squealer Dies Fast!" With issue #5, the book became *Complete True Mystery*.

## CRIME AND JUSTICE

Charlton Comics
1951 March–1955 September
1–26

The detective team of Curtis and Merry Chase were the stars of this comic. Modeled after Nick and Nora Charles of the *Thin Man* movies, the "Mr. and Mrs. Chase Mystery Novelette" series began with Curtis Chase ("a famous mystery writer and amateur sleuth") and his blonde wife at their swank New York City penthouse. The fun-loving couple embarked on a second honeymoon, which turned into an extended journey over several issues involving "adventure, suspense, and murder." From the French Quarter in New Orleans to a jungle port in Chile, Mr. and Mrs. Chase mixed murder and romance: "You'll be all right, Mr. Chase—but if you keep getting your brains knocked around, I'm going to have a punch-drunk husband!" A second series, "Radio Patrol," starred Barry Storm and Tex Carron of the New York Radio Patrol, who pursued criminals by car and over the airwaves. Artists included Bob Forgione, Stan Campbell, Dick Ayers, Lou Morales, Anthony Tallarico, Dick Giordano, and Steve Ditko.

## CRIME AND PUNISHMENT

Comic House/Lev Gleason
1948 April–1955 August
1–74

The companion magazine to *Crime Does Not Pay* took its title from the novel by Dostoyevski and a popular 1935 movie. Officer Common Sense, a disembodied police officer, served as the host for the lead stories. Artists included George Tuska, Dick Rockwell, Al Borth, Mike Esposito, Mike Roy, Bob Fujitani, Fred Guardineer, Al McWilliams, Alex Toth, Joe Certa, Tony DiPreta, and Leonard Starr.

## CRIME CAN'T WIN

Marvel Comics
1950 September–1953 September
41–43, 4–12

This comic boasted true stories about "America's most dangerous criminals." Artists included Jerry Robinson, Dan Loprieno, Paul Cooper, and George Tuska.

## CRIME CASES COMICS

Marvel Comics
1950 August–1952 July
24–27, 5–12

These "crime cases from police files" were drawn by George Tuska, Robert Q. Sale, Bill Everett, Pete Morisi, Jerry Robinson, and others.

## CRIME CLINIC

Ziff-Davis Publishing Company
1951 July–1952 Summer
10, 11, 3–5

Dr. Tom Rogers, prison psychiatrist, worked behind the walls of the big house. When counseling failed to stop a breakout, the doc put aside his Freud for fisticuffs. Other unlikely features included The Padre, a crime-fighting man of the cloth, and Barney Bailey, Private Eye. The third issue had a hoodlum instructing a young boy in the ways of crime: "You always have to slug 'em! Remember that!" Dr. Fredric Wertham was so impressed with that advice, he made the line a chapter title in his anti-comic book manifesto, *Seduction of the Innocent.* Artists included Gerald McCann and John Prentice.

## CRIME DETECTIVE COMICS

Hillman Periodicals
1948 March–1953 May
1–Vol. 3 #8

This second Hillman crime comic book, following *Real Clue Crime Stories,* was named after a "true detective" magazine from the same publisher. Artists included Bill Ely, Bernard Krigstein, Al McWilliams, Arthur Peddy, Gerald McCann, Rudy Palais, Bob Powell, Dick Briefer, Michael Suchorsky, Mort Lawrence, and Leonard Starr. Writers included Warren Kuhn and Carl Wessler.

*Crime Detective Comics Vol. 3 #6 © 1953 Hillman Periodicals*

*Crime and Justice #7 © 1952 Charlton Comics. Art by Lou Morales.*

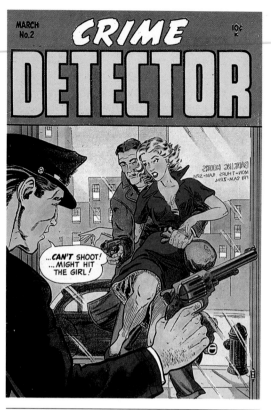

*Crime Detector #2 © 1954 Timor Publications. Art by Vince Fodera.*

## CRIME DETECTOR

Timor Publications
1954 January–1954 September
1–5

The third and fourth issues featured private eye Mike Danger, who had been created by Mickey Spillane nearly seven years earlier. The character became the basis for Spillane's popular detective Mike Hammer after the comic book stories did not make it into print as originally planned. Artists included Arthur Peddy, Paul Parker, Bruno Premiani, Jay Disbrow, Pete Morisi, and Ed Smalle. Issue #5 loosely adapted the 1949 movie *Gun Crazy* as "Gun Happy."

## CRIME DOES NOT PAY

Comic House/Lev Gleason
1942 June–1955 July
22–147

The premier "true crime" comic book that was responsible for the birth of a genre. Charles Biro—writer, editor, artist—drew the early covers. Other artists included Creig Flessel, Harry Lucey, Bob Montana, Dick Briefer, Bob Wood, Paul Parker, Fred Kida, Vern Henkel, Bob (Fuje) Fujitani, Dan Barry, Dick Rockwell, Fred Guardineer, Mike Roy, Gene Colan, George Tuska, Norman Maurer, Rudy Palais, Bob Q. Siege, Bob Powell, Jack Alderman, Frank Giacoia,

*Crime Exposed #4 © 1951 Marvel Entertainment Group*

Al Borth, Vic Carrabotta, Paul Parker, Richard Hall, Alan Mandel, Joe Certa, Tony Dipreta, Dick Giordano, Lou Silver, Lee Teaford, Al Wentzel, Pete Morisi, Howard O'Donnell, and Joe Kubert. Writers included Bob Wood, Dick Wood, Charles Biro, Ken Fitch, Carl Wessler, and Red Woodbury. Mr. Crime, the white-fanged host for the lead story in each issue, was eventually replaced by a pipe-smoking private eye, J. Chippendale "Chip" Gardner (May 1950). Initially drawn by George Tuska, the adventures of Chip and his secretary Wendy were thereafter handled by Bob Fujitani.

## CRIME EXPOSED

Marvel Comics
1948 June–1952 June
1–14

This comic promised to expose "criminals as the vicious rats they really are." Artists included George Tuska, Robert Q. Sale, Jerry Robinson, Bernard Krigstein, Dick Rockwell, and John Romita.

## CRIME FIGHTERS ALWAYS WIN

Marvel Comics
1954 September–1955 January
11–13

From the publishers who brought you *Lawbreakers Always Lose* came its corollary. Artists included Joe Maneely, Paul Reinman, John Severin, and Mac Pakula.

## CRIME FIGHTING DETECTIVE

Star Publications
1950 April–1952 June
11–19

Formerly *Criminals on the Run,* this title (with art by L. B. Cole) became *Shock Detective Cases* with issue #20. A "Young King Cole" detective story appeared in issue #12.

## CRIME FILES

Standard Magazines
1952 September–1952 November
5, 6

Artists included Alex Toth and Mike Sekowsky.

## CRIME ILLUSTRATED

EC Comics
1955 November–1956 Spring
1, 2

Publisher William Gaines attempted to

reach a mature audience by publishing crime comic stories ("picto-fiction") in a magazine format which bypassed the code's restrictions. The stories were printed in black and white with the text beneath each panel to create an illustrated story effect. Artists included Johnny Craig, Reed Crandall, George Roussos, George Evans, Jack Davis, Graham Ingels, Joe Orlando, and Bernard Krigstein.

## CRIME INCORPORATED

Fox Features Syndicate
1950 June–1951 August
12, 2, 3

This anthology of "true crime stories and actual crime cases" was probably named after the 1945 movie *Crime, Inc.* A. C. Hollingsworth, a prolific crime comic artist, contributed to this title as well.

## CRIME MACHINE

Skywald
1971 February–1971 May
1, 2

Black-and-white magazine reprinted crime comics from the 1950s, with original stories as well. Artists included Joe Kubert, Angelo Torres, and Doug Wildey.

## CRIME MUST LOSE!

Marvel Comics
1950 October–1952 April
4–12

These "startling cases which prove crime must lose" were drawn by Ann Brewster, Jerry Robinson, and others. Issue #5 featured the story of Pretty Boy Floyd.

## CRIME MUST PAY THE PENALTY

Ace Magazines
1948 February–1955 August
33, 2–46

Artists who worked on this long-running title included Gene Colan, Mike Sekowsky, Rocco Mastroserio, Ken Battlefield, Dick Beck, Lou Cameron, Warren Kremer, Rudy Palais, Kenneth Rice, Mario Rizzi, John Rosenberger, Frank Sieminsky, Chic Stone, Lin Streeter, and Louis Zansky. With issue #47, the comic was retitled *Penalty*.

## CRIME MUST STOP

Hillman Periodicals
1952 October
1

This crime comic, with art by Mort Lawrence and Bernard Krigstein, added a heaping helping of horror to its stories of murder and intrigue.

## CRIME MYSTERIES

Ribage Publishing Corp.
1952 May–1954 September
1–15

This anthology (which was combined with *Crime Smashers* with issue #7) featured Jerry Jasper (Brilliant Criminologist), Queenie Star (Glamour Girl of Hollywood), Lance Storm (Crime-Fighter), and Sally the Sleuth. Many stories had elements of horror. Artists included John Belfi, Angelo Torres, Art Gates, A. C. Hollingsworth, Myron Fass, George Woodbridge, Morris Marcos, Tony Tallarico, and Pierre Charpentier. Writers included Ray McClelland, Albert Tyler, Richard Kahn, and Paul S. Newman.

## CRIME ON THE RUN

St. John Publications
1954 June
8

These "startling cases of the men who defied the law" were drawn by Bob Powell and others for the Approved Comics line.

*Crime Mysteries #11*
© *1954 Ribage Publishing Corp.*

*Crime Must Pay the Penalty #27 © 1952 Ace Magazines*

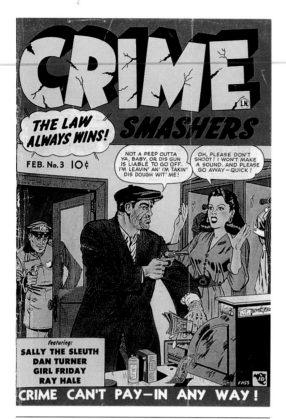

*Crime Smashers #3 © 1951 Trojan Publishing Corp.* Art by Myron Fass.

These brutal stories on the crime beat reprinted a story from *Dynamic Comics* (January 1946) which caught the eye of Fredric Wertham. He reproduced a panel from the story in *Seduction of the Innocent* that showed a woman tied in a chair with her legs suggestively spread. A man shoved a glowing, red-hot poker toward her open thighs. Wertham showed this illustration to his disturbed juvenile patients and announced that the "children told me what the man was going to do with the red-hot poker." Artists included George Tuska and Matt Baker.

## CRIME SMASHER

Fawcett Publications
1948 Summer
1

Alan Turner, a wealthy Virginia sportsman, became a costumed aviator known as the Spy Smasher in *Whiz Comics* (February 1940). After finishing off World War II spies, Turner changed his name to Crime Smasher in the July 1946 issue and fought crime on the streets as a plainclothes detective. This comic book featured three Crime Smasher stories and a secondary feature, "Richard Richard, Private Dick."

## CRIME ON THE WATERFRONT

Realistic Publications
1952 May
4

Formerly published as *Famous Gangsters,* this retitled comic focused on the exploits of "harbor racketeers and waterfront bosses who control the shipment of drugs."

## CRIME SMASHERS

Trojan/Ribage Publishing Corp.
1950 October–1953 March
1–15

The comic book's cast of characters included Sally the Sleuth, Gail Ford ("Girl Friday"), Ray Hale ("News Ace"), and Dan Turner ("Hollywood Detective"). Some stories were reprinted from pulp magazines such as *Hollywood Detective* and *Private Detective* which featured eight-page comic strips (in black and white) along with their mystery fiction. Robert Leslie Bellem, for example, wrote both the prose and comic strip adventures of "Dan Turner." Later issues featured all-new stories. Artists included Max Plaisted, Ray McClelland, Newt Alfred, Bill Fraccio, Anthony Tallarico, Wally Wood, Henry C. Kiefer, and Myron Fass.

## CRIME PATROL

EC Comics
1948 Summer–1950 February
7–16

Formerly published as *International Crime Patrol,* EC's second "true crime" title had art by Johnny Craig, Al Feldstein, Graham Ingels, Sheldon Moldoff, George Roussos, John Alton, Stanely Aschmeier, H. C. Kiefer, and Fred Peters. Captain Crime appeared in early issues, while the last two issues featured the first appearances of the Crypt Keeper as the host of a horror comic story. The title became *Crypt of Terror* with issue #17, and was later retitled *Tales from the Crypt*—the most famous horror comic of all time.

## CRIME REPORTER

St. John Publications
1948 August–1948 December
1–3

## CRIME SUSPENSTORIES

EC Comics
1950 October–1955 February
15, 1–27

The comic book that elevated ménage à trois to a high crime with spouses, boyfriends, and betrayed lovers engaging in petty viciousness and elaborate murders. Dr. Fredric Wertham objected to the amoral stance of many of the

*Crime Patrol #13 © 1949 William M. Gaines.* Art by Johnny Craig.

stories in which criminals often escaped traditional criminal punishment. Artists included Johnny Craig, Reed Crandall, Jack Davis, Jack Kamen, Graham Ingels, Bill Elder, Harvey Kurtzman, George Evans, Joe Orlando, Fred Peters, Al Williamson, Wally Wood, and Bernard Krigstein. Stories by Ray Bradbury were adapted by writers Al Feldstein (#15) and Johnny Craig (#17).

## CRIMEFIGHTERS

Marvel Comics
1948 April–1949 November
1–10
    The March 1949 issue carried an early editorial response to the growing criticism of crime comics. By that month, Marvel Comics was one of the largest publishers of crime comics, with six titles on the newsstands.

## CRIMES BY WOMEN

Fox Features Syndicate
1948 June–1951 August; 1954
1–15; 54
    Publisher Victor Fox may have gotten the concept for this comic from a "true detective" magazine called *Women in Crime*. Full of catfights, spanking scenes, and hot pistol-packing mamas in lingerie, the title was a lightning rod for comic book critics. Dr. Wertham mentioned two issues in his *Seduction of the Innocent* as a corrupting influence on the morals of youth. He was especialy distressed by the role models the women in the comic provided his teenage girl patients: "Scantily dressed, thighs and breasts exposed . . . she shoots at the policeman with a revolver and mutters, 'Here's one for luck.'" Some scripts were written by veteran crime comic writer Ken Fitch.

## CRIMINALS ON THE RUN

Novelty Press
1948 August–1949 December
1–10
    Formerly published as *Young King Cole*, the title continued the adventures of the "detective agency mastermind," with art by L. B. Cole and Al McWilliams.

## DAKOTA NORTH

Marvel Comics
1986 June–1987 February
1–5
    Dakota North, a dashing redhead who affects blue-black bodysuits and red motorcycles, runs North Security, an international troubleshooting agency consisting of her brother Ricky and her assistant "Mad Dog." Written by Martha Thomases and drawn by Tony Salmons.

## DANGER

Comic Media
1953 January–August 1954
1–11
    Soviet spies, Arabian conspiracies, and New York counterfeiters faced off against Duke Douglas, U.S. Secret Agent. Artists include Don Heck, Pete Morisi, and Bill Discount.

## DANGER

Charlton Comics
1955 June–October 1955
12–14
Leftover war yarns and spy tales from defunct comic book publishers made up most of these "dangerous" stories.

## DANGER

IW/Super
1964
10, 11, 12, 15–18
Reprints of 1940s–50s comics. Crime-related

*Dakota North #1 © 1986 Marvel Entertainment Group. Art by Tony Salmons.*

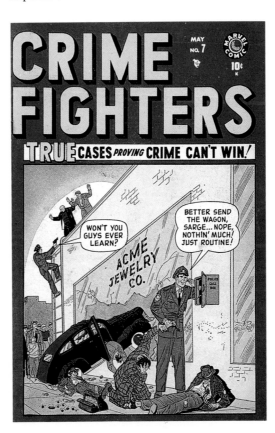

*Crimefighters #7 © 1949 Marvel Entertainment Group*

*Dead End Crime Stories #1 © 1949 Kirby Publishing Co.*

issues included #11 (reprints *Johnny Danger* #1), #15 (*Spy Cases* #26), and #18 (*Guns Against Gangsters* #5).

## DANGER MAN

Dell Publishing Co.
1961 November
1231

Based on the 1961 CBS television show starring Patrick McGoohan as John Drake, an international security investigator.

## DANGER TRAIL

DC Comics
1950 July–1951 March
1–5

International intrigue from Paris to Trinidad took place in this series, which starred world-traveler King Faraday. Johnny Peril, the host of a series of suspense stories in *Comic Cavalcade* during the late 1940s, was featured in the last issue. Artists included Frank Giacoia and Alex Toth. Robert Kanigher was the writer behind the title.

## DATE WITH DANGER

Standard Magazines
1952 December–1953 February
5, 6

*Detective Comics #16 © 1938 DC Comics, Inc. Art by Creig Flessel.*

Johnny Miller, U.S. Counter-Intelligence Agent, chases after spies in "sweltering Central American ports." Meanwhile, his comic book cohort, U.S. intelligence agent Joe Krammer, tracks down traitors in "the icy wastes of northern Alaska."

## DC SPECIAL

DC Comics
1971 February
10

This 64-page anthology entitled "Stop . . . You Can't Beat the Law!" reprinted crime and adventure stories from various 1950s DC comics, including *Showcase* #1 and #5. Artists included Mort Meskin, Curt Swan, Ruben Moreira, and John Prentice.

## DEAD END CRIME STORIES

Kirby Publishing Co.
1949 April
1

"Crime is the game of fools: Death is the scorekeeper." With this message blazoned across the top of every page, readers got a double dose of morality in this hard-nosed, shoot 'em-up comic book. The comic was the premiere title of publisher Allen Kirby, a former comic book artist who drew Amazing Man in the early 1940s. Kirby (no relation to artist Jack Kirby) employed such artists as Wally Wood, Bob Powell, Graham Ingels, and George Roussos. Powell and Roussos each had a story in this title.

## DEFENDERS, THE

Dell Publishing Co.
1962 September–1963 February
12–176–211, 12–176–304

Based on the 1961 CBS television show starring E. G. Marshall and Robert Reed as the father and son lawyer team, Preston & Preston.

## DETECTIVE COMICS

DC Comics
1937 March–1961 June
1–292

The second comic book devoted to detective stories is best known as the birthplace of Batman—the quintessential costumed crime fighter who premiered in the May 1939 issue. Before the Caped Crusader, however, more mundane detectives got their start here, such as Slam Bradley, Speed Saunders, Spy, Brad Nelson, Cosmo the Phantom of Disguise, and Larry

Steele. With the growing popularity of televison in the 1950s, a new detective feature was added in the November 1953 issue: Roy Raymond, TV Detective.

## DETECTIVE DAN, SECRET OPERATIVE 48

Humor Publishing Co.
1933
1

Before launching the "Dan Dunn" newspaper comic strip, artist Norman Marsh tried out his detective in this black-and-white comic magazine.

## DETECTIVE EYE

Centaur Publishing
1940 November–1940 December
1, 2

This comic featured a flying costumed hero known as the Airman as well as more conventional crime fighters such as Dean Denton (Scientific Detective), Pack Morgan (Super Detective), and Dick Hurston (Detective).

## DETECTIVE PICTURE STORIES

Comics Magazine Company
1936 December–1937 April
1–5

This first all-detective comic book featured art by William Allison, Joe Buresch, Will Eisner, George Brenner, and Bob Kane.

## DETECTIVES, INC.

Eclipse Comics
1985 April
1, 2

Art by Gene Colan.

## DETECTIVES, INC.: A TERROR OF DYING DREAMS

Eclipse Comics
1987 June–1987 December
1–3

Art by Gene Colan.

## DETECTIVES, THE

Dell Publishing Co.
1961 March–1961 November
1168, 1219, 1240

Based on the 1959 ABC television series starring Robert Taylor as Captain Holbrook. Like the TV show, the comic book (which was written by TV playwright Eric Freiwald with Robert

Schaffer) rotated its stories around Holbrook and one of his three detectives: Lt. Jim Conway of Homicide, Lt. Johnny Russo of Burglary, and Lt. Otto Lindstrom of the Bunco squad.

## DICK TRACY

Harvey Publications
1950 March–1961 April
25–145

Harvey Publications picked up the rights to the *Dick Tracy* comic book from Dell Publishing just months before the ABC television series began with Ralph Byrd as the square-jawed detective. The comic book reprinted Chester Gould's newspaper strip, and some stories reprinted after the Comics Code took effect in late 1954 had to be edited in order to meet the new restrictions.

## DICK TRACY

Blackthorne Publishing
1984 December–1989 June
1–24

Reprinted daily and Sunday strip reprints from December 31, 1945, to April 5, 1949 (#s 1–12), and July 19, 1941, to February 20, 1944 (#s 13–24).

*Detectives, The #1240*
*© 1961 Four-Star*
*Hastings*

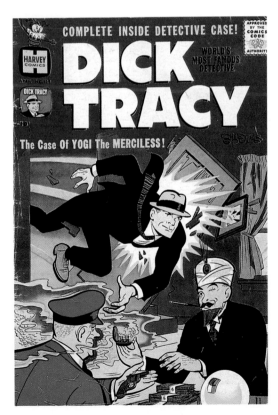

*Dick Tracy #139*
*© 1960 Chicago*
*Tribune*

*Dick Tracy Monthly #3*
*© 1948 Chicago*
*Tribune*

These oversize comics (8½" by 11⅜") reprinted the "Dick Tracy" newspaper strips in black and white.

## DICK TRACY MONTHLY

Dell Publishing Co.
1948 January–1949 December
1–24

The first issue of this regularly published *Dick Tracy* comic book began reprinting newspaper strips from 1934. A secondary series drawn by Bill Ely featured plainclothes detective Jim O'Brien, who is known as "the Iron Man because of his preference for always operating alone."

## DICK TRACY MONTHLY/WEEKLY

Blackthorne Publishing
1986 May–1989
1–99

Reprinted newspaper strip from March 10, 1940, to July 13, 1941 (#s 1–10); April 6, 1949, to December 31, 1955 (#s 10–51); December 26, 1956, to April 26, 1964 (#s 52–99). Black and white. Became *Weekly* with issue #26.

## DICK TRACY SPECIAL

Blackthorne Publishing
1988 January–1989 August
1–3

Reprinted origin of Dick Tracy from the newspaper strips October 12, 1931, to March 30, 1932.

## DICK TRACY: THE EARLY YEARS

Blackthorne Publishing
1987 August–1989
1–4

These 72-page issues (which reprinted the strips from 1931 through 1934) featured the first appearances of many villains and secondary characters that made Dick Tracy an American classic.

## DICK TRACY: THE UNPRINTED STORIES

Blackthorne Publishing
1987 September–1988 June
1–4

These issues reprinted Dick Tracy adventures from 1944 to 1945.

## DICK TRACY

WD Publications
1990
1–3

Adaptation of the 1990 movie with Warren Beatty. Art by Kyle Baker.

## DICK TRACY ADVENTURES

Gladstone
1991 September
1

This 76-page book reprinted (in color) the "Dick Tracy" comic strips from February 1, 1942, to April 18, 1942.

## DICK TRACY COLOR SERIES

Dell Publishing Co.
1939–1948
1, 4, 8, 11, 13, 15, 1, 6, 8, 3, 21, 34, 56, 96, 133, 163, 215

This irregularly issued series of Dell Comics (referred to as the Large Feature comic series and the Four-Color series) reprinted "Dick Tracy" newspaper strips from the 1935–41 period.

## DICK TRACY FEATURE BOOK

David McKay
1937 May–1938 January
nn, 4, 6, 9

## DOWN WITH CRIME

Fawcett Publications
1952 November–1953 November
1–7

"See the violent end for cowards who choose a life of crime!" Issue #6 featured the true story of "Jack Dillon," better known as John Dillinger. Art by Bob Powell in #s 2 and 4.

## DYNAMITE

Comic Media
1953 May–1954 September
1–9

The first two issues featured government agents, arctic explorers, and crime syndicates in stories of "high explosive action," with art by Don Heck and Pete Morisi. The third issue began the adventures of Chicago private eye Johnny Dynamite by artist Pete Morisi and writer Ken Fitch (under the pen name William Waugh).

## 87TH PRECINCT

Dell Publishing Co.
1962 April–1962 July
1309, 2

Adaptation of the 1961 NBC television series based on the police procedural stories of mystery novelist Ed McBain (Evan Hunter). The jagged art by Bernard Krigstein in the first issue captured the grim violence surrounding the team of detectives that operated out of Manhattan's 87th precinct.

## ELLERY QUEEN

Superior Comics
1949 May–1949 November
1–4

This comic book version had the detective encountering werewolves, haunted houses, and drug pushers. Artists included John Forte, Jack Kamen, and L. B. Cole.

## ELLERY QUEEN

Ziff-Davis Publishing Company
1952 January–1952 Summer
1, 2

This series may have been inspired by the 1950 *Adventures of Ellery Queen* television show.

## ELLERY QUEEN

Dell Publishing Co.
1961 March–1962 March
1165, 1243, 1289

Ellery Queen and his father, Inspector Richard Queen, solved two crimes each issue in this third attempt at a comic book series.

## ESCAPE FROM DEVIL'S ISLAND

Avon Periodicals
1951
1

This comic about "convicts condemned to a living death in a penal colony" was reprinted (circa 1964) in *Dynamic Comics* #9.

## ESPIONAGE

Dell Publishing Co.
1964 May–1964 August
1, 2

This anthology title of "true" spy stories was based on the 1963 NBC television show which adapted actual espionage cases from World War I to the present.

## EXPOSED

D.S. Publishing Co.
1948 March–1949 July
1–9

Artists included John Rosenberger, Graham Ingels, Bob Jenney, Paul Reinman, Dan Loprieno, Ken Battlefield, Myron Fass, Red Holmdale, and Bob Jenny.

*Exposed #8 © 1949
D.S. Publishing Co.*

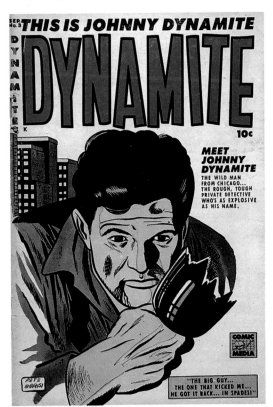

*Dynamite #3 © 1953
Comic Media. Art by Pete
Morisi.*

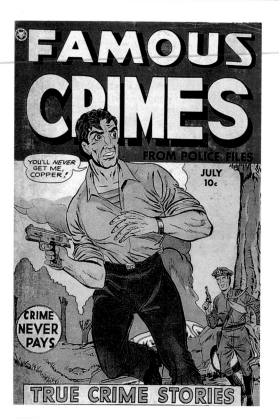

*Famous Crimes #18 © 1950 Fox Features Syndicate*

## FBI STORY, THE

Dell Publishing Co.
1959 November
1069

Based on the 1959 movie about the history of the FBI as seen through the career of an agent played by James Stewart. Art by Alex Toth and script by Eric Freiwald with Robert Schaffer.

## FBI, THE

Dell Publishing Co.
1965 April
1

Produced in cooperation with the Federal Bureau of Investigation, this comic book told the history of the nation's law enforcement agency in documentary style. The comic book, drawn by Joe Sinnot, featured real-life villains like Machine-Gun Kelly and Al Capone, as well as a bigger-than-life hero, FBI chief J. Edgar Hoover.

## FAMOUS CRIMES

Fox Features Syndicate/M.S. Dist.
1948 June–1951 August/1953
1–20, 51, 52

These "famous crimes and true stories of cold-blooded killers" (such as Alvin Karpis and "Legs" Diamond) attracted the ire of anticrime comic book crusader Dr. Fredric Wertham. The

*Fight Against Crime #3 © 1951 Story Comics. Art by Edward Goldfarb.*

psychiatrist worried about stories that make a hero out of a criminal "who robs a bank and shoots five men to death." Ken Fitch wrote some stories. Artists included Pete Morisi, Paul Parker, and A. C. Hollingsworth.

## FAMOUS GANGSTERS

Avon Periodicals
1951 April–1952 February
1–3

Famous gangsters immortalized here included Al Capone (#1), John Dillinger (#1, 2), Lucky Luciano (#1, 3), and Dutch Schultz (#1). Issue #2 reprinted a *Saint* comic book story, with the character renamed Mike Strong.

## FEDERAL MEN COMICS

Gerard Publishing Co.
1945
2

Reprints Jerry Siegel and Joe Shuster's 1930s Federal Men series from *New Adventure Comics* starring G-Man hero Steve Conrad.

## FIGHT AGAINST CRIME

Story Comics
1951 May–1954 September
1–21

The crime format was changed to horror with issue #9. Later issues were full of decapitations, homicidal maniacs, and gratuitous skulls. Artists included A. C. Hollingsworth, Don Cameron, Hy Fleishman, Edward Goldfarb, Ross Andru, and Doug Wildey.

## FIGHT AGAINST THE GUILTY

Story Comics
1954 December–1955 March
22, 23

Formerly published as *Fight Against Crime*, the title was changed before the Comics Code took effect to escape the growing stigma attached to "crime" comics. The second issue (#23) was one of the first crime comics to be approved by the Comics Code and featured a "Dragnet" style detective. Artists included Ross Andru, A. C. Hollingsworth, and Steve Ditko.

## FIRST ISSUE SPECIAL (LADY COP)

DC Comics
1975 July
4

After witnessing the murder of her roommates, Liza Warner became a police officer to bring the killer to justice. The title *Lady Cop* was inspired by the 1974 NBC television series *Police Woman* starring Angie Dickinson. Writer Robert Kanigher made the comic book a realistic and sympathetic treatment of the new 1970s woman police officer. In addition to handling domestic disputes and preventing rapes, Officer Warner told kids about venereal disease: "VD's deceptive! Girls may not have symptoms! But it's a secret destroyer—poisoning you like an underground river! It can cause blindness! Insanity! Death—if not arrested in time!" This one-time appearance of Lady Cop was drawn by John Rosenberger.

## FOREIGN INTRIGUES

Charlton Comics
1956 March–1956 August
13–15

Johnny Dynamite, the hard-nosed detective from Chicago, went abroad in this new series as a government agent who mixed it up with East German spies.

## FOX GIANTS

Fox Features Syndicate
1948–1950
unnumbered (10 crime issues)

Publisher Victor Fox squeezed every dollar he could out of this line of crime, romance, jungle, and western comic books. A favorite trick was to rebind three random ten-cent comic books of roughly the same genre under a new cover and then sell the resulting "giant" for twenty-five cents. Fox recycled leftover issues of *Murder Incorporated; Crimes By Women; Famous Crimes;* and other crime comics as "giant" editions under these titles: *Album of Crime, All Famous Crimes, All Great Crime Stories, Almanac of Crime, Crimes Incorporated, Journal of Crime, March of Crime,* and *Truth About Crime.*

## FREEDOM AGENT

Gold Key
1963 April
1

John Steele began his "secret agent" career here before appearing in his own 1964 comic book.

## FUGITIVES FROM JUSTICE

St. John Publications
1952 February–1952 October
1–5

True to the title, the comic featured stories of criminals on the lam. Artists included Matt Baker and George Tuska. Issues #s 2–5 reprinted the detective comic strip "Vic Flint."

## GANG BUSTERS

McKay/Dell Publishing
1938–1943
17, 10, 17, 7, 23, 24

Based on Phillips H. Lord's long-running radio show (1936–57), these issues featured original stories as well as reprints of the "Gang Busters" series from *Popular Comics*. Artists included Al McWilliams, Jim Chambers, and Erwin Hess.

## GANG BUSTERS

DC Comics
1947 December–1958 December
1–67

The popular "true crime" radio series was adapted into a successful comic book which outlasted the radio show by a year. Artists included Mort Meskin, Ramona Fradon, Joe Maneely, Dan Barry, Ralph Mayo, Jay McArdle, Nick Cardy, Bill Ely, George Papp, and Howard Purcell. Regular series included "A Perfect Crime Mystery" and "Federal Agent."

*Gang Busters #1 © 1947 DC Comics, Inc.*

*Fox Giants (All-Famous Crime) © 1949 Fox Features Syndicate*

*Girl From UNCLE, The #4 © 1967 Gold Key*

## GANG BUSTERS FEATURE BOOK

David McKay
1938 September
17

The popular 1936 radio show, which was based on "actual police records," inspired this seventy-six-page comic book adaptation.

## GANG WORLD

Standard Magazines
1952 November–1953 January
5, 6

Artists included Ralph Mayo, Jay McArdle, Rocco Mastroserio, and George Tuska.

## GANGSTERS AND GUN MOLLS

Avon/Realistic Comics
1951 September–1952 June
1–4

Bonnie Parker and other "molls" starred in this comic, with stories by Wally Wood, Sid Check, and Jack Kamen.

## GANGSTERS CAN'T WIN

D.S. Publishing Co.
1948 February–1949 June
1–9

*Gang World #6 © 1952 Standard Magazines*

Artists included Al McWilliams, Fred Bell, Harry Anderson, Edd Ashe, Ken Battlefield, Bill Fraccio, Graham Ingels, and Paul Parker. Ken Fitch and Bob Jenney wrote some scripts.

## GIANT COMICS EDITION (POLICE CASE BOOK)

St. John Publications
1949 April
5

This large-size comic consisted of four (or sometimes five) leftover crime comics which were rebound under a new cover and sold for twenty-five cents.

## GIRL FROM UNCLE, THE

Gold Key
1967 January–1967 October
1–5

This spinoff from the *Man from UNCLE* television show featured secret agents April Dancer (played by Stefanie Powers) and Mark Slate (Noel Harrison). Although the NBC show lasted for only one season (1966–67), it produced this comic book adaptation, with art by Al McWilliams and Bill Lignante and scripts by Paul Newman.

## GUNS AGAINST GANGSTERS

Novelty Press
1948 September–1949 November
1–8

Gregory Gayle the Gunmaster was an expert marksman who hunted down the criminal element. He was assisted by Toni Gayle (from *Young King Cole* comics), a private investigator in her own right. Artists included L. B. Cole and Alex Schomburg.

## HARDY BOYS, THE

Dell/Gold Key
1957–1959; 1970–1971
760, 830, 887, 964, 1–4

The popular juvenile novels starring teenage detectives Joe and Frank Hardy inspired a TV serial which was broadcast on Walt Disney's Mickey Mouse Club television show in the 1950s. The TV show prompted four comic book adaptations (1957–59) from Dell Publishing, with art by Dan Spiegel. When the young sleuths returned as an animated television series in 1970, there was a second comic book adaptation by Gold Key comics.

## HAWAIIAN EYE

Gold Key
1963 July
1

In this 1959 television series, private detectives Tom Lopaka (Bob Conrad) and Tracy Steele (Anthony Eisley) fought crime from their poolside office at the Hawaiian Village Hotel. They were aided by a terminally cute singer-photographer named Cricket Blake (played by Connie Stevens) and taxi driver Kazuo Kim, who wore wild straw hats and carried a ukulele. For the final season (1962–63), actor Troy Donahue joined the cast as Lopaka's new partner, Philip Barton. The comic book played up the roles of Barton (Donahue) and Cricket (Stevens) and also featured a secondary feature about a surfing detective called Beach Boy.

## HEADLINE COMICS

Prize Publications
1947 March–1956 October
23–77

Originally the home of superhero and adventure strips, the comic's format was changed to "true crime" when Joe Simon and Jack Kirby set up a studio to supply new stories. Other artists included Mort Meskin, Mart Bailey, John Severin, Rudy Palais, A. C. Hollingsworth, Bruno Premiani, Vic Donahue, John Prentice, Marv Stein, Mo Marcus, and Jack Abel.

## HOMICIDE

Dark Horse
1990 April
1

Detective series by Gray Morrow originally begun in *Dark Horse Presents* #54.

## HONEY WEST

Gold Key
1966 September
1

Based on the 1965–66 ABC television show starring Anne Francis, this comic book adaptation featured female private detective Honey West and her partner, Sam Bolt. Influenced by the James Bond movies, Honey had a fondness for spy gadgets, tricky weapons, and martial arts. Operating out of a mobile spy van, the sexy sleuth was often seen in the company of Bruce, her pet ocelot.

## HORRORS OF THE UNDERWORLD

Star Publications
1954–April 1954
14, 15

The bitter fruit that awaits all criminals was grimly detailed in stories of wayward youth ("No—no! That'll never happen to me—just give me one more chance!") and cheap hoods ("I'll show them all! I'm going to be a real *big-shot*!!").

## HUNTED

Fox Features Syndicate
1950 July–1950 September
13, 2

Dr. Fredric Wertham singled out this title for criticism in *Seduction of the Innocent* for its contemptuous treatment of police officers. One scene which particularly bothered Wertham showed a criminal murdering a policeman who simply asked him for his driver's license. The doctor sadly confided that "I was asked to help in the defense of a youth who had committed exactly the same crime in Connecticut."

## I SPY

Gold Key
1966 August–1968 September
1–6

Based on the NBC espionage television series (1965–68), these book-length stories (some adapted by writer Paul Newman and artist Mike

*I Spy #4 © 1968 Three F Productions*

*Headline Comics #40 © 1950 Headline Publications*

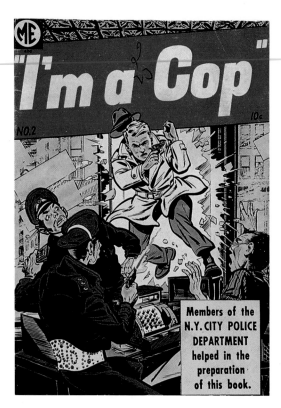

*I'm A Cop #2 © 1954 Magazine Enterprises.* Art by Bob Powell.

Members of the N.Y. CITY POLICE DEPARTMENT helped in the preparation of this book.

Roy) remained faithful to the TV characters portrayed by Robert Culp and Bill Cosby.

## I'M A COP

Magazine Enterprises
1954
1–3

Although *Dragnet* was the most popular police TV show in history, there were no comic books based on the series. During the height of its popularity from 1953 to 1954, however, a comic book appeared that was obviously inspired by the show and even borrowed its title from Jack Webb's classic opening line: "My name's Friday—I'm a cop." In this series, drawn by Bob Powell, police procedural work was emphasized: "My name is Rogers—Richie Rogers. I'm a detective assigned to homicide. My partner is Mike Flynn, one of the greatest and toughest cops ever to carry a badge." Like the television show, the comic was told from a first-person view: "1:12 P.M. . . . We arrived at the scene. It's a small neighborhood grocery, the kind that sells everything from socks to salami. The proprietor is dead, shot through the chest three times. No witnesses. The lab boys are just wrapping up as we arrive."

*Informer, The #1 © 1954 Sterling Comics*

## IDEAL, A CLASSIC COMICS

Marvel Comics
1948 September
2

Along the lines of *Classic Comics* and *Classic Illustrated*, this title purported literary merit, with such adaptations as "Anthony and Cleopatra," "Joan of Arc," and "Richard the Lion-Hearted." For the growing crime comic market, the second issue featured the mystery thriller "The Corpses of Dr. Sacotti"("The case that shook Scotland Yard").

## IN THE DAYS OF THE MOB

Hampshire Dist. Ltd.
1971 Fall
1

Jack Kirby wrote and drew stories about Al Capone, Ma Barker, and Pretty Boy Floyd for this fifty-two-page black-and-white comic magazine. A second issue was drawn but not published.

## INFORMER, THE

Sterling Comics
1954 April–1954 December
1–5

Detective Sergeant Mark Fabian, who worked with his partner Pat Polo, often sounded like Sergeant Joe Friday from the television show *Dragnet.* "It was 6:20 when Homer Waring, top society jeweler, stopped a slug in his Park Avenue apartment . . . 6:23 P.M.—Pat Polo and I are working the night watch out of homicide. The call came in to us." The similarity to the popular TV show (number two in the nation that year) was intentional, even down to the comic book's subtitle: "From the files of the police DRAGNET!" A secondary series featured Kenny Cogan as The Cop, whose beat is the slum where he grew up. Mike Sekowsky drew the majority of the stories.

## INSIDE CRIME

Fox Features Syndicate
1950 July–1950 August
3, 2

The first issue (#3) of this comic book featured art by Wally Wood, while the second issue earned a mention in Fredric Wertham's *Seduction of the Innocent* for pandering to "latent fetishistic tendencies" and "sexual masochism."

## INSPECTOR WADE FEATURE BOOK

David McKay
1938 May
13

This oversize comic book reprinted the "Inspector Wade" newspaper strips in black and white. The Scotland Yard detective was taken from Edgar Wallace's mystery novel *The India*

*Rubber Man* (1929) and adapted for the comics by writer Sheldon Stark and artist Lyman Anderson. Although the comic strip ran from 1935 to 1941, this was the only comic book.

## INTERNATIONAL CRIME PATROL

EC Comics
1948 Spring
6

Formerly published as *International Comics*, the title became a crime comic with this issue that introduced the "International Crime-Busting Patrol." The title was shortened to *Crime Patrol* with the next issue.

## JAMES BOND: FOR YOUR EYES ONLY

Marvel Comics
1981 October–1981 November
1, 2

Adaptation of 1981 James Bond movie, with art by Howard Chaykin. Previously published as *Marvel Super Special #19*.

## JAMES BOND: LICENSE TO KILL

Eclipse Comics
1989
1

Adaptation of James Bond movie with Timothy Dalton.

## JAMES BOND: PERMISSION TO DIE

Eclipse Comics
1989–1990
1–3

Mike Grell wrote and drew this adaptation of Ian Fleming's James Bond.

## JANE ARDEN CRIME REPORTER

St. John Publications
1948 March–1948 June
1, 2

Jane Arden, an investigative reporter, mixed it up with big-city crime in this comic book which reprinted the newspaper comic strip drawn by Russell Ross and written by Monte Barrett.

## JEFF JORDAN, U.S. AGENT

D.S. Publishing Co.
1947 December
1

Publisher Richard Davis made this postwar spy comic the first title of a comic book lineup that included *Gangsters Can't Win, Pay-Off, Exposed, Public Enemies,* and *Underworld.*

## JET DREAM

Gold Key
1968 June
1

"Jet Dream and Her Stunt-Girl Counterspies" originally appeared as a backup series in the *Man from UNCLE* comic book and was written by comic book veteran Dick Wood. Jet's all-girl air squadron consisted of martial arts experts and daredevil pilots who worked as international freelance agents. The series was probably inspired by the all-woman stunt plane squadron headed by Pussy Galore in the 1964 James Bond movie *Goldfinger.*

## JOHN LAW DETECTIVE

Eclipse Comics
1983 April
1

Contained three previously unpublished stories of a detective drawn in 1948 by Will Eisner, creator of the Spirit.

## JOHN STEELE SECRET AGENT

Gold Key
1964 December
1

*Inside Crime #3 © 1950 Fox Features Syndicate*

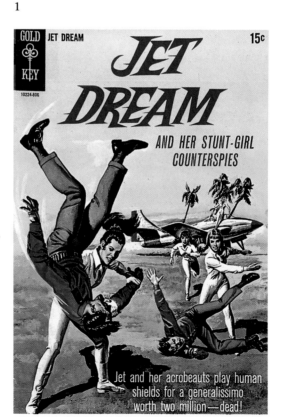

*Jet Dream #1 © 1968 Western Publishing Company, Inc.*

*Ken Shannon #6 © 1952
Quality Comics*

One of the first comic books to take
advantage of the James Bond secret agent craze.
Written by Paul Newman. Previously published
as *Freedom Agent*.

## JOHNNY DANGER PRIVATE EYE

Toby Press
1954 August
1

Johnny Danger's first case took him to an
opium den where he was tortured, branded, and
finally seduced. His "meek, retiring secretary
Debbie Shaw" stood up for her boss when the
going got hot. Reprinted in 1964 by Super
Comics as *Danger #11*.

## JOHNNY DYNAMITE

Charlton Comics
1955 June–1955 October
10–12

Formerly published as *Dynamite*, this title
continued the adventures of hard-hitting Chicago
detective, Johnny Dynamite. Pete Morisi supplied
both script and art for several stories.

## JUSTICE COMICS

Marvel Comics
1947 Fall–1955 March
7–52

*Justice Traps the Guilty
#24 © 1951 Headline
Publications.* Art by
Marvin Stein.

Early issues were based on "real FBI" cases.
Artists included Russ Heath, Bob Brown, Hy
Rosen, Tony Dipreta, Mac Pakula, Louis Ravielli,
Jerry Robinson, George Tuska, and Doug Wildey.

## JUSTICE TRAPS THE GUILTY

Prize Publications
1947 October–1958 April
1–92

The second-longest running "true crime"
comic book (after *Crime Does Not Pay*) was
created by Joe Simon and Jack Kirby. The early
issues were packaged by Simon and Kirby from
their studio, where they were also creating crime
stories for *Headline Comics* and *Real Clue Crime
Cases*. Simon wrote some stories and Kirby even
found time to pose as a gangster for a photograph that was used later as a cover. Other artists
who worked on the title included Bill Draut,
Rudy Palais, Bruno Premiani, John Prentice, Marv
Stein, Mort Meskin, Bernard Krigstein, John
Severin, Mart Bailey, Jerry Robinson, Joe Orlando,
and Al Feldstein.

## KEEN DETECTIVE FUNNIES

Centaur Publishing
1938 July–1940 September
8–24

Superheroes like the Masked Marvel and
TNT Todd shared this comic book with Crane of
Scotland Yard and a trio of alliterative private
eyes: Dean Denton (Scientific Detective), Dan
Dennis (F.B.I.), and Dan Dix (Ship's Detective).

## KEN SHANNON

Quality Comics
1951 October–1953 April
1–10

Ken Shannon, a handsome, hulking private
eye, used his fists as well as his wits to solve a
caper. He was accompanied by Dee-Dee Dawson
("my girl Friday and any other day of the week")
and mixed it up with white slavers, Oriental
masterminds, and vampires, as well as the usual
run-of-the-mill urban rats. The fighting Irish
detective, who bore a passing resemblance to
movie actor Fred MacMurray, originally appeared
in *Police Comics* (December 1950).

## KENT BLAKE OF THE SECRET SERVICE

Marvel Comics
1951 May–1953 July
1–14

This comic book, with "real behind the
scene stories of how U.S. secret agents track
down dangerous enemy spies," featured Kent

Blake behind the Iron Curtain. Marvel artist Joe Sinnot made his company debut in the second issue. As the Korean War continued, later issues emphasized battlefield stories and "action behind enemy lines."

## KERRY DRAKE

Argo Publishing
1956 January–March 1956
1, 2

Reprinted the newspaper strip adventures by Alfred Andriola of the "chief investigator for the D.A.'s office."

## KERRY DRAKE DETECTIVE CASES

Magazine Enterprises/Harvey Publications
1944–1952 August
1–33

Reprinted the "Kerry Drake" newspaper comic strips by Alfred Andriola.

## KILLERS, THE

Magazine Enterprises
1947–1948
1, 2

Murderers were the heroes in this comic book which drew the criticism of Dr. Fredric Wertham for one scene which he cited as a "graphic description of sexual flagellation on the buttocks." Artists included Vernon Henkel and Paul Parker.

## LAW AGAINST CRIME

Essenkay Publishing Co.
1948 April–1948 August
1–3

A disembodied policeman known as "Officer Law" narrated stories of infamous criminals, such as Clyde Barrow. One story ("Crimson Trail of the Lipstick Slayer") warranted mention in Fredric Wertham's *Seduction of the Innocent* for pandering to the "truly dangerous perversion of wishing to hurt or kill couples making love to each other." For the kiddies, there were funny animal stories mixed in with the murder and mayhem. L. B. Cole supplied artwork for covers and some stories.

## LAWBREAKERS

Charlton Comics
1951 March–1952 October
1–9

Homicide detective Sergeant Force worked the city beat in this crime comic anthology drawn by Stan Campbell, Lou Morales, Bob Forgione, and Dick Giordano.

## LAWBREAKERS ALWAYS LOSE!

Marvel Comics
1948 Spring–1949 October
1–10

In addition to the "true-to-life" stories, each issue featured a "Wanted By The F.B.I." page with mugshots and descriptions ("nude girl tattoo on left arm . . . horizontal scar left index finger . . . bald in front . . . wanted for violation of the white slave traffic act . . . "). Alert comic book readers could earn a hundred dollars by identifying and turning in one of these public enemies.

## LAWBREAKERS SUSPENSE STORIES

Charlton Comics
1953 January–1953 November
10–15

Formerly published as *Lawbreakers,* the comic was retitled with more emphasis on horror. Artists included Lou Morales, Dick Giordano, and Al Bellman.

## LIMITED COLLECTORS' EDITION

DC Comics
1976 January
40

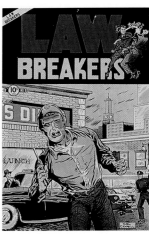

*Lawbreakers #9 © 1952 Charlton Comics. Art by Stan Campbell.*

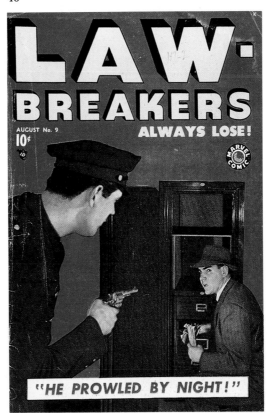

*Lawbreakers Always Lose! #9 © 1949 Marvel Entertainment Group*

*Man From UNCLE, The #15 © 1967 Metro-Goldwyn-Mayer, Inc.*

This oversize (10" by 13½") 60-page comic book reprinted the "Dick Tracy" strips from December 21, 1943, to May 17, 1944.

## LITTLE AL OF THE FBI

Ziff-Davis Publishing Company
1950–1951 April
10, 11

Little Al Conway ("the shortest but toughest agent") somehow ducked the agency's height requirements to fight communists and government terrorists. Mike Sekowsky handled some of the art chores.

## LITTLE AL OF THE SECRET SERVICE

Ziff-Davis Publishing Company
1951 July–1951 Winter
10, 2, 3

Evidently, the FBI wasn't thrilled about having a diminutive agent in the field, even if only in a comic book, so the title was changed to reflect Al's new role as an international government agent. Leonard Starr, who drew the newspaper strip "On Stage" (1957–79), had a story in the first issue.

## LITTLE GIANT DETECTIVE FUNNIES

Centaur Publishing
1938 October–1939 January
1–4

*Little Al of the Secret Service #10 © 1951 Ziff-Davis Publishing Company*

This early anthology of mystery stories earned its name from its small digest size (6¾" by 4½") and lengthiness (128 pages). Stories were printed in black and white.

## MALTESE FALCON FEATURE BOOK

David McKay
1946
48

Dashiell Hammett's 1929 novel was adapted into comic book format by artist Rodlow Willard. Before the comic appeared, the novel had already been filmed three times, the last in 1941 with Humphrey Bogart.

## MAN FROM UNCLE, THE

Gold Key
1965 February–1969 April
1–22

Based on the 1964–68 NBC television spy spoof series with Robert Vaughn as Napoleon Solo and David McCallum as Illya Kuryakin. Mr. Waverly, THRUSH, and all the UNCLE gadgets found their way into the comic book series, which featured art by Mike Roy, Werner Roth, Mike Sekowsky, George Tuska, and Bill Lignante. Writers included Dick Wood and Marshal McClintock. A secondary series, "Jet Dream and Her Stunt-Girl Counterspies," began in issue #7.

## MAN FROM UNCLE, THE

Entertainment Publishing
1987 January–1988 September
1–11

Napoleon Solo, Illya Kuryakin, and Mr. Waverly appeared in this second comic book treatment of the 1964 television show. While the action took place in the 1980s, Solo and Kuryakin kept their 1960s looks. Writer David Lynch also added new UNCLE agents to this black-and-white series.

## MANHUNT

Magazine Enterprises
1947 October–1953
1–14

This anthology featured such action-detective series as "Undercover Girl" by Ogden Whitney, "Kirk of Scotland Yard" by Paul Parker, "Fallon of the F.B.I." by Ogden Whitney, and "Red Fox of the Northwest Mounted Police" by L. B. Cole.

## MARCH OF CRIME

Fox Features Syndicate
1950 July–1951 September
7, 2, 3

The title of this comic book (which was a takeoff on the popular movie newsreel series "The March of Time") aptly described the succession of violent "true crime" stories that made up each issue ("Reach for the sky! Get your claws in the air! I'm walking out with every buck in the joint!"). Wally Wood and Harry Harrison contributed their artistic efforts.

## MARTIN KANE PRIVATE EYE

Fox Features Syndicate
1950 June–1950 August
4, 2

Martin Kane, a radio private eye, made his NBC television debut in 1949. William Gargan, who played Ellery Queen in three 1942 movies, starred as this early TV detective. Artists Wally Wood and Joe Orlando struggled mightily to capture Gargan's likeness for their readers. The comic book was the first to be based on a TV detective show.

## MARVEL PREVIEW

Marvel Comics
1976 April–1976 Spring
5, 6

Sherlock Holmes starred in this two-part adaptation of *Hound of the Baskervilles* by writer Doug Moench and artist Val Mayerik. Magazine size. Black and white.

## MASTER DETECTIVE

IW/Super
1964
17

Reprinted two *Young King Cole* stories from 1947–48, with art by Al McWilliams.

## MAZE AGENCY, THE

Comico/Innovation
1988 December–1991 August
1–23

Private eye Jennifer Mays and true-crime writer Gabriel Webb starred in this series created and written by Mike Barr. Art initially by Adam Hughes and later by Joe Staton. Issue #9 featured Ellery Queen in a tribute to the character's 60th anniversary.

## MEN AGAINST CRIME

Ace Magazines
1951 February–1951 October
3–7

The "men against crime" in this series included Mr. Risk and private investigator Kirk Mason, as drawn by Gene Colan.

## MIKE BARNETT, MAN AGAINST CRIME

Fawcett Publications
1951 December–1952 October
1–6

The comic book was based on the popular television show *Man Against Crime* starring Ralph Bellamy as Mike Barnett, a rough-knuckled New York City private eye. The TV series (1949–56) eventually appeared on three networks. The steely eyed comic book detective bore a passing resemblance to Ralph Bellamy and featured the same tough-guy talk as on the screen: "I could have handled Al—but that heater in Claire's hand looked ready to bark any second! I decided to reason with them . . ."

## MIKE MIST MINUTE MYSTERIES

Eclipse Comics
1981 April
1

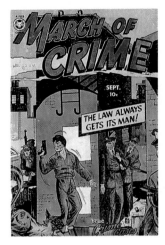

*March of Crime #2*
*© 1950 Fox Features*
*Syndicate*

*Mike Barnett, Man*
*Against Crime #4 © 1952*
*Fawcett Publications*

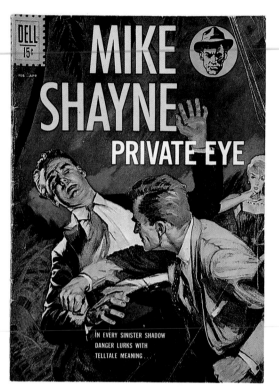

*Mike Shayne Private Eye #2 © 1962 Dell Publishing Company*

These solve-it-yourself mini-mysteries, complete with clues and solutions, were hosted by Mike Mist, a crime solver created by mystery writer Max Allan Collins.

## MIKE SHAYNE PRIVATE EYE

Dell Publishing Co.
1961 November–1962 September
1–3

Mike Shayne, a debonair private eye created in 1934 by David Dresser under the pen name of Brett Halliday, was the hero of nearly one hundred novels, twelve movies (1940–47), a radio show (1949), and a newsstand magazine launched in 1956. In 1960, NBC made the Miami-based investigator the star of a television series (*Michael Shayne, Private Detective*) with Richard Denning in the title role. The show provided the impetus for the 1961 comic book which was released just as the television series was canceled. Writer Ken Fitch helped bring the suave detective to the comic books, while veteran crime comic artists Lee Ames (*Crime Does Not Pay*) and Edd Ashe (*Gangsters Can't Win*) provided the artwork.

## MISS CAIRO JONES

Croyden Publishers
1945
1

*Mission Impossible #4 © 1968 Paramount Pictures Corp.*

Miss Cairo Jones, a gun-toting and globe-trotting adventuress, appeared in a Sunday newspaper comic strip in 1945. The tough-talking blonde investigator (originally envisioned as a man) was created by Bob Oskner, a comic book artist whose early work included "Terry Vance, School Boy Sleuth" for *Marvel Mystery Comics* in 1940. Oskner's heroine eventually starred in both a daily and Sunday comic strip that ran until 1947. Her adventures reprinted in this comic book were written by Gerald Albert, editor of *Rare Detective Cases*.

## MISSION: IMPOSSIBLE

Dell Publishing Co.
1967 May–1969 October
1–5

Based on the 1966 CBS television series that featured a team of highly specialized government agents who receive instructions from a self-destructing tape recorder ("Your mission, should you decide to accept it . . ."). Writer Joe Gill attempted to duplicate the suspense and pacing of the TV show in the comic book.

## MOD SQUAD

Dell Publishing Co.
1969 January–1971 April
1–8

Based on the 1968–73 ABC television series that featured a youth squad of three undercover "hippie cops" (Pete, Linc, and Julie) who infiltrated the counterculture in order to solve crimes.

## MOLLY O'DAY (SUPER SLEUTH)

Avon Periodicals
1945 February
1

Molly O'Day, another of the female comic book crime fighters who proliferated during the mid-1940s, solved her cases with a snub-nosed revolver while wearing an ankle-length evening gown.

## MOON GIRL (FIGHTS CRIME)

EC Comics
1949 May–1949 Winter
7, 8

With the growing popularity of crime comics, publisher William Gaines changed Moon Girl, a superheroine drawn by Sheldon Moldoff, into a crime-fighting detective and added a "True Crime Feature" in issue #8. In the next issue, however, the book was turned into a romance comic.

## MR. DISTRICT ATTORNEY

Dell Publishing Co.
1942
13

The popular *Mr. District Attorney* radio crime show (1939–53) inspired an early comic book series in *The Funnies* (September 1939–May 1942). This comic book was the first devoted entirely to the "champion of the people."

## MR. DISTRICT ATTORNEY

DC Comics
1948 January–1959 January
1–67

The popular radio show with District Attorney Paul Garrett was adapted into a comic book series with art by Bill Ely, Sheldon Moldoff, Howard Purcell, and others. Two television series were also produced in the early 1950s. The comic book, however, outlasted both its radio and TV counterparts by almost five years.

## MR. MONSTER'S SUPER DUPER SPECIAL

Eclipse Comics
1986 September–1986 November
3, 4

Michael T. Gilbert's Mr. Monster played host to classic crime comics by Jack Cole reprinted from *True Crime Comics* (May 1947 and July 1948).

## MR. RISK

Ace Magazines
1950 October–1950 December
7, 2

"The fact that I don't carry a gun isn't as strange as it sounds. I've found out that two fists and a brain are a lot more effective! What I do carry is my card. It has my name, address and phone number: Dangerfield 7-7777. If a person is in trouble he's free to call. It makes no difference how great the trouble nor how great the risk!" Mr. Risk originally appeared in *Super Mystery Comics* (1942–45) and made his last appearance in *Men Against Crime*. Kirk Mason, "The Tough Dick," also appeared here before moving over to *Men Against Crime*.

## MS. TREE QUARTERLY

DC Comics
1990 Summer–1992
1–8

The continuing adventures of the woman private eye created by writer Max Collins and artist Terry Beatty as she entered motherhood.

## MS. TREE'S THRILLING DETECTIVE ADVENTURES

Eclipse/Aardvark/Renegade
1983 February–1989 June
1–50

Writer Max Collins and artist Terry Beatty created one of the most successful women comic book detectives ever in the character of Ms. Michael Tree. The widow of a private eye, Ms. Tree was loosely based on Velda, Mike Hammer's secretary from the Mickey Spillane novels.

## MURDER INCORPORATED

Fox Features Syndicate
1948 January–1951 August
1–9, 9, 5, 2, 3

The comic's title came from the notorious crime syndicate run by Bugsy Siegel and Meyer Lansky in the 1930s. The comic featured "true" stories about such gangsters as Machine-Gun Kelly, Pretty Boy Floyd, and Dutch Schultz. The first two issues were marked "For Adults Only" and were the first newsstand comic books to carry such a prohibition. Ken Fitch wrote some stories; artists included Pete Morisi and Don Rico.

*Mr. Risk #7 © 1950 Ace Magazines*

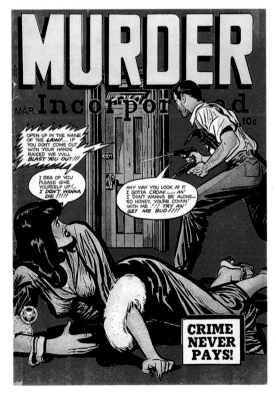

*Murder Incorporated #9 © 1949 Fox Features Syndicate*

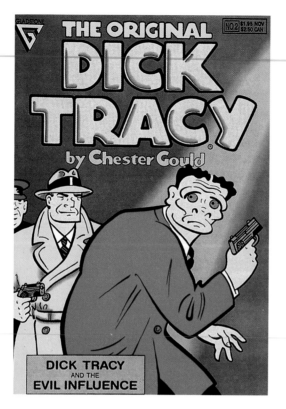

*Original Dick Tracy #2 © 1990 Tribune Media Services*

## MURDER TALES

World Famous Periodicals
1970 November–1971 January
10, 11

Magazine-size comic book reprinted fifty-two pages of 1940s crime stories in black and white from *Crime Does Not Pay* (May 1946) and other issues.

## MURDEROUS GANGSTERS

Avon/Realistic Comics
1951 July–1952 June
1–4

The "murderous gangsters" included Pretty Boy Floyd, Baby Face Nelson, Legs Diamond, and the "Mad Dog" Esposito brothers. Artists included Wally Wood, Mike Becker, and Mort Lawrence.

## MYSTERIES OF SCOTLAND YARD

Magazine Enterprises
1954
121

Inspector Kirk of Scotland Yard from *Manhunt* comics appeared in these stories drawn by Paul Parker.

*New Adventures of Charlie Chan #6 © 1959 DC Comics, Inc.*

## NATHANIEL DUSK

DC Comics
1984 Feb–1984 May; 1985 October–1986 January
1–4; Vol. 2 #1–4

Nathaniel Dusk was a tough New York City private detective, circa 1934, who became involved in a murder case. The series, written by Don McGregor and drawn by Gene Colan, was awash with authentic period touches, brutal violence, and grotesque villainy.

## NEW ADVENTURES OF CHARLIE CHAN

DC Comics
1958 May–1959 March
1–6

The comic book was a spin-off from the 1957 syndicated television series "The New Adventures of Charlie Chan" from A.T.V. Studios of London with J. Carrol Naish in the lead role. The comic book was written by John Broome, with art by Gil Kane and Sid Greene.

## NEW ADVENTURES OF SHERLOCK HOLMES

Dell Publishing Co.
1961 March–1962 November
1169, 1245

These two issues presented stories beyond the Arthur Conan Doyle canon, with art by Bob Fujitani and the team of Mike Sekowsky and Frank Giacoia.

## OFFICIAL TRUE CRIME CASES

Marvel Comics
1947 Fall–1947 Winter
24, 25

Along with *Justice*, Marvel's first crime comic books; later retitled *All-True Crime Cases*. Artists included Carl Burgos and Michael Becker.

## ON THE SPOT

Fawcett Publications
1948 Fall
1

The life and death of 1930s gangster Pretty Boy Floyd was detailed in a forty-nine-page comic book story.

## ORIGINAL DICK TRACY

Gladstone
1990 September–1991 May
1–5

These large-size books reprinted complete

story sequences in color from the Dick Tracy newspaper strips, circa 1943–47.

## ORIGINAL DICK TRACY COMIC ALBUM

Gladstone
1990
1–3

These large-size books reprinted complete story sequences in color from the Dick Tracy newspaper strips.

## P.I.S, THE

First Comics
1985 January–1985 May
1–3

The adventures of private investigators Michael Mauser and Ms. Tree were written by Max Allan Collins and drawn by Joe Staton.

## PAROLE BREAKERS

Avon/Realistic Comics
1951 December–1952 July
1–3

The star of this crime comic was the recalcitrant criminal who refuses to reform. Readers thrilled to the exploits of Pete Loris and the Notorious Flathead Gang, Helen Willis the Gun-Crazed Gun-Moll, and an assortment of repeat offenders like Lou "Limpy" Savatto, John "Slicer" Berry, and Clarence "Gunny" Smith ("Though the ordinary citizen may laugh at such queer nicknames, the police officer frequently finds them useful in tracking down his man . . ."). Artists included Syd Shores, Edward Goldfarb, Joe Kubert, and Everett R. Kinstler.

## PAY-OFF

D.S. Publishing Co.
1948 July–1949 March
1–5

Artists included John Rosenberger, Dan Loprieno, Harry Anderson, Myron Fass, Red Holmdale, Bob Jenny, and Walter Johnson.

## PENALTY

Ace Magazines
1955 October–1956 January
47, 48

With New York State's 1955 restriction against using the word "crime" in a comic book title, *Crime Must Pay the Penalty* was renamed for its two final issues. Bert and Sue, the husband-and-wife detective team from *Super Mystery Comics,* make an appearance.

## PERFECT CRIME

Cross Publications
1949 October–1953 May
1–33

Although the comic book often reminded readers that "there is NO perfect crime," one issue came under attack by comic critic Dr. Frederic Wertham for showing readers the details of a "nearly foolproof scheme" for robbing a neighborhood drugstore. Issues #s 7–30 featured the adventures of "famous Licensed Investigator" Steve Duncan, college graduate and ex-lieutenant of the O.S.S. The series was drawn by 23-year-old Cal Massey as one of his first comic book assignments. Other artists included Jerry Buckley, Howard Nostrand, Bob Powell, James Reilley, and Doug Wildey.

## PERRY MASON FEATURE BOOK

David McKay
1946
49, 50

The popularity of the Perry Mason radio show, which premiered on CBS in 1943, provided the impetus for these comic book adaptations of two Erle Stanley Gardner novels. *The Case of The Lucky Legs* (originally published in 1934) was adapted by artist Vernon Greene for issue #49, while Gardner's 1938 novel *The Case of the*

*Perfect Crime #20*
*© 1952 Cross Publications*

*Penalty #47 © 1955 Ace Magazines*

TOPS IN SUSPENSE, MYSTERY, ADVENTURE AND INTRIGUE!

**POLICE** COMICS

10¢ DECEMBER No.122

KEN SHANNON
CRIME-BUSTING PRIVATE EYE
in
**THE LONELY HEARTS KILLER**

Also-
T-MAN
in
THE RED
ROBBERS

*Police Comics #122*
*© 1952 Quality Comics*

*Shoplifter's Shoes* was adapted by artist/writer Paul Norris for issue #50.

### PERRY MASON MAGAZINE

Dell Publishing Co.
1964 June–1964 October
1, 2

The popular television show starring Raymond Burr as Erle Stanley Gardner's court-room lawyer was in its seventh season when this comic book appeared. The comic's front covers featured photos of Burr as Mason. Art by Stephen Addeo and Ernie Colan.

### PETER GUNN

Dell Publishing Co.
1960 April
1087

*TV Guide* described the new 1958 detective series starring Craig Stevens as "hot jazz, hot action, hot women. And the coolest private eye ever." The *Peter Gunn* TV show bounced along for three years to a musical score by Henry Mancini. When he wasn't preventing a murder (usually involving a glamorous woman), Gunn hung out at a "beat" club known as Mother's with Edie Hart, his jazz-singing girlfriend. In the comic book adaptation drawn by Mike Sekowsky, however, Gunn's womanizing and nightclub

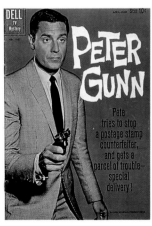

*Peter Gunn #1087*
*© 1960 Spartan*
*Productions*

lifestyle are played down in favor of more action-oriented stories with Lieutenant Jacoby.

### POLICE ACTION

Atlas/Seaboard Publishing
1975 February–1975 June
1–3

The star of this series, police officer Lomax, was drawn by Larry Lieber, Mike Sekowsky, and Frank Thorne. Mike Ploog drew the secondary feature: Luke Malone, Manhunter.

### POLICE ACTION

Marvel Comics
1954 January–1954 November
1–7

"Police Strike Back Against Gangland" in this series with art by Joe Maneely, Gene Colan, Dick Ayers, John Forte, Mort Lawrence, Paul Reinman, Robert Q. Sale, and Bob Powell.

### POLICE AGAINST CRIME

Premier Magazines
1954 April–1955 August
1–9

The second issue (June 1954) was one of the last crime comic books published without the Comics Code seal of approval. While later code-approved issues (#s 3–9) featured tame tales of heroic police action, the early issues exhibited a fascination for violent knife-wielding maniacs. Artists included Jay Disbrow and A. C. Hollingsworth.

### POLICE BADGE #479

Marvel Comics
1955 September
5

Jim Hudson, Patrolman, was the wearer of badge #479 and the rookie cop hero of this police comic.

### POLICE COMICS

Quality Comics
1950 December–1953 October
103–127

Originally the home of such 1940s cos-tumed crime-fighters as Plastic Man, Phantom Lady, and the Spirit, *Police Comics* finally lived up to its name in 1950 when it changed to a format of police action stories. The new stars were Pete Trask, a government agent known as "T-Man," and a hard-boiled private eye named Ken

Shannon. Both characters would star in their own comics the following year. Reed Crandall drew stories for many issues.

## POLICE LINE-UP

Realistic/Avon Comics
1951 August–1952 July
1–4

Mugshots of criminals adorned the front cover of every issue. Artists included Wally Wood, Joe Kubert, Everett R. Kinstler, Mort Lawrence, and Howard Larsen.

## POLICE TRAP

IW/Super
1963–1964
11, 16–18

Reprints crime comics from the late 1940s and early 1950s such as *Police Trap, Justice Traps the Guilty,* and *Inside Crime.*

## POLICE TRAP

Mainline/Charlton Comics
1954 August–1955 September
1–6

Artists included Mort Meskin, Bill Draut, W. G. Harris, John Prentice, Joe Simon, and Jack Kirby. Simon also wrote several stories. "Kelly Green, Private Eye" appeared in some issues.

## PRISON BREAK

Avon/Realistic Comics
1951 September–1952 September
1–5

These jail-busting stories were drawn by Wally Wood, Joe Orlando, Joe Kubert, Sid Check, Carmine Infantino, Joe Kubert, and others.

## PRISON RIOT

Avon Periodicals
1952
1

Lockup in the Big House turned ugly when the trustees staged a mutiny at Bradburn Prison.

## PRIVATE EYE

Marvel Comics
1951 January–1952 March
1–8

Rocky Jorden, a red-headed private eye, may have been inspired by the popular 1950 television show *Rocky King, Inside Detective.* Rocky

gained a loyal secretary in the second issue after he rescued Lisa Brown from her "coked-up drummer" boyfriend. Artists included George Tuska, Sol Brodsky, Joe Sinnot, Pete Morisi, and Vern Henkel.

## PRIZE MYSTERY

Key Publications
1955 May–1955 September
1–3

This crime suspense title was issued immediately after the Comics Code took effect.

## PUBLIC DEFENDER IN ACTION

Charlton Comics
1956 March–1957 October
7–12

The comic was probably inspired by the 1954–55 CBS television show *The Public Defender,* which was based on files from public defenders who help exonerate wrongly accused and destitute individuals. Most of the adventures of the pipe-smoking attorney Richard Manning were drawn by Rocco Mastroserio and Charles Nicholas.

*Private Eye #4 © 1951 Marvel Entertainment Group. Art by Vernon Henkel.*

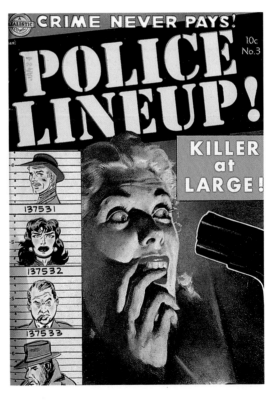

*Police Line-Up #3 © 1952 Realistic Publications*

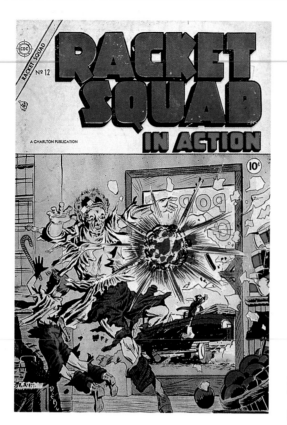

*Racket Squad in Action #12 © 1954 Charlton Comics. Art by Steve Ditko.*

## PUBLIC ENEMIES

D.S. Publishing Co.
1948–1949 June
1–9

These "stories of the fight for law and order" featured art by Chu Hing, Dan Loprieno, Art Gates, Al Wentzel, Ken Battlefield, and others.

## PUBLIC ENEMIES

Eternity Comics
1989 November–1989 December
1, 2

The comic book accounts of Pretty Boy Floyd, John Dillinger, Machine-Gun Kelly, and Legs Diamond were reprinted in black and white from such 1950s comics as *All-True Detective Cases*, *Law Against Crime*, and *Crimes By Women*.

## RACKET SQUAD IN ACTION

Charlton Comics
1952 May–1958 March
1–29

Inspector J. J. O'Malley exposed the rackets of swindlers, con men, crooked gamblers, and bunco artists in stories drawn by George Tuska, Steve Ditko, Dick Giordano, Frank Frollo, Bob Forgione, Joe Shuster, and Charles Nicholas.

*Public Enemies #1 © 1989 Malibu Graphics, Inc. Art by Madman.*

Some bunco-busting scripts were written by veteran comic writer Ken Fitch. The comic may have been inspired by the 1951 television show *Racket Squad*, with Reed Hadley starring as Capt. John Braddock, who protected people from shady operators who ran confidence rackets.

## REAL CLUE CRIME STORIES

Hillman Periodicals
1947 June–1953 May
Vol. 2 #4–Vol. 8 #3

Formerly published as *Clue Comics*, the format was changed to all-true crime stories ("Commit a Crime and the World Is Made of Glass!"). Artists included Jack Kirby, Joe Simon, Dan Barry, Mort Lawrence, Bob Powell, Carmine Infantino, Dick Briefer, Bob Fujitani, Bernard Krigstein, Bill Ely, Gerald McCann, Bernard Sachs, Rudy Palais, Paul Parker, Arthur Peddy, and Michael Suchorsky. Writers included Warren Kuhn, Carl Wessler, and Joe Simon.

## RECORD BOOK OF FAMOUS POLICE CASES

St. John Publications
1949
1

This 132-page comic book (with reprints of earlier St. John comics) sold for twenty-five cents.

## REFORM SCHOOL GIRL

Realistic Publications
1951
1

Juvenile delinquency never looked better in this "graphic story of boys and girls running wild in the violence-ridden slums of today." Readers could find out what happened to "pretty girls who fall victim to unscrupulous men, their own wayward emotions, and the other hidden pitfalls of a sensation-crazed society!" Dr. Frederic Wertham attacked the comic for blending "sex, violence, and torture," as well as for its advertisement of a figure-enhancing device called the "Bulge-Master." The comic book borrowed its title and front cover from a 1948 paperback novel of the same name.

## RIP KIRBY FEATURE BOOK

David McKay
1947
51, 54

Alex Raymond, the original artist on the *Flash Gordon* and *Secret Agent X-9* comic strips, began his comic strip about a cerebral sleuth in March 1946. Rip Kirby, who lived in a swank Manhatten apartment, was often seen in the company of Honey Dorian, a slender blonde fashion model. Raymond's early strips were reprinted in these two comic books.

## RIP KIRBY (HARVEY HITS)

Harvey Publications
1952 May
57

Reprinted the newspaper comic strip by Alex Raymond which tells the story of how "Rip Kirby Exposes the Kidnap Racket."

## ROOKIE COP

Charlton Comics
1955 November–1957 August
27–33

Patrolman Sam Barton learned on the job as he rescued errant youths and fought urban corruption under the command of Police Captain Lane. Out of uniform, the rookie cop passed time with girlfriend Ellen Banks and her kid brother Danny, who played ball in the Police Athletic League. Artists included Joe Maneely and Rocco Mastroserio, with early stories written by Ken Fitch.

## RUSTY, BOY DETECTIVE

Good Comics/Lev Gleason
1955 March–1955 November
1–5

With the advent of the Comics Code, publisher Lev Gleason (*Crime Does Not Pay*) tried a gentler approach to crime fighting with Rusty and his friends, Spunky and Tubby. Carl Hubbel and Bob Wood drew the stories. Virginia Hubbel was the likely author.

## SAINT, THE

Avon Periodicals
1947 August–1952 March
1–12

Simon Templar (aka, the Saint), the urbane detective of novels, screen, and radio created by Leslie Charteris, was adapted as a comic book in 1947 and then as a comic strip in 1948. The first seven issues contained original stories done for the comic book while the later issues reprinted the "Saint" newspaper strips drawn by Mike Roy and John Spranger. "Lucky Dale, Girl Detective" appeared as a secondary feature in early issues.

## SAM HILL PRIVATE EYE

Archie Comics
1950–1952
1–7

Sam Hill, "America's hard-boiled, wise-cracking sleuth," was drawn by Harry Lucey, who had also worked for *Crime Does Not Pay* and drawn a few stories featuring "America's favorite teenager," Archie Andrews. Sam, who had a stylish white streak down the middle of his blue/black hair, had a helpful secretary named Roxy and worked with Lieutenant Dugan, "Ireland's gift to the homicide department."

## SARGE STEEL

Charlton Comics
1964 December–1966 April
1–8

This 1960s private detective (named in part for his artificial steel left hand) was written by Joe Gill and drawn by Dick Giordano. With the 1960s super-spy craze, the character became a secret agent in the ninth issue (which was retitled *Secret Agent*).

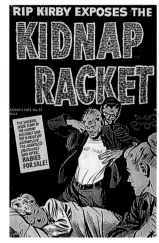

*Rip Kirby (Harvey Hits)*
© 1952 King Features Syndicate

*Sam Hill Private Eye #7*
© 1951 Close-Up Publications. Art by Harry Lucey.

*Secret Missions #1 © 1950 St. John Publications.* Art by Joe Kubert.

## SCARLET IN GASLIGHT

Eternity Comics
1988
1–4

Sherlock Holmes met Count Dracula in this series written by Martin Powell and illustrated by Seppo Makinen. The famous detective and enduring vampire teamed up to combat the evil genius of Professor Moriarty, who had managed to pit the two against each other.

## SCOTLAND YARD

Charlton Comics
1955 June–1956 March
1–4

Inspector Farnsworth of Scotland Yard, moustachioed and prematurely gray, worked with a red-headed, freckle-faced assistant known as Chipp. A secondary feature starred Stephen Hammish, "master detective and crime raconteur."

## SECRET AGENT

Charlton Comics
1966 October–1967 October
9, 10

Government agent Sarge Steel and CIA operative Tiffany Sinn appeared in this comic book drawn by Bill Montes, Frank McLaughlin, and Jim Aparo, with scripts by Joe Gill.

*Secret Agent #9 © 1966 Charlton Comics*

## SECRET AGENT

Gold Key
1966 November–1968 January
1, 2

The British television series *Danger Man,* with Patrick McGoohan, grew into a 1965 CBS show called "Secret Agent." Like the TV show, the comic book adaptation written by Dick Wood had secret agent John Drake blowing up his enemies and seducing gullible women to "preserve world peace and promote brotherhood." Although the TV series lasted only until September 1966, the last comic book issue came out over a year later.

## SECRET AGENT X-9 FEATURE BOOK

David McKay
1937 December
8

This oversize comic book (8½" by 11⅜") reprinted the *Secret Agent X-9* newspaper strips. Art was by Charles Flanders, who succeeded Alex Raymond on the feature, and writing was by Max Trell.

## SECRET MISSIONS

St. John Publications
1950 February
1

The Cold War heated up in these "all true and authentic" stories about U.S. intelligence agents fighting communists from Red China to Romania. "The Red Army was planning a blitz attack on a Baltic nation in defiance of the Atlantic Pact. To verify this tip, a young U.S. intelligence agent was dispatched on a dangerous mission into the red police-infested city of Prague. There he met a blonde who took him on a midnight rendevouz with police-state treachery . . ."

## SELECT DETECTIVE

D.S. Publishing Co.
1948 August–1948 December
1–3

Artists included Al McWilliams, Bob Jenny, Walter Johnson, and Frank Sieminsky.

## SENSATION COMICS/SENSATION MYSTERY

DC Comics
1952 January–1953 July
107–116

Originally the home of Wonder Woman, Wildcat, and Mr. Terrific, the comic book's superhero lineup was dropped in favor of mystery stories beginning in 1952. The resident star was Johnny Peril, a worldwide adventurer, detective, and journalist from the pages of *Danger Trail*. The title was officially changed to *Sensation Mystery* with issue #110. Artists included Alex Toth, Gil Kane, Gene Colan, and John Giunta, with scripts by John Broome and Robert Kanigher.

## SENSATIONAL POLICE CASES

Avon Periodicals
1952; 1954 March–1954 July
no number; 2–4
The first issue was a giant-size (100-page), unnumbered edition which sold for twenty-five cents. Artists included Joe Kubert and Everett R. Kinstler.

## SENSATIONAL POLICE CASES

IW/Super
1964
5
Reprinted *Prison Break* #5.

## 77 SUNSET STRIP

Dell/Gold Key
1960 January–1963 February
1066, 1106, 1159, 1211, 1263, 1291, 01-742-209, 1, 2
The first "glamorous" private-eye television show (1958) featured the detective team of Stu Bailey (played by Efrem Zimbalist, Jr.) and Jeff Spencer (Roger Smith), who operated out of their Hollywood office on 77 Sunset Strip. They were soon joined by "Kookie" Kookson (Edward Byrnes), a youthful parking lot attendant from the restaurant next door. Kookie, who had ambitions of becoming a private detective, spent much of his time combing his hair. In the comic book, he spouted such hipster lingo as: "I'm Mr. Bailey's associate in this international intrigue jazz! What's cooking in troublesville, doll? My ears are all bent for you! I'm hip . . . your problem is my problem!" The comic book paralleled the TV series, with Kookie eventually becoming a partner in the detective firm. The comic book's faithfulness to the TV show can be attributed to writer Eric Freiwald, who also wrote for the television series. Alex Toth drew the first three issues and Russ Manning was the artist for the rest of the series.

## SHERLOCK HOLMES

Charlton Comics
1955 October–1956 March
1, 2
In this unauthorized adaptation of Arthur Conan Doyle's detective, the famous London sleuth was removed from his Baker Street digs and plopped down in New York City, where he had to work with a dull-witted sergeant named Flaherty and an officious assistant called Frothingham.

## SHERLOCK HOLMES

DC Comics
1975 September
1
Adaptation of Arthur Conan Doyle's "The Final Problem" by writer Dennis O'Neil and artist E. R. Cruz.

## SHERLOCK HOLMES

Eternity Comics
1988 August–1989 July
1–12+
Reprinted the 1954–56 "Sherlock Holmes" newspaper comic strip by Mike Sekowsky and Frank Giacoia.

*Select Detective #2 © 1948 D.S. Publishing Co.*

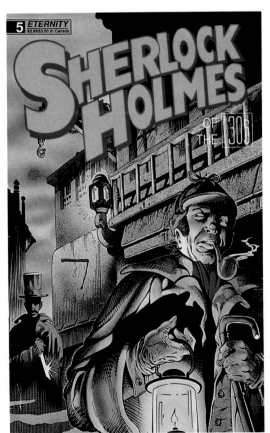

*Sherlock Holmes of the '30s #5 © 1990 Malibu Graphics, Inc. Art by Ron Wilber.*

*Sherlock Holmes #12 © 1989 Malibu Graphics, Inc. Art by Frank Giacoia.*

## SHERLOCK HOLMES OF THE '30S

Eternity Comics
1990 January–July 1990
1–7

Reprinted the 1930–32 "Sherlock Holmes" newspaper comic strip by Leo O'Mealia.

## SHOCK DETECTIVE CASES

Star Publications
1952 September–1952 November
20, 21

Previously published as *Crime Fighting Detective*, the new title reflected a trend toward more horror in crime comics. Artists included Rudy Palais and L. B. Cole.

## SHOCKING MYSTERY CASES

Star Publications
1952 September–1952 November
50–60

Formerly published as *Thrilling Crime Cases*, this retitled comic featured new stories by George Peltz, Jay Disbrow, Pete Morisi, and A. C. Hollingsworth, as well as reprints from *Murder Incorporated*, and other comics published by Victor Fox.

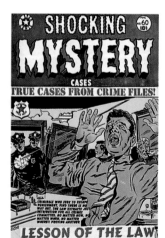

*Shocking Mystery Cases #60 © 1954 Star Publications. Art by L.B. Cole.*

## SHOWCASE

DC Comics
1956 December–1968 November
5, 43, 50, 51, 78

This "tryout" series from DC Comics featured several detective and spy-related titles: *Manhunters* (#5, with art by Mort Meskin, Curt Swan, Bill Ely); *Dr. No* (#43, with art by Norman Nodell); *I Spy* (#s 50, 51, with art by Carmine Infantino); and *Johnny Double* (#78, with art by Jack Sparling). The *Dr. No* issue (April 1963) was the first American comic book to feature James Bond. The comic was originally drawn for the Classics Illustrated series but the company suspended publishing. The comic then became part of the British Classics Illustrated series (#158A) and the European Detective series (#6). The comic was next reprinted as part of DC Comics's *Showcase* series to take advantage of the new James Bond movie. The story was edited to delete racial references, and the Jamaicans, including Quarrel, Bond's right-hand man, were literally whitewashed.

## SKY SHERIFF

D.S. Publishing Co.
1948 Summer
1

Writer/artist Edmond Good created Breeze Larson, Sky Sheriff. With his trusty plane and gal Friday, Tenny, Breeze battled crime in the skies and on the wing.

## SPECIAL AGENT (STEVE SAUNDERS)

Parents' Magazine Institute
1947 December–1949 September
1–8

Produced in cooperation with the Federal Bureau of Investigation, the editors told readers that the "situations and the characters are authentic with the exception of 'Steve Saunders' who has been created as a typical example of the intelligent and courageous men of the FBI." Saunders was the "FBI everyman" who was in on every case, including the capture of John Dillinger. J. Edgar Hoover lent his official likeness to several stories (appearing on the front cover of the first issue), and the "Official Story" of the FBI was serialized as a text feature. The same month the comic started, Steve Saunders also began a series in *True Comics*. Artist Ruben Moreira drew a secondary feature for the comic.

## SPECTACULAR FEATURES MAGAZINE

Fox Features Syndicate
1950 August
3

"They hung the name 'Lucky' on him way back in the Roaring Twenties because of his uncanny ability to survive through the years in the most ruthless business in existence! One of his secrets of his luck was that he avoided the glare of publicity, almost unknown to the public. His power grew with every passing year and then in 1936, when Luciano's luck finally ran out on him, his career as a mobster was emblazoned across the nation's headlines . . . and the tough little character emerged from the obscurity of police files as Lucky Luciano, the Super-Gangster!" Also featured was a story drawn by Carmine Infantino about Charlie Zack, who earned the name "Baby-Face Butcher" for his Prohibition racketeering.

## SPECTACULAR STORIES MAGAZINE

Fox Features Syndicate
1950 July–1950 September
4, 3

Victor Fox, publisher of such esteemed comics as *Crimes By Women* and *Women Outlaws,* carefully cultivated a mix of soft sex and tawdry violence in his comic books. For the cover of this first issue (#4), Fox featured a buxom blonde slugging an equally buxom brunette with the spike of her high-heel shoe. To add the necessary redeeming social value, Sherlock Holmes was engaged to narrate one of the stories inside. The next issue (#3), Fox dropped all literary pretensions and brought forth his version of the St. Valentine's Day Massacre.

## SPICY TALES

Eternity Comics
1988 September–1989 May
1–7

This "naughty anthology" reprinted risqué comic strips such as "Sally the Sleuth" and "Dan Turner, Hollywood Detective" from *Spicy Detective* and other pulp magazines of the 1930s–40s. Black and white.

## SPY AND COUNTERSPY

American Comics Group
1949 August–1949 October
1, 2

Jonathan Kent, Counterspy, starred in this comic book written by Richard Hughes. The series continued as *Spy-Hunters* with the third issue.

## SPY CASES

Marvel Comics
1950 September–1953 October
26–28, 4–19

Like the true-crime comics, these early issues featuring "America's secret soldiers" were all "based on fact." As the Korean war unfolded, later issues (#s 11–14) concentrated on the "battlefield adventures of actual spies." Artists included Bill Everett, Joe Maneely, and George Tuska.

## SPY FIGHTERS

Marvel Comics
1951 March–1953 July
1–15

Federal agent Clark Mason, spy fighter, took to the battlefields of Korea. Artists included Mac Pakula, George Tuska, and Ed Winiarski.

## SPY THRILLERS

Marvel Comics
1954 November–1955 May
1–4

The villains here were "the commies" in these stories of Cold War intrigue.

*Spectacular Features Magazine #3 © 1950 Fox Features Syndicate*

*Showcase #43 © 1963 DC Comics, Inc.* Art by Bob Brown.

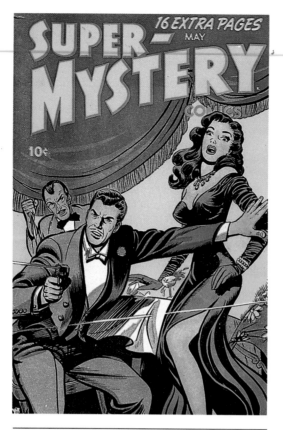

*Super Mystery Vol 7 #5*
*© 1948 Ace Magazines*

## SPY-HUNTERS

American Comics Group
1949 December–1953 June
3–24

"Jonathan Kent, Counterspy" and other espionage features were written by Richard Hughes and illustrated by Leonard Starr, Al Williamson, Mort Drucker, Sam Cooper, Ogden Whitney, and others. The last four issues were devoted almost exclusively to war stories.

## STARTLING CRIME ILLUSTRATED

Caliber Press
1991 January
1

This black-and-white comic featured art by Ken Holewczynski and Peter Krause, with stories by Rafael Nieves, Chris Klein, and Ken Holewczynski.

## STORIES BY FAMOUS AUTHORS

Famous Authors Illustrated
1950 September
7

This series of classic comics was based on such literary works as *Hamlet, Ben-Hur, The Scarlet Pimpernel,* etc. For issue #7, artist H. C. Kiefer drew Cornell Woolrich's 1947 suspense novelette "The Boy Who Cried Murder" as a comic book

story called *The Window*—the same name as the 1949 movie that also adapted the novelette.

## SUPER COPS, THE

Red Circle Productions
1974 July
1

Based on the real-life exploits of New York City policemen Dave Greenberg and Bob Hantz, who earned the title of "super cops" for their teamwork on the job. Written by Marvin Channing with art by Frank Thorne, Gray Morrow, and Carlos Pino.

## SUPER MYSTERY

Ace Magazines
1946 February–1948 July
34–48

Originally the home of such superheroes as Magno, the Black Spider, and the Sword, *Super Mystery* replaced its costumed characters with plainclothes crime fighters and detectives, such as the crime-solving team of Bert and Sue, private eye Mack Martin, and the gun-shunning Mr. Risk. Artists included George Tuska, Mort Meskin, Bill Walton, and Sid Greene.

## SUSPENSE

Marvel Comics
1949 December–1950 February
1, 2

These "Real Life Tales of Suspense" were loosely based on the popular CBS radio-television series. The radio show, which won an award from the Mystery Writers of America, inspired a 1949 TV series featuring famous Hollywood and Broadway actors. Instead of art, the front covers of the comic book featured photographs of such *Suspense* performers as Peter Lorre, Sidney Greenstreet, and Gale Storm. With issue #3, the title changed from mystery and suspense to horror.

## SUSPENSE DETECTIVE

Fawcett Publications
1952 June–1953 March
1–5

Artists included George Evans, Mike Sekowsky, and Bernard Baily.

## T-MAN

Quality Comics
1951 September–1956 December
1–38

*Suspense Detective #2*
*© 1952 Fawcett*
*Publications*

Pete Trask is a U.S. treasury agent (T-Man) who fights narcotics smugglers, communist extortion rackets, and atomic bomb terrorists from Bangkok to Bavaria. This "world wide trouble shooter" originally appeared in *Police Comics* (December 1950) and was drawn by Jack Cole and Reed Crandall, among others.

## TALES OF JUSTICE

Marvel Comics
1955 May–1957 August
53–67

After the Comics Code put the nix on true-crime comics, *Justice Comics* disappeared with issue #52 and reappeared under this name as a cleaned-up "cops and robbers" comic. Artists included Bob Powell, Bernard Krigstein, Joe Orlando, Angelo Torres, Reed Crandall, Bill Everett, John Severin, Jay Scott Pike, and Doug Wildey.

## TALES OF THE KILLERS

World Famous Periodicals
1970 December–1971 February
10, 11

Robert Farrell, who published crime and horror comics in the 1950s, was the editor and publisher of this magazine-size comic book which reprinted crime stories from the 1940s and 1950s in black and white.

## TARGET: THE CORRUPTERS

Dell Publishing Co.
1962 May–1962 December
1306, 2, 3

Based on the 1961–62 ABC television series with Stephen McNally as Paul Marino, an investigative rackets reporter, and Robert Harland as Jack Flood, his undercover agent.

## THRILLING CRIME CASES

Star Publications
1950 June–1952 July
41–49

For this title, editor/artist Leonard B. Cole mixed new stories with reprints from Fox crime comics and the Chameleon series from *Target Comics* with Pete Stockbridge, private investigator. Gregory Cole, the gunmaster from *Guns Against Gangsters,* also made an appearance. Artists included Jay Disbrow, A. C. Hollingsworth, L. B. Cole, and George Peltz.

## TOP DETECTIVE COMICS

IW/Super
1964
9

Reprinted *Young King Cole* #14.

## TOP SECRETS

Street and Smith
1947 November–1949 July
1–10

This comic book promised to reveal the "top secrets of crime, history, and science" to its readers. Issue #7 achieved minor notoriety for printing a chart that showed the "vulnerable" areas of the human body with such helpful information as: "Eyes—Finger Jab or Thumb Gouge" and "Throat: Adam's Apple, Carotid Arteries, Wind Pipe—Edge of hand, finger jab or hand pressure." Artists included A. C. Hollingsworth, Bob Powell, and Powell's studio of artists.

## TRAPPED!

Ace Magazines
1954 October–1955 April
1–4

Reprinted crime stories from *Men Against Crime* and others. Artists included Gene Colan and Mike Sekowsky.

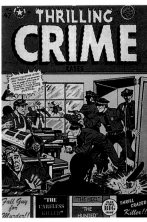

*Thrilling Crime Cases #47 © 1952 Star Publications.* Art by L.B. Cole.

*Top Secrets #8 © 1949 Street & Smith Publishing.* Art by Bob Powell.

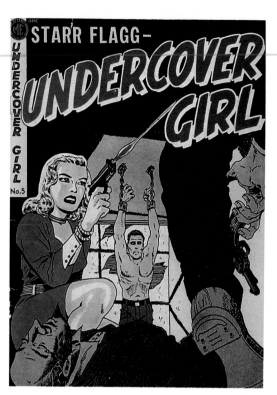

*Undercover Girl #5 © 1952*
*Magazine Enterprises*

## TROUBLE WITH GIRLS, THE

Malibu/Comico/Eternity
1987 August
1–14, Vol. 2#1–10+

"Lester Girls is a man who craves tedium and anonymity but is constantly being thrust into international adventures, gunbattles, and torrid sexual trysts," explained Will Jacobs, the co-creator, with Gerard Jones, of *The Trouble With Girls.* Drawn by Tim Hamilton and others, the adventures of Lester Girls took him from the streets of San Francisco to the Mayan temples of the Yucatan. Wherever the action, however, Girls always found himself besieged by (but, of course) girls.

## TRUE CRIME COMICS

Magazine Village
1947 May–1949 August
2–6; Vol. 2 #1

The first issue was perhaps the single most notorious crime comic book ever published—full of drugs (opium, morphine, marijuana), women ripping off their clothes, and stilettos pressed against eyeballs. Two illustrations from the comic book were reproduced by Wertham in his *Seduction of the Innocent,* in addition to two other mentioned in the text. The same issue was also singled out for criticism by Geoffrey Wagner in a

*Vic Flint #2 © 1954*
*Argo Publishing*

section on comic book censorship in *Parade of Pleasure.* One story ("Murder, Morphine and Me") was reproduced in its entirety in the report issued by the New York State Legislative Commission on censorship in comics. The early issues were packaged by artist, writer, and editor Jack Cole. Other artists included Alex Kotzky, George Roussos, Alex Toth, and Wally Wood.

## UNDERCOVER GIRL

Magazine Enterprises
1952–1954
5–7

Starr Flag, a glamorous undercover agent for the Central Intelligence Agency, appeared in *Manhunt* comics as drawn by Ogden Whitney. Her adventures (which included an obligatory swim suit, bath shower, or lingerie scene) were reprinted in these three issues.

## UNDERWORLD

D.S. Publishing Co.
1948 February–1949 June
1–9

Artists included John Rosenberger, Graham Ingels, Louis Ravielli, Robert Q. Sale, Harry Anderson, George Appel, Sam Cooper, Red Holmdale, Bob Jenny, Frank Sieminsky, and Leonard Starr.

## UNDERWORLD CRIME

Fawcett Publications
1952 June–1953 September
1–7

"Follow the frantic fugitives from the law into their secret hiding places! Watch them in their unguarded moments! See them tracked, tormented, and trapped by the police in . . . UNDERWORLD CRIME!"

## UNDERWORLD STORY, THE

Avon Periodicals
1950
1

Based on the 1950 movie of the same name about a reporter who joined a small-town newspaper to expose gangster corruption.

## UNKNOWN MAN, THE

Avon Periodicals
1951
1

Based on the 1951 movie starring Walter Pidgeon, about a lawyer and the "underworld gang lord who controlled the crime syndicate!"

## UNTOUCHABLES, THE

Dell Publishing Co.
1961 October–1962 August
1237, 1286, 01-879-207, 12-879-210

Based on the 1959 ABC television series starring Robert Stack as treasury agent Elliot Ness. While the TV show was criticized as one of the most mindlessly violent programs of the day, the comic book limited its shootouts to usually one per story, with the bad guy neatly wounded by Ness. The comic book, true to the TV show with its 1920s settings, borrowed from a familiar cast of villains such as Al Capone's top lieutenant, Frank "The Enforcer" Nitti.

## VENGEANCE SQUAD

Charlton Comics
1975 July–1976 May
1–6

Included the adventures of "Mike Mauser, Private Eye" as drawn by Joe Staton, with stories by veteran crime comic artist Pete Morisi.

## VIC FLINT

Argo Publishing
1956 February–1956 May
1, 2

Newspaper strip reprints of the hard-boiled detective created in 1946 by artist Ralph Lane and writer Ernest Lynn continued in this second comic book series. The newspaper strip, now drawn by Art Sansom, was appearing only on Sunday since the demise of the daily strip in January 1956.

## VIC FLINT, CRIME BUSTER

St. John Publications
1948 August–1949 April
1–5

The newspaper strip adventures of artist Ralph Lane's tough-guy detective were reprinted here and in other St. John crime comics (*Authentic Police Cases, Fugitives From Justice*).

## WANTED COMICS

Orbit Publishing
1947 September–1953 April
9–53

One of the earliest imitators of *Crime Does Not Pay*, this comic had a host who looked suspiciously like Mr. Crime from that title. There were short-lived series such as "Crime Lab,"

"Anthony Action," and "Mr. D.A.," but most stories were based on true-crime accounts. Writers included Carl W. Smith and William and Dorothy Woolfolk. Artists included Syd Shores, Mort Leav, Mort Lawrence, Bob Rogers, Rudy Palais, John Giunta, John Forte, Charles Miller, and Rafael Astarita.

## WAR AGAINST CRIME

EC Comics
1948 Spring–1950 February
1–11

The first true-crime comic from EC Comics adapted the life stories of infamous gangsters, gun molls, and bank robbers. Artists included Johnny Craig, Al Feldstein, Fred Peters, Lee Ames, H. C. Kiefer, John Alton, Rudy Palais, George Roussos, Leonard Starr, and Graham Ingels. Wally Wood and Harry Harrison also collaborated on a story that Harrison helped write. The last two issues featured a horror story introduced by the Vault Keeper, and the title was soon changed to a horror comic called the *Vault of Horror.*

## WHO IS NEXT?

Standard Magazines
1953 January
5

With criminals running rampant, no one knew "who will be next" in this comic book with

*Wanted Comics #31*
© *1950 Orbit Publishing*

*War Against Crime #6*
© *1949 William M. Gaines. Art by Johnny Craig.*

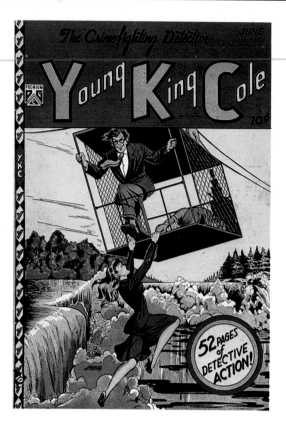

*Young King Cole Vol. 3 #11 © 1948 Novelty Press.* Art by L. B. Cole

art by Alex Toth, Mike Sekowsky, and Ross Andru.

## WHODUNIT

D.S. Publishing Co.
1948 August–1948 December
1–3

This anthology emphasized foreign intrigue and mystery stories over true-crime and gangster tales. Artists included Al Cammarata, Matt Baker, and Red Holmdale.

## WHODUNNIT?

Eclipse Comics
1986 June–1987 April
1–3

You got the clues—whodunnit? Stories by Don Spiegle.

## WOMEN TO LOVE

Avon Periodicals
1953
1

A "book-length" romance-crime comic based on the novel by Sinclair Drago that dared to ask the question: Can a girl find happiness in the underworld?

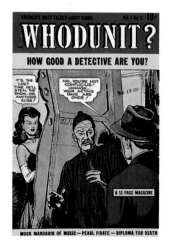

*Whodunit #2 © 1948 D.S. Publishing Co.*

## YOUNG KING COLE

Novelty Press
1945 Fall–1948 July
1–23

Young Kingston Cole, Jr., runs a detective agency. The bespectacled, bow tie-wearing sleuth (assisted by his secretary Iris) usually had mild-mannered adventures without messy bloodshed. Other crime-busting characters included Toni Gayle ("glamorous detective model"), Foxy ("Office Boy in the Detective Bureau"), Larry Briderick ("City Detective"), Homer K. Beagle ("The Demon Detective"), and Dr. Doom ("the resourceful professor of criminology"). Artists included Al McWilliams, L. B. Cole, Joe Certa, Jim Cannon, Will Hammel, Harvey Fuller, Hy Gage, and Nina Albright.

## ZAZA THE MYSTIC

Charlton Comics
1956 April–1956 September
10, 11

Zaza, queen of the Gypsy fortune-tellers, used her "shrewd judgement and woman's intuition" to solve crimes for boyfriend Lt. Bob Nelson, city detective, in stories drawn by Rocco Mastroserio and others. Formerly published as *Charlie Chan,* the title and format were changed when Charlton Comics lost the rights to the character. A leftover Charlie Chan story, however, was slipped into the first issue, with the famous detective crudely disguised by a pair of drawn-on glasses and a hasty name change to "Louie Lue."

# BIBLIOGRAPHY

Bails, Jerry, editor. *The Who's Who of American Comic Books*. St. Claire Shores, Michigan (self-published).

Benton, Mike. *Comic Book Collecting For Fun and Profit*. New York: Crown Publishers, 1985.

_____. *The Comic Book In America: An Illustrated History*. Dallas, Texas: Taylor Publishing Company, 1989.

_____. *Horror Comics: The Illustrated History*. Dallas, Texas: Taylor Publishing Company, 1991.

_____. *Science Fiction Comics: The Illustrated History*. Dallas, Texas: Taylor Publishing Company, 1992.

_____. *Superhero Comics of the Golden Age: The Illustrated History*. Dallas, Texas: Taylor Publishing Company, 1992.

_____. *Superhero Comics of the Silver Age: The Illustrated History*. Dallas, Texas: Taylor Publishing Company, 1991.

California Bureau of Public Administration. *Comic Book Regulation*. Berkeley: University of California, February 1955.

Gaines, William. "Censorship In Comics." *Comics Journal* #77 November. 1982.

Galewitz, Herb, editor. *The Celebrated Cases of Dick Tracy 1931–1951*. New York: Chelsea House, 1980.

Goulart, Ron, editor. *The Encyclopedia of American Comics*. New York: Facts on File, 1990.

Horn, Maurice, editor. *The World Encyclopedia of Comics*. New York: Avon Publishing, 1977.

Kirby, Jack. Interview. *Comics Journal* #134 February. 1990

Kunzle, David. *The Early Comic Strip: Narrative Strips and Picture Stories in the European Broadsheet from c.1450 to 1825*. Berkeley: University of California Press, 1973.

Legman, Gershom. *Love and Death: A Study in Censorship*. New York 1949.

Macek, Carl. "*Film Noir* and Comic Books." *Fanfare* Winter 1978.

Maeder, Jay. *Dick Tracy: The Official Biography*. New York: Penguin Books, 1990.

Nash, Jay Robert. *Bloodletters and Badmen*. New York: M. Evans and Company, 1973.

New York State Legislature. *Report of the New York State Joint Legislative Committee to Study the Publication of Comics*. Albany: Williams Press, March 1951.

*New York Times*. "Police Fight Comic Books." New York Times August 12, 1947.

*New York Times*. "Pupils Burn Comic Books." New York Times December 23, 1948.

*New York Times*. "Publishers to Start Regulation of Comics." New York Times September 10, 1948.

*New York Times*. "Comic Criminals To Burn." New York Times January 7, 1949.

*New York Times*. "Bill Curbs Comic Books." New York Times February 5, 1949.

*New York Times*. "State Senate Acts to Control Crime Comics." New York Times February 24, 1949.

Overstreet, Robert M. *The Overstreet Comic Book Price Guide (22nd Edition)*. Cleveland, Tennessee: Overstreet Publications, 1992.

Penzler, Otto. *The Private Lives of Private Eyes, Spies, Crimefighters, & Other Good Guys*. New York: Grosset & Dunlap, 1977.

Powers, Richard G. *G-Men: Hoover's FBI in American Popular Culture*. Carbondale: Southern Illinois University Press, 1983.

Senate Committee on the Judiciary. *Comic Books and Juvenile Delinquency*. Washington, D.C.: Government Printing Office, 1955.

Special Committee to Investigate Organized Crime in Interstate Commerce. *Juvenile Delinquency*. Washington, D.C.: Government Printing Office, 1950.

Simon, Joe with Jim Simon. *The Comic Book Makers*. New York: Crestwood/II Publications, 1990.

Wertham, Fredric. *Seduction of the Innocent*. New York: Rinehart & Company, 1954.

Wertham, Fredric. Interview. *Inside Comics*. Winter 1974–1975.

Wertham, Fredric. Interview. *Comics Feature*. 1984.

Zone, Ray. "4-Color Frenzy." *Blab!* #5 Summer 1990.

# INDEX

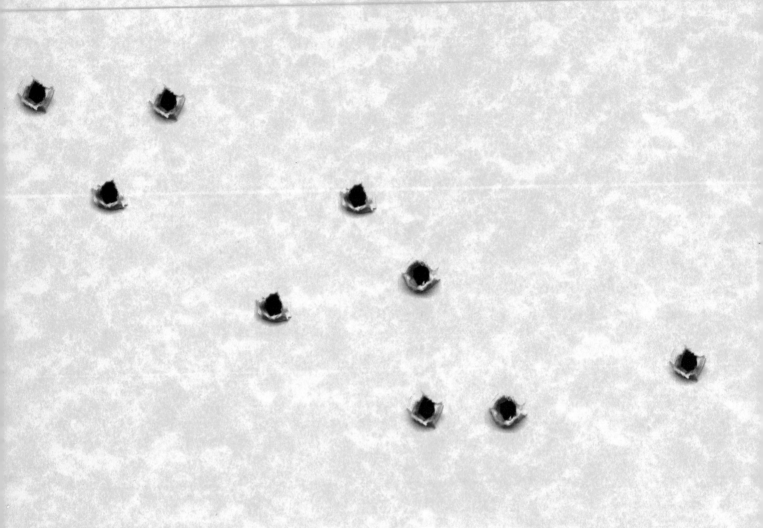